Lecture Notes in Computer Science 9808

Commenced Publication in 1973
Founding and Former Series Editors:
Gerhard Goos, Juris Hartmanis, and Jan van Leeuwen

More information about this series at http://www.springer.com/series/7410

Alessandro Aldini · Javier Lopez
Fabio Martinelli (Eds.)

Foundations
of Security Analysis
and Design VIII

FOSAD 2014/2015/2016 Tutorial Lectures

 Springer

Editors
Alessandro Aldini
University of Urbino
Urbino
Italy

Fabio Martinelli
National Research Council C.N.R.
Pisa
Italy

Javier Lopez
University of Malaga
Malaga
Spain

ISSN 0302-9743   ISSN 1611-3349   (electronic)
Lecture Notes in Computer Science
ISBN 978-3-319-43004-1   ISBN 978-3-319-43005-8   (eBook)
DOI 10.1007/978-3-319-43005-8

Library of Congress Control Number: 2016945140

LNCS Sublibrary: SL4 – Security and Cryptology

Printed on acid-free paper

This Springer imprint is published by Springer Nature
The registered company is Springer International Publishing AG Switzerland

Preface

The International Summer School on Foundations of Security Analysis and Design (FOSAD) has promoted the publication of books in the LNCS series that collect a selection of tutorials presented at FOSAD. We are very proud to present the eighth volume in this series, which includes contributions from three editions of FOSAD from 2014 to 2016. The history of FOSAD goes back to 2000, when it was established as a high education cradle for young researchers in the field of security for computer systems and networks. The overall number of participants since the first edition is now more than 750, and many of them have become well-known and appreciated researchers and FOSAD lecturers. Analogously, thanks to the quality and high standard of the lectures, the FOSAD book series represents a clear and comprehensive reference for graduate students and young researchers from academia and industry.

The first two contributions accompany presentations given at FOSAD 2014. The former is presented by Jonathan Bootle, Andrea Cerulli, Pyrros Chaidos, and Jens Groth from University College London. In the setting of proof systems for cryptographic protocols verification, the authors provide an overview of techniques behind the construction of zero-knowledge proofs. The latter is a work by Steven Van Acker and Andrei Sabelfeld from Chalmers University of Technology, who discuss the security of Web applications executing JavaScript code and the sandboxing systems used to restrict and control JavaScript functionalities. A contribution from FOSAD 2015 is authored by Michael Backes, Pascal Berrang, and Praveen Manoharan from Saarland University. They developed a user-centric privacy framework for quantitatively assessing the exposure of personal information in open environments. The proposed methodology is instantiated in the setting of identity disclosure and validated in a large-scale real-world case study. The last contribution, selected from FOSAD 2016, is by Ankur Taly and Asim Shankar, researchers at Google Inc. They define a fully decentralized authorization model for large and open distributed systems. Such a model is deployed as part of an open-source application framework called Vanadium.

We are grateful to the organizations and institutions that have supported FOSAD in the last few years, among which we would like to mention the IFIP Working Groups 1.7 on Theoretical Foundations of Security Analysis and Design and 11.14 on Secure Engineering. We also thank the EU FP7 project Confidential and Compliant Clouds (CoCoCloud), the EU H2020 project European Network for Cyber Security (NeCS), and the EPSRC CryptoForma network. We finally wish to thank the staff of the University Residential Centre of Bertinoro for the organizational and administrative support.

June 2016

Alessandro Aldini
Javier Lopez
Fabio Martinelli

Contents

Efficient Zero-Knowledge Proof Systems

Jonathan Bootle, Andrea Cerulli, Pyrros Chaidos, and Jens Groth[✉]

University College London, London, UK
j.groth@ucl.ac.uk

Abstract. A proof system can be used by a prover to demonstrate to one or more verifiers that a statement is true. Proof systems can be interactive where the prover and verifier exchange many messages, or non-interactive where the prover sends a single convincing proof to the verifier. Proof systems are widely used in cryptographic protocols to verify that a party is following a protocol correctly and is not cheating.

A particular type of proof systems are zero-knowledge proof systems, where the prover convinces the verifier that the statement is true but does not leak any other information. Zero-knowledge proofs are useful when the prover has private data that should not be leaked but needs to demonstrate a certain fact about this data. The prover may for instance want to show it is following a protocol correctly but not want to reveal its own input.

In these lecture notes we give an overview of some central techniques behind the construction of efficient zero-knowledge proofs.

1 Introduction

Imagine a company is trying to assess a candidate for a highly specialized position. A simple solution would be for them to present her with a task of their choice and rate her performance. The candidate declines, as the assessment might have her doing useful work without compensation. She proposes the choice of the task is left to her, to ensure the company does not unfairly profit from this process. The company is not convinced; the task may be too easy, or selected to hide the candidate's weaknesses.

For the assessment to go forward we need a special set of tasks: on the one hand they must be hard enough such that only qualified candidates are able to accomplish them, on the other hand they should not give away anything else since candidates do not want to function as unpaid workers. In job interviews this often takes the form of logic puzzles.

In cryptographic protocols, we do not have jobs and candidates; but we often have situations where we want to demonstrate some property holds or a statement is true without giving away any other information. Here zero-knowledge proofs are appropriate tools.

Zero-knowledge proof systems, introduced by Goldwasser et al. [GMR85], take place between two parties called prover and verifier. The prover wants to convince the verifier a certain statement is true, but without the verifier gaining

© Springer International Publishing Switzerland 2016
A. Aldini et al. (Eds.): FOSAD VIII, LNCS 9808, pp. 1–31, 2016.
DOI: 10.1007/978-3-319-43005-8_1

any other knowledge during the exchange (e.g. *why* the statement is true). Thus, there are three core requirements in zero-knowledge proofs:

Completeness. For true statements, a prover can convince the verifier.

Soundness. For false statements, a prover cannot convince the verifier (even if the prover cheats and deviates from the protocol).

Zero-Knowledge. The verifier will not learn anything from the interaction apart from the fact that the statement is true.

The statements we will be concerned with here are of the form $u \in L_R$, where L_R is an NP-language defined by a polynomial time decidable binary relation R. For $(u, w) \in R$, we say u is the statement and w is a witness for $u \in L_R$. The prover knows the witness w, and wants to convince the verifier that $u \in L_R$ without revealing anything else. In particular, the prover does not want to reveal the witness w.

1.1   Motivation

Here we will describe a few applications of zero-knowledge protocols. We do not aim to be exhaustive, but rather to provide some context in terms of applications.

e-Voting. Let's consider a simple voting setting: individual voters cast their votes and the electoral authorities produce the tally. To keep their votes private, the voters encrypt their votes. There are encryption schemes with a homomorphic property that allows the addition of the votes in encrypted form. If ballots consist of encrypted 0 s and 1 s (signifying "no" and "yes"), then the authorities can use the homomorphic property to produce an encrypted sum of all the votes. The authorities can then decrypt the ciphertext with the sum of the votes to get the election result, the number of "yes" votes, without the need to decrypt any of the individual ballots.

Unfortunately, this solution is *too* simple. What is to stop a voter from cheating by encrypting a 2 instead of the prescribed 0 or 1? In effect, the voter would be voting twice. We want to prevent voters from deviating from the voting protocol, but at the same time we want their votes to remain private. So, we want to verify that their ballots are valid, i.e., encrypt 0 or 1, but at the same time the voters do not want to reveal which vote they are casting, i.e., whether the plaintext is a 0 or a 1. This can be accomplished by using zero-knowledge proofs between the voters and the electoral authorities. Each voter acts as a prover that demonstrates her encrypted vote is valid. Completeness means that the ballots of honest voters are accepted. Soundness ensures that invalid ballots are rejected. And zero-knowledge keeps the votes secret.

Mix-Nets. Mix-nets [Cha88] are a tool for anonymous messaging given a broadcast channel. Instead of directly addressing messages to their recipients, a sender might opt to use a Mix server as an intermediary. The sender encrypts the message and recipient with the server's public key and addresses the message to the server. Once the server has collected a number of messages, it decrypts all of them and broadcasts the plaintexts in a randomized order. We can expand on this construction by using multiple servers in sequence and threshold decryption: each server removes part of the encryption and randomly reorders the list of ciphertexts. The advantage of this construction is that no single server can determine which input corresponds to which output.

However, this procedure gives dishonest servers too much freedom. In particular, they might opt to drop messages and replace them with their own. Worse, even if the replacement is noticed, it will be hard to attribute it to a single server. Again zero-knowledge proofs come to the rescue. A solution is to ask each server to prove it acted honestly; that is to demonstrate that there exists a reordering such that the server's outputs is a partial decryption (consistent with the server's private key) of the server's inputs. Obviously, this proof should not reveal the concrete reordering or the server's private key, which is why it should be zero-knowledge.

Playing Nicely. In general, we can use zero-knowledge protocols to ensure that parties are following the prescribed protocol for any particular operation. This is a powerful tool since it prevents active attacks where somebody tries to cheat by deviating from the protocol.

1.2   Example: A Zero-Knowledge Proof for Graph Isomorphism

In this section we will use a simple zero-knowledge proof for graph isomorphism [GMW91] as an example to illustrate a common protocol flow. We can think of an undirected graph as a set of vertices V and a set of edges E between the vertices. Two graphs $G_0 = (V, E_0)$ and $G_1 = (V, E_1)$ are isomorphic if there is a permutation of the vertices and edges mapping one graph to the other, see Fig. 1 for an example. More precisely, we say a permutation $f : V \rightarrow V$ is an isomorphism from G_0 to G_1 if for all pairs of vertices $(u, v) \in E_1$ if and only if $(f(u), f(v)) \in E_2$. Graph isomorphisms are transitive, if we have two graph isomorphisms $f : G_0 \rightarrow G_1$ and $g : G_1 \rightarrow G_2$ then $g \circ f : G_0 \rightarrow G_2$ is a graph isomorphism between G_0 and G_2.

Given graphs G_0, G_1 it is easy to check whether a permutation f of the vertices is a graph isomorphism. On the other hand, there is currently no known polynomial time algorithm that given two graphs G_0 and G_1 can determine whether they are isomorphic or not. We will in the following consider the situation where the statement consists of a claim that two graphs are isomorphic to each other. The prover knows an isomorphism between the graphs, but wants to convince the verifier that they are isomorphic without revealing the isomorphism. More precisely, we consider the language of pairs of isomorphic graphs $L_R = \{(G_0, G_1)\}$ defined by the relation $R = \{((G_0, G_1), f) : G_1 = f(G_0)\}$.

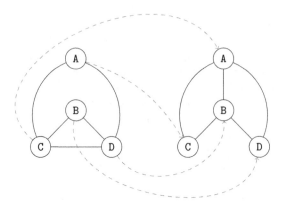

Fig. 1. Two isomorphic graphs: Reordering ABCD to CDAB maps the first graph to the second.

Statement: A pair of graphs G_0, G_1 on the same set of vertices V.
Prover's witness: An isomorphism f between G_0 and G_1.
Protocol:

- The prover picks a random permutation $h : V \to V$ and computes $H = h(G_1)$. She stores h and sends H to the verifier.
- The verifier picks a random challenge $b \leftarrow \{0, 1\}$.
- If $b = 0$ the prover sends $g = h \circ f$ to the verifier.
   If $b = 1$ the prover sends $g = h$ to the verifier.
- The verifier accepts the proof if $g(G_b) = H$.

It is simple to see that our protocol is complete. If G_0 and G_1 are isomorphic to each other, then both of them are isomorphic to H. Furthermore, the prover who knows the isomorphism f can easily compute both the isomorphism between G_0 and H and the isomorphism between G_1 and H. So she can answer both of the possible challenges $b \in \{0, 1\}$ and has 100 % probability of convincing the verifier.

Our protocol is sound in the sense that there is 50 % chance of catching a cheating prover. If G_0 and G_1 are not isomorphic then H cannot be isomorphic to both. So, if the verifier picks b such that G_b is not isomorphic to H, then the prover cannot answer the challenge.

To increase our chance of catching a cheating prover, we can repeat the challenge and response protocol. We modify the protocol to perform n repetitions for the same G_0, G_1 but different H_i, b_i and g_i. In each interaction, we have 50 % chance of catching the cheating prover, so overall the risk of cheating is reduced to 2^{-n}.

In the soundness discussion above, we considered a cheating prover using non-isomorphic G_0, G_1. But what about the case where G_0 and G_1 are isomorphic but the prover might or might not know f? Soundness provides no guarantees: it ensures that a witness w exists, but not that the prover knows it. The graph isomorphism protocol gives a stronger guarantee, which we will refer to as extractability. Suppose the prover after having sent H can answer both challenges $b = 0$ and $b = 1$, then it could actually compute an isomorphism $f = g_1^{-1} \circ g_0$ between G_0 and G_1. We will later define a zero-knowledge protocol to be *extractable* if it is possible to extract a witness from a successful prover, for instance by rewinding it and running it again on a new challenge.

Finally, there is the zero-knowledge property. This can be somewhat puzzling: what does it mean for a run of the protocol not to give the verifier any new information? We will define zero-knowledge through simulation. If the verifier could simulate the protocol transcript himself without interacting with the prover, then he cannot have learned anything new from seeing the transcript.

The graph isomorphism proof can be simulated by first picking a random permutation g, then guessing at random $b \leftarrow \{0, 1\}$, and finally setting $H = g(G_b)$. With 50 % probability the guess b matches what the verifier would send after seeing H, and in that case we have a simulated proof transcript (H, b, g). If our guess is wrong, we just rewind the verifier to the start and try again with a new random g and b until we guess the challenge correctly.

Let us argue that if G_0, G_1 are isomorphic then the transcripts produced by successful simulations are identical to those produced by real executions of the protocol. In both cases we can think of g as a uniformly random renumbering of the vertices of G_0 or G_1, which means that H is uniformly random. We also note that the distribution of b given H is unchanged. Therefore, we see that the probability distributions of real and simulated transcripts are identical. The important thing to notice about the simulation is that we do not use the witness at all to simulate. Therefore, the simulated transcript cannot leak any information about the witness. Since the real proofs have the same probability distribution as the simulated proofs this means they do not leak any information either.

1.3   Security and Performance Parameters

Zero-knowledge proofs come in many flavours depending on the application. The particular choice depends on the desired security properties and performance parameters. We will now discuss some of these options.

Security Properties. Completeness, soundness and zero-knowledge often come in one of three flavours: perfect, statistical and computational. Perfect completeness means that an honest prover will always convince an honest verifier on a true statement, perfect soundness means that it is impossible to prove a false statement, and perfect zero-knowledge means that transcripts can be perfectly simulated and leak no information whatsoever.

In the graph isomorphism example we have perfect completeness and perfect zero-knowledge, but not perfect soundness since a cheating prover has 50 % chance of convincing the verifier on a false statement. Even if we repeat the protocol n times, there is still 2^{-n} chance of cheating and we do not get perfect soundness. However, we get statistical soundness in the sense that there is negligible small probability of cheating the verifier.

Perfect soundness can be relaxed to statistical soundness, where we require a prover has negligible probability of cheating the verifier. We can relax it further to computational soundness, where we admit the possibility of cheating, but are content if it is computationally infeasible to find a way to cheat. We have computational soundness, when it is unlikely that a probabilistic polynomial time prover can cheat.

Perfect zero-knowledge can be relaxed to statistical zero-knowledge, where the simulated transcript just needs to have a probability distribution that is close to that of a real proof. It can be further relaxed to computational zero-knowledge, where a computationally bounded verifier cannot tell whether it is seeing a transcript of an interaction with a real prover or a simulation of its view of such an interaction.

Interaction. The graph isomorphism proof we described needs three messages to be exchanged between the two parties, starting with the prover. In general, we measure the interaction of a zero-knowledge proof in the number of messages or *moves* the parties makes. We will refer to two moves as a *round* consisting of one move from each side.

When expanding the graph isomorphism protocol to n repetitions, we can easily see that the number of moves becomes $2n + 1$ since we can combine the last message of iteration i with the first message of iteration $i + 1$ since both are sent from the prover. Another option would be to perform the multiple iterations in parallel to reduce interaction. However, parallel composition does not always yield the desired result. Parallel composition of zero-knowledge proofs does not necessarily result in a zero-knowledge proof [GK96], or soundness may be less than what we might expect [BIN97].

In general, we aim to restrict the number of rounds used by protocols, as it requires that participants are available and need to remember previous messages for an extended period. One particular class of zero-knowledge proofs are those consisting of a single move from the prover to the verifier. We call these proofs *non-interactive* and will return to them in Sect. 3.

Communication. We consider the communication cost of the protocol to be the total bit-length of all messages exchanged by the two parties. We often compare the communication to the size of the statement as an indication of relative efficiency.

In the graph isomorphism proof, the statement is two graphs of k vertices G_0, G_1, which we can represent with two adjacency matrices using less than k^2 bits since they are symmetric. The communication consists of the graph H (less than $\frac{1}{2}k^2$ bits), the reply b (1 bit) and a description of g (in the order of $k \log k$ bits). The communication cost is thus linear in the size of the statement.

Computation. We usually distinguish between the computation cost of the prover and that of the verifier. We often opt to make verification quicker at the expense of the prover. First, in some settings, such as voting, a non-interactive proof for a ballot being valid is only created once but may be seen and verified multiple times. Second, in applications such as verifiable computation the verifier is much weaker than the prover and it is only natural to try and lessen the computational load of the verifier. Finally, one may argue that being computationally bounded is a core characteristic of the verifier. If the verifier was computationally unbounded, she could check whether a statement $u \in L$ directly. This would eliminate the need for a proof in many cases.

Security Setting. Most protocols do not exist in vacuum; their security is based on a number of assumptions. These assumptions may be computational in nature, where a certain mathematical problem is considered hard to solve. There are also zero-knowledge protocols making stronger assumptions on the underlying primitives, e.g., many zero-knowledge proofs rely on the random oracle model where a cryptographic hash-function is assumed to behave like a truly random function [BR93].

A potential resource but at the same time potential security liability is the environment in which the zero-knowledge proof is executed. Interactive zero-knowledge proofs can be executed without any setup but the availability of a common reference string, e.g., a bit-string with a certain probability distribution, may improve performance. For non-interactive zero-knowledge proofs it is necessary and unavoidable to have a common reference string or some other form of assistance.

1.4   Notation

In the next two sections, we will give an overview of main ideas in Σ-protocols, which yield efficient interactive zero-knowledge proofs, and non-interactive zero-knowledge proofs. It will be useful to establish some common notation.

We write $y = A(x; r)$ when an algorithm A on input x and randomness r, outputs y. We write $y \leftarrow A(x)$ for the process of picking randomness r at random and setting $y = A(x; r)$. We also write $y \leftarrow S$ for sampling y uniformly at random from a set S. We will for convenience assume uniform random sampling from various types of sets is possible; there are easy ways to amend our protocols to the case where the sets are only sampleable with a distribution that is statistically close to uniform.

We assume all algorithms and parties in a cryptographic protocol will directly or indirectly get a security parameter λ as input (which for technical reasons will be written in unary 1^λ to ensure the running time is polynomial). The intuition is that the higher the security parameter the more secure should the scheme be. We will define security in terms of experiments that define the execution of a scheme in the presence of the adversary, and predicates that define whether the adversary succeeded in breaking the scheme. We are interested in the probability that the adversary breaks the scheme, for which we use the notation

$$\Pr[\text{output} \leftarrow \text{Experiment}(1^\lambda) : \text{Predicate}(\text{output})].$$

We will use the notation $\mathcal{A}$ for the adversary and assume it is either unbounded or efficient, where we define an efficient adversary as one that runs in probabilistic polynomial time.

Given two probability functions in the security parameter $f, g : \mathbb{N} \to [0, 1]$ we say that they are *close* and write $f(\lambda) \approx g(\lambda)$ when $|f(\lambda) - g(\lambda)| = O(\lambda^{-c})$ for every constant $c > 0$. We say that f is *negligible* if $f(\lambda) \approx 0$, and we say that f is *overwhelming* if $f(\lambda) \approx 1$. We will in many security definitions want the adversary's success probability to be negligible in the security parameter.

2 Σ-Protocols

In the previous section we discussed an interactive proof system for graph isomorphism. In the example the verifier picks a random challenge in $\{0, 1\}$ and the prover has probability $\frac{1}{2}$ of convincing the verifier of a false statement. The protocol needs to be iterated many times in order to reduce this probability and achieve good soundness. In this section we describe 3-move interactive proof systems in which the verifier picks a uniformly random challenge from a much larger space. This means a cheating prover has small probability of guessing the verifier's challenge in advance. The size of the challenge space is made big enough so that a single execution of the protocol suffice to convince the verifier. This kind of interactive proof systems often goes under the name of Σ-protocols.

2.1   Definitions

Σ-protocols are 3-move interactive proof systems that allow a prover to convince a verifier about the validity of a statement. The prover sends an initial message a to the verifier, the verifier replies with a random challenge x, and the prover answers with a final response z. The verifier finally checks the transcript (a, x, z) and decides whether to accept or reject the statement.

A Σ-protocol is *public coin*, which means that the verifier picks the challenge x uniformly at random and independently of the message sent by the prover.

Definition 1 (Σ-protocol). *Let R be a polynomial time decidable binary relation and let L_R be the language of statements u for which there exists a witness w such that $(u, w) \in R$. A Σ-protocol for a relation R is a tuple $(\mathcal{P}, \mathcal{V})$ of probabilistic polynomial time interactive algorithms such that*

- $a \leftarrow \mathcal{P}(u, w)$: *given a statement u and a witness w such that $(u, w) \in R$, the prover computes initial message a and sends it to the verifier.*
- $x \leftarrow S$: *the verifier picks a uniformly random challenge x from a large set S and sends it to the prover.*
- $z \leftarrow \mathcal{P}(x)$: *given challenge x the prover computes a response z and sends it to the verifier.*
- $1/0 \leftarrow \mathcal{V}(u, (a, x, z))$: *the verifier checks the transcript (a, x, z) and returns 1 if she accepts the argument and 0 if she rejects it.*

A pair of efficient algorithms $(\mathcal{P}, \mathcal{V})$ is a Σ-protocol if is complete, special sound and special honest verifier zero-knowledge in the sense of the following definitions.

Completeness guarantees that if both prover and verifier are honest, then the verifier accepts when $u \in L_R$ and the prover knows the corresponding witness.

Definition 2 (Completeness). *$(\mathcal{P}, \mathcal{V})$ is computationally complete if for all probabilistic polynomial time adversaries $\mathcal{A}$*

$$\Pr\left[(u, w) \leftarrow \mathcal{A}(1^\lambda); a \leftarrow \mathcal{P}(u, w); x \leftarrow S; z \leftarrow \mathcal{P}(x) : \mathcal{V}(u, (a, x, z)) = 1\right] \approx 1,$$

where $\mathcal{A}$ outputs $(u, w) \in R$.

If this holds for unbounded adversaries $\mathcal{A}$, we say that $(\mathcal{P}, \mathcal{V})$ is statistically complete. If the probability above is also exactly equal to 1 we says that $(\mathcal{P}, \mathcal{V})$ is perfectly complete.

A Σ-protocol is a form of proof of knowledge, in the sense that a prover should be able to answer random challenges only if she *knows* a witness for a statement u. This is formalised via *special soundness* which says that given two accepting transcripts corresponding to two distinct challenges and the same initial message it is possible to extract a witness for the statement.

Definition 3 (Special Soundness). *$(\mathcal{P}, \mathcal{V})$ is computationally special sound if there exists an efficient extractor algorithm $\mathcal{E}$ such that for all probabilistic polynomial time adversaries $\mathcal{A}$*

$$\Pr\left[\begin{array}{l}(u, a, x, z, x', z') \leftarrow \mathcal{A}(1^\lambda); w \leftarrow \mathcal{E}(a, x, z, x', z'): \\ \mathcal{V}(u, (a, x, z)) = 0 \text{ or } \mathcal{V}(u, (a, x', z')) = 0 \text{ or } (u, w) \in R\end{array}\right] \approx 1.$$

If this holds for unbounded adversaries $\mathcal{A}$, we say that $(\mathcal{P}, \mathcal{V})$ is statistically special sound. If the probability above is also exactly equal to 1 we says that $(\mathcal{P}, \mathcal{V})$ is perfectly special sound.

A Σ-protocol is zero-knowledge if it does not leak information about the witness beyond the membership of u in the language L_R. The definition of zero-knowledge follows the simulation paradigm, which says that if it is possible to simulate an accepting transcript without knowing a witness, then the protocol is not leaking information about the witness. At first, this might seem in contradiction with the soundness requirement, which says that is should be hard to produce an accepting transcript without knowing a witness. However, the simulator is not taking part in the real execution of the protocol, and therefore we can assume it to be less restricted than the parties directly involved in the protocol. We can for example allow the simulator to produce messages forming the transcript in a different order than it happens during the real interaction. In case of special honest verifier zero-knowledge, we restrict the verifier to be a public coin verifier that picks random challenges independently from the messages she receives from the prover. In this setting the simulator is given the verifier's challenge x and has to simulate a conversation between prover and verifier without knowing a witness.

Definition 4 (Special Honest Verifier Zero-Knowledge). *A public coin argument* $(\mathcal{P}, \mathcal{V})$ *is computationally special honest verifier zero-knowledge (SHVZK) if there exists a probabilistic polynomial time simulator $\mathcal{S}$ such that for all probabilistic polynomial time stateful adversaries $\mathcal{A}$*

$$\Pr\left[(u, w, x) \leftarrow \mathcal{A}(1^\lambda); a \leftarrow \mathcal{P}(u, w); z \leftarrow \mathcal{P}(x) : \mathcal{A}(a, x, z) = 1\right]$$

$$\approx \Pr\left[(u, w, x) \leftarrow \mathcal{A}(1^\lambda); (a, z) \leftarrow \mathcal{S}(u, x) : \mathcal{A}(a, x, z) = 1\right]$$

If this holds for unbounded adversaries $\mathcal{A}$, we say that $(\mathcal{P}, \mathcal{V})$ is statistically special honest verifier zero-knowledge. If the probabilities above are also exactly equal we says that $(\mathcal{P}, \mathcal{V})$ is perfectly special honest verifier zero-knowledge.

The above definition of zero-knowledge might not be strong enough for many applications since it is assuming a semi-honest verifier that does not deviate from the protocol. However, there are efficient transformations [DGOW95, Dam00, GMY06] for SHVZK Σ-protocols to obtain full zero-knowledge against malicious verifiers with a small overhead in communication and computation.

2.2 Σ-Protocol for the Equivalence of Discrete Logarithm

Consider two group elements $s, t \in \mathbb{G}$, such that they share the same discrete logarithm with respect to two different generators $g, h \in \mathbb{G}$. We now give a simple Σ-protocol for the equality of discrete logarithms of s and t. More precisely we describe a Σ-protocol for the following relation

$$R = \{(u, w) | u = (\mathbb{G}, p, g, h, s, t); g, h, s, t \in \mathbb{G}; s = g^w; t = h^w\}$$

where $\mathbb{G}$ is a group of prime order p with $|p| = \lambda$.

The prover starts by picking a random field element r from $\mathbb{Z}_p$ and then computes two *blinding* elements $a = g^r, b = h^r$ and sends them to the verifier. The verifier picks a uniformly random challenge $x \leftarrow \mathbb{Z}_p$ and sends it back to the prover. The prover computes the field element $z = wx + r$ and sends it to the verifier. The verifier checks if both of the following verification equations hold

$$g^z = s^x a \qquad\qquad h^z = t^x b$$

in which case accept the proof and otherwise rejects it. The argument is summarised in Fig. 2.

The idea behind the protocol is that if the prover knows the discrete logarithm of s and t, then she can compute the discrete logarithm of s^x and t^x with respect to base g and h. Moreover, if a and b have the same discrete logarithm, then so will $s^x a$ and $t^x b$.

The protocol above is clearly complete. If both the prover and the verifier are honest, the verifier will always accept statements in the language.

For special soundness consider two accepting transcripts (a, b, x, z) and (a, b, x', z') for distinct challenges x, x' and the same initial message (a, b). Dividing the verification equation $g^z = s^x a$ by $g^{z'} = s^{x'} a$ we obtain $g^{z-z'} = s^{x-x'}$.

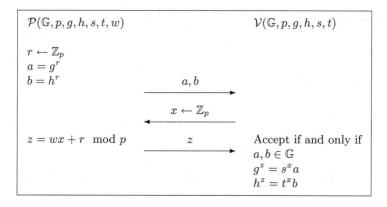

Fig. 2. Σ-protocol for equivalence of discrete logarithm.

Therefore we have that the discrete logarithm of s with respect to g is $w = \frac{z-z'}{x-x'}$ mod p. Similar calculations on the other verification equations tells us that the discrete logarithm of t with respect to base h is w too.

For SHVZK we need to show a simulator that given a uniformly random challenge x as input can produce a transcript indistinguishable from a real transcript. The simulator can pick a uniformly random field element z and compute the first message as $a = g^z s^{-x}$ and $b = h^z t^{-x}$. Note that x and z have the same distribution as in the real execution of the protocol and that a, b are uniquely determined given x and z. Therefore the transcript (a, b, x, z) output by the simulator has the same distribution as an honestly generated transcript.

2.3 Commitment Schemes

Commitment schemes are key primitives for the construction of many cryptographic protocols. They allow a sender to create a commitment to a secret value. The sender may later decide to open the commitment and reveal the value in a verifiable manner. We require two main properties to commitment schemes:

- *Hiding:* a commitment should not reveal the secret value it contains.
- *Binding:* the sender should not be able to open the commitment to a different value.

Non-interactive commitments are a particularly useful type of commitment scheme, for which both committing and verifying the opening of a commitment can be done locally, without any interaction with other parties.

Formally, a non-interactive commitment scheme is a pair of probabilistic polynomial time algorithms (Gen, Com). The setup algorithm $ck \leftarrow \text{Gen}(1^\lambda)$ generates a commitment key ck. The commitment key specifies a message space $\mathcal{M}_{ck}$, a randomness space R_{ck} and a commitment space $\mathcal{C}_{ck}$. The commitment algorithm combined with the commitment key specifies a function $\text{Com}_{ck} : \mathcal{M}_{ck} \times R_{ck} \rightarrow \mathcal{C}_{ck}$. Given a message $m \in \mathcal{M}_{ck}$ the sender picks uniformly at random $r \leftarrow R_{ck}$ and computes the commitment $c = \text{Com}_{ck}(m; r)$.

Definition 5 (Hiding). *A non-interactive commitment scheme* (Gen, Com) *is computationally hiding if for all probabilistic polynomial time stateful interactive adversaries* $\mathcal{A}$

$$\Pr\left[\begin{array}{l} ck \leftarrow \text{Gen}(1^\lambda); (m_0, m_1) \leftarrow \mathcal{A}(ck); b \leftarrow \{0,1\}; \\ r \leftarrow R_{ck}; c \leftarrow \text{Com}_{ck}(m_b; r) : \mathcal{A}(c) = b \end{array}\right] \approx \frac{1}{2}$$

where $\mathcal{A}$ *outputs* $m_0, m_1 \in \mathcal{M}_{ck}$. *If this holds for unbounded adversaries* $\mathcal{A}$, *we say that* (Gen, Com) *is unconditionally hiding. If the probability above is also exactly equal to* $\frac{1}{2}$, *we says that* (Gen, Com) *is perfectly hiding.*

Definition 6 (Binding). *A non-interactive commitment scheme* (Gen, Com) *is computationally binding if for all probabilistic polynomial time adversaries* $\mathcal{A}$

$$\Pr\left[\begin{array}{l} ck \leftarrow \text{Gen}(1^\lambda); (m_0, r_0, m_1, r_1) \leftarrow \mathcal{A}(ck) : \\ \text{Com}_{ck}(m_0; r_0) = \text{Com}_{ck}(m_1; r_1) \text{ and } m_0 \neq m_1 \end{array}\right] \approx 0$$

where $\mathcal{A}$ *outputs* $m_0, m_1 \in \mathcal{M}_{ck}$ *and* $r_0, r_1 \in R_{ck}$. *If this holds for unbounded adversaries* $\mathcal{A}$, *we say that* (Gen, Com) *is unconditionally binding. If the probability above is also exactly equal to 0, we says that* (Gen, Com) *is perfectly binding.*

Many examples of commitment schemes have been proposed in the literature. Two well-known examples are Pedersen [Ped91] and Elgamal [EG85] commitments, which are based on the discrete logarithm assumption. In addition to the above properties, both commitment schemes are also additively homomorphic, which means that multiplying two commitments produces a commitment to the sum of the openings. More precisely, we say a commitment scheme is additively homomorphic if for all valid keys ck the message, randomness and commitment spaces are abelian groups and for all messages $m_0, m_1 \in \mathcal{M}_{ck}$ and randomness $r_0, r_1 \in R_{ck}$ we have

$$\text{Com}_{ck}(m_0; r_0) \cdot \text{Com}_{ck}(m_1; r_1) = \text{Com}_{ck}(m_0 + m_1; r_0 + r_1).$$

Pedersen Commitments. Consider a group $\mathbb{G}$ of prime order p and let g, h be random generators of the group. Message and randomnesses are in $\mathbb{Z}_p$ and the commitment space is the group $\mathbb{G}$. The sender commits to an element $m \in \mathbb{Z}_p$ by picking a uniformly random r from $\mathbb{Z}_p$ and computing $c = g^m h^r$. The scheme is perfectly hiding and computationally binding, assuming that the discrete logarithm assumption holds (Fig. 3).

ElGamal Commitments. The commitment key, the message space and the randomness space are defined as for Pedersen commitments. The commitment space is $\mathbb{G} \times \mathbb{G}$. Commitments are generated by picking a random $r \leftarrow \mathbb{Z}_p$ and computing $(g^r, g^m h^r)$. The ElGamal commitment scheme is perfectly binding and computationally hiding given that the decision Diffie-Hellman assumption holds (Fig. 4).

$\mathsf{Gen}(1^\lambda) \to ck$	$\mathsf{Com}_{ck}(m) \to c$
$\cdot\ p \leftarrow \{0,1\}^\lambda$ s.t. p is prime	$\cdot$ If $m \notin \mathbb{Z}_p \to \bot$
$\cdot\ \mathbb{G}$ of order p	$\cdot\ r \leftarrow \mathbb{Z}_q$
$\cdot\ h \leftarrow \mathbb{G}$ s.t. $\langle h \rangle = \mathbb{G}$	$\cdot\ c := g^m h^r$
$\cdot\ g = h^x$ for $x \leftarrow \mathbb{Z}_p$	
$\cdot\ ck := (\mathbb{G}, p, g, h)$	

Fig. 3. Pedersen commitment.

$\mathsf{Gen}(1^\lambda) \to ck$	$\mathsf{Com}_{ck}(m) \to c$
$\cdot\ p \leftarrow \{0,1\}^\lambda$ s.t. p is prime	$\cdot$ If $m \notin \mathbb{Z}_p \to \bot$
$\cdot\ \mathbb{G}$ of order p	$\cdot\ r \leftarrow \mathbb{Z}_q$
$\cdot\ h \leftarrow \mathbb{G}$ s.t. $\langle h \rangle = \mathbb{G}$	$\cdot\ c := (g^r, g^m h^r)$
$\cdot\ g = h^x$ for $x \leftarrow \mathbb{Z}_p$	
$\cdot\ ck := (\mathbb{G}, p, g, h)$	

Fig. 4. ElGamal commitment.

After seeing the above examples one might wish to build a commitment scheme that achieves both hiding and binding properties unconditionally. Unfortunately, this is not achievable. The reason is that an unbounded adversary $\mathcal{A}$ is always able to compute an opening to a commitment. If the scheme is such that there exists only one possible opening, then the scheme cannot be hiding. On the other hand, if there are several distinct openings to a commitment then an unbounded adversary can compute all of them and break the binding property.

2.4   Two Useful Examples of Σ-Protocols

Commitment schemes and Σ-protocols are closely related. It is possible in fact to construct commitment schemes out of Σ-protocols for hard relations as described in [Dam90]. It is also convenient to rethink the interaction of Σ-protocols in terms of committing and opening. A general way to build Σ-protocols is to let the prover commit to some values in the first move, and to open some commitments depending on the challenge in the last move.

We try to illustrate this general approach by showing two examples of Σ-protocols. The first one is a protocol for showing that a commitment opens to 0. The second protocol is for proving that a commitment opens to the product of the openings of two other commitments.

Σ_{zero}. Consider a commitment A opening to 0 to be part of the statement. The prover computes a random commitment $B = \mathsf{Com}_{ck}(0; s)$ and sends it to the verifier, which answer with a random challenge x. The prover then sends opening information z to the verifier, which checks the commitment $A^x B$ opens to 0 using randomness z. The full description of the protocol is in Fig. 5.

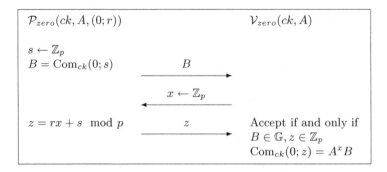

Fig. 5. Σ-protocol for opening a commitment to 0.

This protocol could be used also to prove equality of openings of commitments. Given two commitments A_1 and A_2 it suffices to use Σ_{zero} to show that $A_1 A_2^{-1}$ opens to zero. In the protocol we only require the commitment scheme to be homomorphic, therefore it can be instantiated with both Pedersen and ElGamal commitments. In both cases we get perfect completeness, perfect soundness and perfect special honest verifier zero-knowledge.

Σ_{prod}. For this protocol we focus on the case of Pedersen commitments and refer to [CD98] for the more general case. Let A, B, C be commitments opening to a, b and ab, respectively. Consider a commitment key $ck = (\mathbb{G}, p, g, h)$. The main idea is for the prover to prove knowledge of opening of A and B and showing that C opens to the same value of A when replacing g with B in the commitment key. Let $ck' = (\mathbb{G}, p, B, h)$ be the modified key, thus

$$C = \text{Com}_{ck}(ab; r_c) = g^{ab} h^{r_c} = B^a h^{r_c - ar_b} = \text{Com}_{ck'}(a; r_c - ar_b)$$

The full description of the protocol is in Fig. 6. The protocol, Σ_{prod} achieves perfect completeness, perfect SHVZK and computational special soundness.

2.5   Composition of Σ-Protocols

One of the characteristics that makes Σ-protocols very appealing is that it is easy to combine several of them together to obtain a Σ-protocol for compound relations. This allows a very modular design of complex Σ-protocols starting from simple building blocks.

For example, Σ-protocols are closed under parallel composition, therefore we can combine many Σ-protocols together using a unique verifier's challenge to prove that many statements hold simultaneously. Completeness, special soundness and SHVZK of the combined protocol are directly implied by the respective properties of the singular protocols. In particular for special soundness and SHVZK, we can define an extractor and a simulator respectively running in parallel the extractors and simulators of the constituent Σ-protocols on the same challenge.

$\mathcal{P}_{prod}(ck, A, (a; r_a), B, (b; r_b), C, (ab; r_c))$ $\qquad\qquad\qquad$ $\mathcal{V}_{prod}(ck, A, B, C)$

$d, e, s, s', t \leftarrow \mathbb{Z}_p$
$ck' := (\mathbb{G}, p, B, h)$
$D = \text{Com}_{ck}(d; s)$
$D' = \text{Com}_{ck'}(d; s')$
$E = \text{Com}_{ck}(e; t)$

$\xrightarrow{\qquad D, D', E \qquad}$

$\xleftarrow{\qquad x \leftarrow \mathbb{Z}_p \qquad}$

$f_1 = ax + d \mod p$
$z_1 = r_a x + s \mod p$
$f_2 = bx + e \mod p$
$z_2 = r_b x + t \mod p$
$z_3 = (r_c - ar_b)x + s' \mod p$

Accept if and only if

$\xrightarrow{\quad f_1, f_2, z_1, z_2, z_3 \quad}$ $\quad$ $D, D', E \in \mathbb{G}$
$f_1, f_2, z_1, z_2, z_3 \in \mathbb{Z}_p$
$\text{Com}_{ck}(f_1; z_1) = A^x D$
$\text{Com}_{ck}(f_2; z_2) = B^x E$
$\text{Com}_{ck'}(f_1; z_3) = C^x D'$

Fig. 6. Σ-protocol for the product of openings of Pedersen commitments.

Given two protocols Σ_0 and Σ_1 for relations R_0 and R_1, it is possible to combine them to show that one statement out of u_0, u_1 holds, without disclosing which one. This transformation was first introduced in [CDS94] and could be easily extended to prove the validity of one statement out of many. The idea is to allow prover $\mathcal{P}_{OR}$ to *simulate* the transcript for at most one of the two statements. Without loss in generality, consider a prover knowing a witness w_0 for u_0. Then the prover can pick a random challenge x_1 and simulate an accepting transcript (a_1, x_1, z_1) for u_1 by invoking simulator $\mathcal{S}_1$ for Σ_1. In the first move the prover sends to the verifier a_0 generated as in Σ_0 and simulated a_1. Upon receiving a challenge x form the verifier, the prover computes $x_0 = x \oplus x_1$. The prover computes responses z_0 using challenge x_0 and sends z_0, z_1, x_0, x_1 to the verifier. Then, the verifier checks that $x = x_0 \oplus x_1$ and accepts if both transcripts (a_0, x_0, z_0) and (a_1, x_1, z_1) are accepting. As above, completeness special soundness and SHVZK of the combined protocol are directly implied by the respective properties of the individual protocols. In particular for SHVZK, the simulator $\mathcal{S}_{OR}$ receives a challenge x as input, picks a random x_1 and computes x_0 such that $x = x_0 \oplus x_1$. Then, $\mathcal{S}_{OR}$ invokes $\mathcal{S}_0$ and $\mathcal{S}_1$ respectively on x_0 and x_1. The simulated transcript has the same distribution as a real transcript.

2.6 Arithmetic Circuits

To illustrate the capabilities of Σ-protocols, we show how to build a protocol for a more general relation combining several simpler protocols. For example using many parallel executions of the zero and product Σ-protocols in Sect. 2.4 we can provide Σ-protocols for the satisfiability of arithmetic circuits. To prove

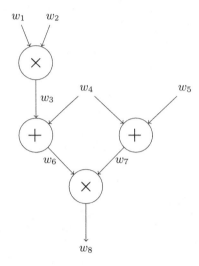

Fig. 7. Example of an arithmetic circuit.

satisfiability of an arithmetic circuit the prover has to commit to all the w_i corresponding to wire assignments and then prove consistency of inputs and outputs of addition gates using Σ_{zero} and multiplication gates using Σ_{prod}.

Consider for instance a very simple arithmetic circuit over $\mathbb{Z}_p$ consisting of fan-in-2 addition and multiplication gates, as the one pictured in Fig. 7. The prover computes commitments $W_i = \mathrm{Com}_{ck}(w_i, r_i)$ for random r_i and then shows that both commitments $W_1 \cdot W_2 \cdot W_3^{-1}$ and $W_4 \cdot W_5 \cdot W_7^{-1}$ open to 0 and that W_3 and W_8 open to $w_1 \cdot w_2$ and $w_6 \cdot w_7$, respectively.

For an arithmetic circuits with N addition and multiplication gates we need to combine N parallel executions of Σ_{zero} and Σ_{prod}. The resulting communication amounts to $O(N)$ commitments and field elements.

2.7   Batching

When proving the same relation many times, there are more efficient solutions than executing many Σ-protocols in parallel. As a simple example, if we have several commitments $A_1, \ldots, A_n$ and want to prove all of them contain zero, we can use the protocol in Fig. 8. The underlying idea is to use the homomorphic property to build a committed degree n polynomial in the challenge x, with the committed values as coefficients. This committed polynomial has negligible probability of evaluating to 0 in the random challenge x unless it is the zero polynomial, i.e., all the committed values are 0. Using this protocol we only communicate a constant number of elements to prove a statement of size n elements is true.

Another way to batch arguments together is to commit to many values at once. We can build commitments to vectors rather than single elements and

$\mathcal{P}_{batch}(ck, A_1, \ldots, A_n, r_1, \ldots, r_n)$ $\qquad\qquad$ $\mathcal{V}_{batch}(ck, A_1, \ldots, A_n)$

$s \leftarrow \mathbb{Z}_p$
$B = \mathrm{Com}_{ck}(0; s)$ $\qquad\qquad\qquad B \qquad\longrightarrow$

$\qquad\qquad\qquad\qquad x \leftarrow \mathbb{Z}_p$
$\qquad\qquad\qquad\longleftarrow$

$z = s + \sum_{i=1}^{n} r_i x^i \mod p$ $\qquad\qquad z \qquad\longrightarrow$ Accept if and only if
$\qquad\qquad\qquad\qquad\qquad\qquad\qquad\qquad B \in \mathbb{G}, z \in \mathbb{Z}_p$
$\qquad\qquad\qquad\qquad\qquad\qquad\qquad\qquad \mathrm{Com}_{ck}(0; z) = B \prod_{i=1}^{n} A_i^{x^i}$

Fig. 8. Batch Σ-protocol for opening of many commitments to 0.

$\mathrm{Gen}(1^\lambda) \to ck$	$\mathrm{Com}_{ck}(m) \to c$
$\cdot\ p \leftarrow \{0,1\}^\lambda$ s.t. p is prime	$\cdot$ If $m \notin \mathbb{Z}_p^n \to \perp$
$\cdot\ \mathbb{G}$ of order p	$\cdot\ m = (m_1, \ldots, m_n)$
$\cdot\ h \leftarrow \mathbb{G}$ s.t. $\langle h \rangle = \mathbb{G}$	$\cdot\ r \leftarrow \mathbb{Z}_q$
$\cdot\ (x_1, \ldots, x_n) \leftarrow \mathbb{Z}_p^n$	$\cdot\ c := h^r \prod_{i=1}^{n} g_i^{m_i}$
$\cdot\ g_i = h^{x_i}$ for $i \in [n]$	
$\cdot\ ck := (\mathbb{G}, p, h, g_1, \ldots, g_n)$	

Fig. 9. Pedersen commitment for vectors of length n.

extend the previous techniques to vector commitments. We can for instance extend Pedersen commitments to allow openings in $\mathbb{Z}_p^n$, as described in Fig. 9. This extension preserves the same properties of the standard Pedersen commitment scheme but committing to n elements only requires sending a single group element.

Groth [Gro09] used batching techniques and vector commitments together to give zero-knowledge arguments for linear algebra relations over vectors. These techniques make it possible to give arguments for the satisfiability of arithmetic circuits with an overall communication of $O(\sqrt{N})$ group and field elements. So arithmetic circuit satisfiability and many other relevant relations can be proved with sublinear communication.

3   Non-interactive Zero-Knowledge Proofs

In interactive zero knowledge proofs, the prover and the verifier interact over multiple rounds, and can vary their responses depending on the messages that they have received so far. By contrast, non-interactive zero knowledge proofs consist of a single message sent by the prover to the verifier. Non-interactive proofs are typically more difficult to construct than interactive proofs, and often rely on stronger assumptions. However, they are useful in settings where interaction cannot or should not take place, such as digital signatures and encryption schemes.

Non-interactive zero-knowledge proofs were introduced by Blum et al. [BFM88], who produced a proof for the 3-colourability of graphs under a number-theoretic assumption.

3.1 Formal Definitions

A non-interactive proof system for a relation R consists of three probabilistic polynomial time algorithms. There are the common reference string generator Gen, the prover $\mathcal{P}$, and the verifier $\mathcal{V}$. The common reference string generator takes the security parameter as input and produces a common reference string σ. The prover takes (σ, x, w) as input and produces a proof π. The verifier takes (σ, x, π) as input and outputs 1 if accepting the proof as valid, and 0 if rejecting the proof.

We call $(\text{Gen}, \mathcal{P}, \mathcal{V})$ a non-interactive proof system for R if it has the completeness and perfect soundness properties to be defined below. If $(\text{Gen}, \mathcal{P}, \mathcal{V})$ has completeness and computational soundness, we call it a non-interactive argument system.

Completeness. As with interactive proofs, completeness states that a prover should be able to prove a true statement.

Definition 7 (Completeness). *We say the proof system is perfectly complete if for all $(u, w) \in R$*

$$\Pr\left[\sigma \leftarrow \text{Gen}(1^\lambda); \pi \leftarrow \mathcal{P}(\sigma, u, w) \; : \; \mathcal{V}(\sigma, u, \pi) = 1\right] = 1.$$

For statistical completeness, the definition is changed so that the probability is close 1 when an unbounded adversary outputs (u, w) after seeing σ. For computational completeness, we restrict to probabilistic polynomial time adversaries $\mathcal{A}$ outputting (u, w), and change the definition so that the probability close to 1.

Soundness. Soundness states that a cheating prover should not be able to prove a false statement; even when deviating from the protocol.

Definition 8 (Soundness). *We say the proof system has (adaptive) perfect soundness if for all adversaries $\mathcal{A}$*

$$\Pr\left[\sigma \leftarrow \text{Gen}(1^\lambda); (u, \pi) \leftarrow \mathcal{A}(\sigma, u) \; : \; u \notin L_R \text{ and } \mathcal{V}(\sigma, u, \pi) = 1\right] = 0.$$

The definition can be relaxed to statistical soundness by changing the definition such that the probability is close from 1 instead of requiring exact equality. For computational soundness, we restrict to probabilistic polynomial time adversaries $\mathcal{A}$, and change the definition so that the probability is close 1.

A weaker definition is that of *non-adaptive* soundness. Here the adversary $\mathcal{A}$ is given a false statement $u \notin L_R$ independently of the common reference string σ. Adaptively sound proofs are harder to construct, but are more versatile since in many cases the false statement could be chosen after seeing the common reference string. Adaptively sound proofs also have the advantage that the same common reference string can be reused to prove different statements u from the same language.

Proof of Knowledge. A non-interactive proof system is a proof of knowledge if it is possible to recover the witness w from the proof. More formally, we say that a non-interactive proof system is a proof of knowledge if there exists a probabilistic polynomial time knowledge extractor $E = (E_1, E_2)$ such that E_1 produces a correctly generated common reference string with extraction key ξ, which E_2 uses to extract a valid witness from a proof.

Definition 9 (Knowledge Extraction). *We say the proof system has perfect knowledge extraction if for all adversaries $\mathcal{A}$*

$$\Pr\left[\sigma \leftarrow \mathrm{Gen}(1^\lambda) \ : \ \mathcal{A}(\sigma) = 1\right] \ = \ \Pr\left[(\sigma, \xi) \leftarrow \mathcal{E}_1(1^\lambda) \ : \ \mathcal{A}(\sigma) = 1\right]$$

and

$$\Pr\left[(\sigma, \xi) \leftarrow E_1(1^\lambda); (u, \pi) \leftarrow \mathcal{A}(\sigma); w \leftarrow E_2(\sigma, \xi, u, \pi) \ : \ (u, w) \in R \,\text{if}\, V(\sigma, u, \pi) = 1\right] = 1.$$

For statistical knowledge extraction, the definition is changed so that the first two probabilities are close to each other, and the third is close to 1. For the computational version, we restrict to probabilistic polynomial time adversaries $\mathcal{A}$.

Perfect knowledge extraction implies perfect soundness. This is because if a valid proof π is given for statement u, we can extract a witness w with $(u, w) \in R$, so in particular, $x \in L_R$.

Zero-Knowledge. The zero-knowledge property ensures that a non-interactive proof reveals nothing except for the truth of the statement being proved. As with interactive zero-knowledge proofs, this is achieved using the simulation paradigm. There must be an efficient simulator for the proof, so that any information computed from a real proof could also be computed from a simulated proof. There is no witness available when simulating the proof, so no information about the witness is leaked. However, the simulator must have access to more than just the statement u and a common reference string σ when simulating a proof. Otherwise, anybody would be able to create a convincing proof, even without the witness! To this end, the simulator is allowed to produce the common reference string for itself, along with some extra information τ, the 'simulation trapdoor'. This trapdoor is used by the simulator, but is unavailable to an adversary against the protocol.

Definition 10 (Zero-Knowledge). *We call* $(\mathrm{Gen}, \mathcal{P}, \mathcal{V})$ *an NIZK proof for R with perfect zero-knowledge if there exists a simulator* $\mathcal{S} = (\mathcal{S}_1, \mathcal{S}_2)$ *such that for all adversaries* $\mathcal{A}$

$$\Pr\left[\sigma \leftarrow \mathrm{Gen}(1^\lambda); (u, w) \leftarrow \mathcal{A}(\sigma); \pi \leftarrow \mathcal{P}(\sigma, u, w) \; : \; \mathcal{A}(\sigma, \pi) = 0\right]$$

$$= \Pr\left[(\sigma, \tau) \leftarrow \mathcal{S}_1(1^\lambda); (u, w) \leftarrow \mathcal{A}(\sigma); \pi \leftarrow \mathcal{S}_2(\sigma, \tau, u) \; : \; \mathcal{A}(\sigma, \pi) = 0\right]$$

For statistical zero-knowledge, the definition is changed so that the probabilities are close to each other. For computational zero-knowledge, we restrict to probabilistic polynomial time adversaries $\mathcal{A}$, *and change the definition so that the probabilities are close to each other.*

3.2   The Common Reference String

The definitions of an NIZK proof system require a common reference string to be available to the prover and verifier. It would be desirable to try and remove this requirement and obtain a proof system where the prover sends a single message to the verifier, with no setup. Unfortunately, it can be shown that any such proof system can only be used for languages that are easy to decide [Gol01] so the verifier does not need the prover to be convinced that $u \in L_R$. In order to construct NIZK proof systems for non-trivial languages, a common reference string or some other type of assistance is necessary.

A common reference string can be made up of uniformly random bits. In this case, it is often referred to as a common random string. However, in many NIZK proof systems, a more structured common reference string is generated according to a different probability distribution.

The common reference string can be honestly generated by a trusted party. Another solution is to use the multi-string model of Groth and Ostrovsky [GO14], where random strings are produced by several authorities, and a majority of strings are assumed to be honestly generated. This removes the need to completely trust any single party. Secure multi-party computation can also be used to ensure that the common reference string is generated correctly.

3.3   Public and Private Verifiability

In the original definitions, the verification algorithm takes σ, u and π as input. This means that the proof can be verified by anybody. One variation is a designated-verifier proof system. In this case, the setup algorithm Gen outputs a verifier key ω as well as the common reference string, and the verification algorithm takes ω, u and π as input. Now, proofs can only be privately verified. Public verifiability corresponds to the special case where $\omega = \sigma$.

Designated-verifier non-interactive proof systems are generally easier to construct, and can be more efficient than publicly verifiable proofs. This is because unlike publicly verifiable proofs, the verifier has ω, which is not available to the prover. Designated verifier proofs can only be used to convince somebody in posession of ω. This is in contrast with publicly-verifiable proofs, where a single proof can be copied and sent to other recipients, and suffices to convince everybody.

Private verifiability is sufficient for some applications, such as CCA-secure encryption schemes including the Cramer-Shoup cryptosystem. However, public-verifiability is necessary for many other applications such as signatures, and universally-verifiable voting systems.

3.4   The Fiat-Shamir Heuristic

The Fiat-Shamir heuristic is a method for converting public coin interactive zero-knowledge arguments into NIZK proofs. The first step is to include the description of a cryptographic hash function H in the common reference string. The prover computes their messages as they would in the interactive proof, but replaces the verifier's messages with a hash of the protocol transcript up to that point (Fig. 10).

The method yields highly efficient NIZK arguments in practice. By modelling the hash function as a truly random function, or 'random oracle', it is possible argue that the resulting arguments are sound [BR93]. Further, in the random oracle model, even if the initial interactive proof only has honest verifier zero-knowledge, the resulting argument will have full zero-knowledge.

However, in reality, hash functions are deterministic. It has been shown [CGH00, GK03] that there are interactive protocols which have soundness when H is modelled as a truly random function, but which are insecure for *any* choice of hash function H. Despite this theoretical problem, the Fiat-Shamir heuristic is still used to produce arguments for practical applications, where the hope is that it does give sound arguments for "natural" problems.

3.5   The Hidden Bits Model

In the hidden bits model, described in [FLS99], the prover uses the common reference string in a particular way that produces some secret bits known only to the prover. She can then choose to reveal individual bits to the verifier in a verifiable manner.

One way the hidden bits model can be implemented is as follows [FLS99, BY96, Gro10a]: The prover chooses a public key for an encryption scheme. She then interprets the common reference string as a sequence of ciphertexts. Since only she knows the secret decryption key, only she knows the corresponding plaintexts. If the encryption scheme allows revealing a plaintext in a verifiable manner, she can now selectively disclose some plaintexts and let other plaintexts remain secret.

A structured hidden bit-string is often more useful than a uniformly random string. In order to create a structured hidden bit-string the prover may discard or reveal certain bits in order to obtain, with good probability, a string with a particular structure. As a simple example, if the prover orders the bits in pairs

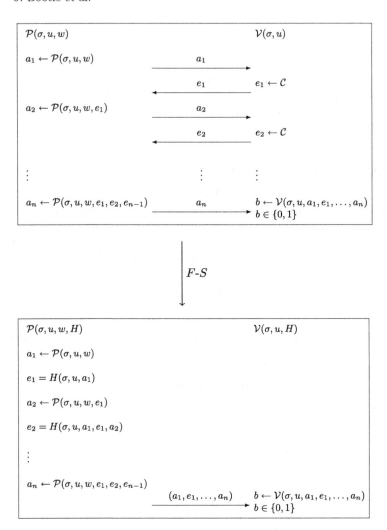

Fig. 10. The Fiat-Shamir Heuristic. The first box shows an interactive zero knowledge proof. The second box shows the non-interactive zero knowledge proof resulting from applying the Fiat-Shamir transformation.

and reveals the bits in all pairs of the form '00' or '11', then the verifier knows that statistically speaking the remaining hidden bits are structured such that almost all pairs are '01' or '10'.

One technique to use a structured hidden bit string [KP98] is to group bits in pairs, and reveal at most one bit from each pair. We refer to '11' and '00' as 'R' for random, and '10' and '01' as 'W' for wildcard. From 'W', the prover can choose whether to reveal a '0' or a '1'. From an 'R' pair, the prover has no choice in what to reveal since both bits are the same. Using this, and more sophisticated structures, it is possible to set up equations the revealed bits should satisfy. When the statement is true, the structure allows the prover to reveal bits such that all equations are satisfied. When the statement is false, no choice of bits to reveal will satisfy all equations. We will now give a simple example to provide some intuition how this can work.

Example. Consider the formulae

$$x_1 \vee x_2 = 1, \qquad (\neg x_1) \vee x_3 = 1, \qquad (\neg x_2) \vee (\neg x_3) = 1$$

This is a very simple instance of the satisfiability problem and will form the statement for an NIZK proof. Note that each variable and its negation appear exactly once. We will consider blocks of four bits, and assume that every block has exactly one 'W'; we only use the blocks 'WR' and 'RW'. A proof of satisfiability for these formulae will require one block for each variable, 3 blocks in this case.

The idea behind the proof is as follows. For each variable x_i, exactly one of the literals x_i or $\neg x_i$ is equal to 1. This will be assigned to the 'W' part of the block, while the other will be assigned the 'R' part of the block. This means that the prover can choose whether to reveal a '0' or '1' for the true value, which will be the key to completeness, but has no choice about which bit to reveal for the false value, which will help to enforce soundness.

The assignment $x_1 = 1, x_2 = 0, x_3 = 1$ is a solution to the satisfiability problem. This is the witness for the proof.

Suppose for example that the prover receives hidden bits in blocks 'WR', 'WR', 'RW'. Variables are assigned to blocks as follows.

$$\begin{matrix} \text{W} & \text{R} & \text{W} & \text{R} & \text{R} & \text{W} \\ x_1 & \neg x_1 & \neg x_2 & x_2 & \neg x_3 & x_3 \end{matrix}$$

Now, the prover reveals one bit from each pair. For the false values, the prover is forced to reveal a particular bit, and randomly chooses between the first and the second bit from the pair. For the true values, the prover chooses whether to reveal a '0' or a '1' in order to make each formula from the statement have odd parity. In this example, the prover could reveal bits as follows.

$$\begin{matrix} \text{W} & \text{R} & \text{W} & \text{R} & \text{R} & \text{W} \\ x_1 & \neg x_1 & \neg x_2 & x_2 & \neg x_3 & x_3 \\ 1? & ?1 & 1? & 0? & ?1 & 0? \end{matrix}$$

The verifier now checks that the formulae are satisfied when the revealed bits are substituted for each variable. The prover can always reveal bits consistent with the formulae, because at least one 'W' has been assigned to each formula.

The proof does not give away any information about the witness, because the pairs such as '1?' that the verifier sees can originate from several different bit-strings and possible witnesses.

In this example, the statement was true. But to argue soundness, let us consider what would happen for an unsatisfiable set of formulae. Then no matter which assignment the prover chooses, there is at least one formulae where all the variables have been assigned an 'R' pair. Now for each pair in this formulae the prover has only one choice of bit to reveal and there is 50 % chance of the revealed bits having even parity.

In the example shown above, it is very easy to work out a witness. For more complicated satisfiability problems it is possible to design a similar proof where, if there is no solution, then a large fraction of the verifier's checks will fail [KP98, Gro10a]. By increasing the size of blocks, and imposing further conditions, the prover can only succeed with negligible probability in the case where the statement is an unsatisfiable set of formulae.

3.6   Boneh-Goh-Nissim Encryption

Many public-key cryptosystems have homomorphic properties, but only recently have we seen the emergence of encryption schemes that are homomorphic with respect to both addition and multiplication. Partial progress was made by Boneh et al. [BGN05], who designed a public-key encryption scheme based on pairings, which are bilinear maps arising from the study of algebraic geometry and elliptic curves. This cryptosystem allows arbitrary additions on the encrypted plaintexts, but only allows a single multiplication.

The BGN encryption scheme, described in Fig. 11, uses a group with an element g of order n, where n is a product of two primes p and q, and an efficiently computable pairing. Let $\mathbb{G}$ be the group of order n generated by g. Let h be a random, non-trivial element of order p. The message space is chosen to be small so that it is easy to take discrete logarithms and find the message m, given the element g^{pm}. For example, we could use $\{0, 1, \ldots, t\}$ with t sufficiently small.

Let $e : \mathbb{G} \times \mathbb{G} \to \mathbb{G}_T$ be the bilinear pairing map.

The public key of the scheme is $\mathbb{G}, n, g, h$, and the secret key is p.

A message m is encrypted with randomness $r \leftarrow \mathbb{Z}_n$ as the ciphertext $c = \mathsf{Enc}(m; r) = g^m h^r$.

Decryption is performed by raising the ciphertext to the power of the secret key, p. Since h has order p, this removes the randomness from the ciphertext. We have $c^p = g^{mp} h^{rp} = g^{pm}$. Then, since the message space is small, it is easy to take discrete logarithms and recover m.

It is easy to see that the scheme is homomorphic with respect to addition:

$$\mathsf{Enc}(m_1; r_1)\mathsf{Enc}(m_2; r_2) = (g^{m_1} h^{r_1}) \cdot (g^{m_2} h^{r_2}) = g^{m_1+m_2} h^{r_1+r_2} = \mathsf{Enc}(m_1+m_2; r_1+r_2)$$

To do a multiplication of encrypted plaintexts, we apply the bilinear map to two ciphertexts. Let $e(g, g) = G$, which has order n, and let $e(h, h) = H$, which has order p. The elements $e(g, h)$ and $e(h, g)$ turn out to be powers of H by properties of the pairing map. This means that

$$e\left(g^{m_1} h^{r_1}, g^{m_2} h^{r_2}\right) = e(g, g)^{m_1 m_2} e(g, h)^{m_1 r_2} e(h, g)^{r_1 m_2} e(h, h)^{r_1 r_2} = G^{m_1 m_2} H^{r'},$$

which is an encryption of $m_1 m_2$ in $\mathbb{G}_T$ with some randomness r'.

KeyGen$(1^\lambda) \rightarrow (pk, sk)$	Enc$(pk, m) \rightarrow c$	Dec$(sk, c) \rightarrow m$
$\cdot$ $p, q \leftarrow \{0,1\}^\lambda$ s.t. p, q are prime	$\cdot$ If $m \notin \{0, \ldots, t\}$	$\cdot$ If $c \notin \mathbb{G}$ return $m = \bot$
$\cdot$ $\mathbb{G}, \mathbb{G}_T$ of order $n = pq$	$\cdot$ return $c = \bot$	$\cdot$ For $m \in \{0, 1, \ldots, t\}$
$\cdot$ $e : \mathbb{G} \times \mathbb{G} \rightarrow \mathbb{G}_T$, bilinear	$\cdot$ $r \leftarrow \mathbb{Z}_n$	$\cdot$ If $c^p = (g^p)^m$ return m
$\cdot$ $g, u \leftarrow \mathbb{G}$ s.t. $\langle g \rangle = \langle u \rangle = \mathbb{G}$	$\cdot$ Return $c = g^m h^r$	$\cdot$ Return $m = \bot$
$\cdot$ $h = u^q$		
$\cdot$ $t = \text{poly}(\lambda)$		
$\cdot$ $pk := (n, \mathbb{G}, \mathbb{G}_T, e, g, h, t)$		
$\cdot$ $sk := p$		

Fig. 11. The BGN cryptosystem.

3.7   NIZK Proof for Circuit Satisfiability

By using the homomorphic properties of the BGN cryptosystem, we can obtain a zero-knowledge proof of satisfiability for a Boolean circuit. Let $\mathcal{C}$ be a boolean circuit, with $\mathcal{W}$ wires.

The prover begins by encrypting the values of the wires for the circuit to produce $|\mathcal{W}|$ BGN ciphertexts. To show that the encrypted wire values satisfy the circuit, each wire value must be either 0 or 1, and the output of each NAND gate must be correct with respect to the two inputs. Figure 12 provides an example.

Let $c = g^m h^r$ be a ciphertext. Then m is a bit if and only if $m(m - 1) = 0$. We get an encryption of $m - 1$ by computing cg^{-1}, and then an encryption of $m(m - 1)$ by computing $e(c, cg^{-1})$, which should be an encryption of 0.

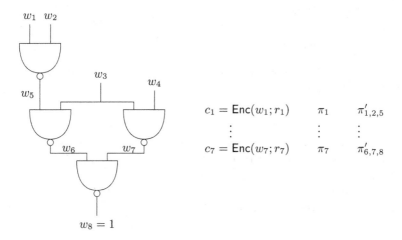

Fig. 12. A simple Boolean circuit. To demonstrate satisfiability using the BGN cryptosystem, the prover encrypts each w_i, and produces an additional group element to prove that they are bits. A further group element per gate used to prove that the wire values respect the logic gates.

The prover sends $\pi = (g^{2m-1}h^r)^r \in \mathbb{G}$ as part of the proof. The verifier then checks that $e(c, cg^{-1}) = e(\pi, h)$. As shown in [GOS12], this demonstrates that $e(c, cg^{-1})$ has order p, which means that it must be an encryption of 0. There are $|\mathcal{W}|$ extra group elements which must be added to the proof.

Finally, the prover must demonstrate that the wire values are correct with respect to each NAND gate. For values $m_1, m_2, m_3 \in \{0, 1\}$, we have that $m_1 = \neg(m_2 \wedge m_3)$ if and only if $2m_1 + m_2 + m_3 - 2 \in \{0, 1\}$. The prover uses the homomorphic property of the commitment scheme again to form an encryption of $2m_1 + m_2 + m_3 - 2$. Then, the prover uses the same technique as for the wire values to show that this value is a bit. This adds another $|\mathcal{C}|$ group elements to the proof.

The total communication of the proof is therefore $2|\mathcal{W}| + |\mathcal{C}|$ group elements. The proof has perfect completeness and perfect soundness. It has computational zero-knowledge relying on the semantic security of the BGN encryption scheme.

Boolean circuit satisfiability is an NP-complete language. Therefore, this example shows that every language in NP has a non-interactive zero-knowledge proof.

3.8 Succinct Non-interactive Arguments and Applications

Having seen a few examples of techniques for constructing NIZK proofs, it is natural to ask how efficient they can be. Micali [Mic00] introduced the notion of computationally sound proofs, which can be much smaller than the statement. Motivated by applications such as verifiable computation, there has recently been a lot of research on reducing the size of the proofs and making the verification process very efficient.

A succinct non-interactive argument (SNARG) is a non-interactive argument system that satisfies an additional succinctness property. SNARGs which are also arguments of knowledge are referred to as SNARKs.

Definition 11 (Succinctness). *A non-interactive argument system is succinct if all proofs π satisfy*

$$|\pi| = \text{poly}(\lambda)\,\text{polylog}\,(|u| + |w|)$$

The development of SNARGs has culminated in pairing-based constructions [Gro10b, Lip12, BCCT12, PHGR13, BCCT13, GGPR13, BSCTV14] which use only a constant number of group elements and are extremely efficient to verify. All arguments rely on very strong assumptions, but there is some evidence that this may be unavoidable [GW11].

Applications of Succinct Arguments. SNARGs and SNARKs are extremely useful in practical applications due to their high efficiency, and in theoretical constructions which use the succinctness property in a crucial way.

Verifiable Computation. Verifiable computation is a practical application which benefits from SNARKs. In a verifiable computation scheme, a client with a small amount of computing power would like to outsource a task involving heavy computation to a worker, who has a large amount of computing power. However, the client would like some assurance that the worker performed the task correctly and delivered the correct result. The assurance takes the form of a non-interactive proof produced by the worker to convince the client. The security of a verifiable computation scheme was first formalised by Gennaro et al. [GGP10].

If it was feasible for the client to perform a large computation to verify a non-interactive proof, then they might already have enough resources to perform the task by themselves, leaving no need to use a verifiable computation scheme in the first place. Therefore, in a verifiable computation scheme, it is essential that the computational cost of verifying a proof should be significantly lower than the cost of completing the task. SNARKs fulfill this requirement.

Pinocchio [PHGR13] is a practical implementation of a verifiable computation scheme. Using Pinnocchio, one can produce schemes to convince the client that a C code was outsourced correctly. Pinocchio takes a program written in C, computes conditions for correct execution in the quadratic arithmetic program model of [GGPR13], and outputs a SNARK which can then be used to verify computation. The system has been tested in applications such as image matching, gas simulations, and computing SHA-1 hashes to provide benchmarking data.

Composition of Arguments. The succinctness property means that SNARKs are well suited for composition. A simple example of composition of SNARKs is as follows. Given a statement and a witness, we can apply a SNARK and obtain a proof that we know a witness for the statement. We can then apply a second SNARK to the proof. This produces a proof, that we know a proof, that we know a witness for the statement! This idea is developed further in [CT10, BCCT13], where the process is repeated recursively, leading to the concept of proof-carrying data systems.

For some non-interactive argument systems, the size of a proof is bigger than the original statement. This makes composition inefficient, because the size of a proof grows after each composition. However, SNARKs are succinct, with proofs that can be much smaller than the original statement.

Composition allows for the construction of multi-party computation schemes with extremely low communication between different parties. The basic idea is that at each stage in the computation, a single party sends on the results of their computation, and attaches a proof that everything was done correctly, as well as forwarding the proofs that were sent by previous parties. The number of proofs grows at each step in the computation. As soon as the size of the message passes a certain point, a SNARK is applied, giving a proof that the party has seen all of the previous proofs. This proof is much shorter than the message that would have been sent, due to the succinctness of SNARKs. Further, by applying composition cleverly, [BCCT13] constructs a non-interactive argument system where the size of the CRS does not depend on the size of the statement to be proved.

3.9   Efficiency

We compare the efficiency of some different NIZK proofs and arguments for circuit satisfiability.

NIZK Proofs. By definition, NIZK proofs have perfect or statistical soundness, which means that they are secure against even a computationally unbounded prover. Table 1 shows the efficiency of some NIZK proofs for circuit satisfiability.

Let λ be the security parameter. Define $k_T = \text{poly}(\lambda)$ to be the size of a trapdoor permutation, $k_G \approx \lambda^3$ to be the size of a suitable group element, and $|C| = \text{poly}(\lambda)$ to be the size of the circuit. Let $|w| \leq |C|$ be the size of the witness for satisfiability of the circuit.

All the essential details of the proof from [GOS12] were presented earlier in Sect. 3.7. This proof uses the BGN cryptosystem. The proofs from [Gro10a] using techniques from the hidden bits model, implemented using either trapdoor permutations or the Naccache-Stern cryptosystem.

The proof of [GGI+14] assumes the existence of a fully homomorphic encryption scheme. Fully homomorphic encryption allows for the multiplication and addition of ciphertexts to produce encrypted multiplications and additions of the plaintexts within. At a high level, the idea of this proof is to simply encrypt the witness, and evaluate the circuit on the witness in encrypted form. The prover then gives an NIZK proof that the resulting ciphertext contains a 1.

NIZK Arguments. By definition, NIZK arguments have computational soundness, which means that they are secure assuming a computationally bounded prover. Table 2 shows the efficiency of some NIZK arguments for circuit satisfiability.

Table 1. Performance comparison of NIZK proofs for circuit SAT

	CRS in bits	Proof in bits	Assumption
[GOS12]	$O(k_G)$	$O(|C|k_G)$	Pairing-based
[Gro10a]	$|C|k_T\text{poly}\log(\lambda)$	$|C|k_T\text{poly}\log(\lambda)$	Trapdoor Permutations
[Gro10a]	$|C|\text{poly}\log(\lambda)$	$|C|\text{poly}\log(\lambda)$	Naccache-Stern
[GGI+14]	$\text{poly}(\lambda)$	$|w| + \text{poly}(\lambda)$	FHE and NIZK

Table 2. Performance comparison of NIZK arguments for circuit SAT

	CRS in group elements	Argument in group elements
[Gro10b]	$O\left(|C|^2\right)$	$O(1)$
[Lip12]	$O\left(|C|^{1+o(1)}\right)$	$O(1)$
[GGPR13]	$O\left(|C|\log|C|\right)$	$O(1)$
[BCCT13]	$O(1)$	$O(1)$

All of the arguments in the table are SNARKs that rely on strong assumptions and bilinear pairings. In each case, the size of the argument is a constant number of elements in a suitable bilinear group. The final entry, due to [BCCT13], results in arguments where a constant-sized CRS suffices for all polynomial-sized statements. This work makes use of SNARKs which have been composed repeatedly.

References

[BCCT12] Bitansky, N., Canetti, R., Chiesa, A., Tromer, E.: From extractable collision resistance to succinct non-interactive arguments of knowledge, and back again. In: Proceedings of the 3rd Innovations in Theoretical Computer Science Conference (2012)

[BCCT13] Bitansky, N., Canetti, R., Chiesa, A., Tromer, E.: Recursive composition and bootstrapping for SNARKS and proof-carrying data. In: Proceedings of the 45th Annual ACM Symposium on Theory of Computing - STOC 2013, p. 111 (2013)

[BFM88] Blum, M., Feldman, P., Micali, S.: Non-interactive Zero Knowledge and Its Applications (Extended Abstract), pp. 103–112. MIT (1988)

[BGN05] Boneh, D., Goh, E.-J., Nissim, K.: Evaluating 2-DNF formulas on ciphertexts. In: Kilian, J. (ed.) TCC 2005. LNCS, vol. 3378, pp. 325–341. Springer, Heidelberg (2005)

[BIN97] Bellare, M., Impagliazzo, R., Naor, M.: Does parallel repetition lower the error in computationally sound protocols? In: Proceedings of 38th Annual Symposium on Foundations of Computer Science, pp. 374–383. IEEE (1997)

[BR93] Bellare, M., Rogaway, P.: Random oracles are practical: a paradigm for designing efficient protocols. In: Proceedings of the 1st ACM Conference on Computer and Communications Security, 1–21 November 1993

[BSCTV14] Ben-Sasson, E., Chiesa, A., Tromer, E., Virza, M.: Scalable zero knowledge via cycles of elliptic curves. In: Garay, J.A., Gennaro, R. (eds.) CRYPTO 2014, Part II. LNCS, vol. 8617, pp. 276–294. Springer, Heidelberg (2014)

[BY96] Bellare, M., Yung, M.: Certifying permutations: noninteractive zero-knowledge based on any trapdoor permutation. J. Cryptol. 9(3), 149–166 (1996)

[CD98] Cramer, R., Damgård, I.B.: Zero-knowledge proofs for finite field arithmetic or: can zero-knowledge be for free? In: Krawczyk, H. (ed.) CRYPTO 1998. LNCS, vol. 1462, pp. 424–441. Springer, Heidelberg (1998)

[CDS94] Cramer, R., Damgård, I.B., Schoenmakers, B.: Proof of partial knowledge and simplified design of witness hiding protocols. In: Desmedt, Y.G. (ed.) CRYPTO 1994. LNCS, vol. 839, pp. 174–187. Springer, Heidelberg (1994)

[CGH00] Canetti, R., Goldreich, O., Halevi, S.: The random oracle methodology. Revisited, p. 31 (2000)

[Cha88] Chaum, D.: The dining cryptographers problem: unconditional sender and recipient untraceability. J. Cryptol. 1(1), 65–75 (1988)

[CT10] Chiesa, A., Tromer, E.: Proof-carrying data and hearsay arguments from signature cards. In: ICS, vol. 10, pp. 310–331 (2010)

[Dam90] Damgård, I.B.: On the existence of bit commitment schemes and zero-knowledge proofs. In: Brassard, G. (ed.) CRYPTO 1989. LNCS, vol. 435, pp. 17–27. Springer, Heidelberg (1990)

[Dam00] Damgård, I.B.: Efficient concurrent zero-knowledge in the auxiliary string model. In: Preneel, B. (ed.) EUROCRYPT 2000. LNCS, vol. 1807, pp. 418–430. Springer, Heidelberg (2000)

[DGOW95] Damgård, I.B., Goldreich, O., Okamoto, T., Wigderson, A.: Honest verifier vs dishonest verifier in public coin zero-knowledge proofs. In: Coppersmith, D. (ed.) CRYPTO 1995. LNCS, vol. 963, pp. 325–338. Springer, Heidelberg (1995)

[EG85] El Gamal, T.: A public key cryptosystem and a signature scheme based on discrete logarithms. In: Blakely, G.R., Chaum, D. (eds.) CRYPTO 1984. LNCS, vol. 196, pp. 10–18. Springer, Heidelberg (1985)

[FLS99] Feige, U., Lapidot, D., Shamir, A.: Multiple noninteractive zero knowledge proofs under general assumptions. SIAM J. Comput. **29**(1), 1–28 (1999)

[GGI+14] Gentry, C., Groth, J., Ishai, Y., Peikert, C., Sahai, A., Smith, A.: Using fully homomorphic hybrid encryption to minimize non-interative zero-knowledge proofs. J. Cryptol. **28**(4), 1–22 (2015)

[GGP10] Gennaro, R., Gentry, C., Parno, B.: Non-interactive verifiable computing: outsourcing computation to untrusted workers. In: Rabin, T. (ed.) CRYPTO 2010. LNCS, vol. 6223, pp. 465–482. Springer, Heidelberg (2010)

[GGPR13] Gennaro, R., Gentry, C., Parno, B., Raykova, M.: Quadratic span programs and succinct NIZKs without PCPs. In: Johansson, T., Nguyen, P.Q. (eds.) EUROCRYPT 2013. LNCS, vol. 7881, pp. 626–645. Springer, Heidelberg (2013)

[GK96] Goldreich, O., Krawczyk, H.: On the composition of zero-knowledge proof systems. SIAM J. Comput. **25**(1), 169–192 (1996)

[GK03] Goldwasser, S., Kalai, Y.T.: On the (in)security of the Fiat-Shamir paradigm. In: Proceedings of 44th Annual IEEE Symposium on Foundations of Computer Science, 2003 (2003)

[GMR85] Goldwasser, S., Micali, S., Rackoff, C.: The knowledge complexity of interactive proof-systems. In: Proceedings of the Seventeenth Annual ACM Symposium on Theory of Computing, pp. 291–304. ACM (1985)

[GMW91] Goldreich, O., Micali, S., Wigderson, A.: Proofs that yield nothing but their validity or all languages in NP have zero-knowledge proof systems. J. ACM (JACM) **38**(3), 690–728 (1991)

[GMY06] Garay, J.A., MacKenzie, P.D., Yang, K.: Strengthening zero-knowledge protocols using signatures. J. Cryptol. **19**(2), 169–209 (2006)

[GO14] Groth, J., Ostrovsky, R.: Cryptography in the multi-string model. J. Cryptol. **27**(3), 506–543 (2014)

[Gol01] Goldreich, O.: The Foundations of Cryptography. Basic Techniques, vol. 1. Cambridge University Press, Cambridge (2001)

[GOS12] Groth, J., Ostrovsky, R., Sahai, A.: New techniques for noninteractive zero-knowledge. J. ACM (JACM) **59**, 11 (2012)

[Gro09] Groth, J.: Linear algebra with sub-linear zero-knowledge arguments. In: Halevi, S. (ed.) CRYPTO 2009. LNCS, vol. 5677, pp. 192–208. Springer, Heidelberg (2009)

[Gro10a] Groth, J.: Short non-interactive zero-knowledge proofs. In: Abe, M. (ed.) ASIACRYPT 2010. LNCS, vol. 6477, pp. 341–358. Springer, Heidelberg (2010)

[Gro10b] Groth, J.: Short pairing-based non-interactive zero-knowledge arguments. In: Abe, M. (ed.) ASIACRYPT 2010. LNCS, vol. 6477, pp. 321–340. Springer, Heidelberg (2010)

[GW11]   Gentry, C., Wichs, D.: Separating succinct non-interactive arguments from all falsifiable assumptions. In: Proceedings of the Forty-Third Annual ACM Symposium on Theory of Computing (2011)

[KP98]   Kilian, J., Petrank, E.: An efficient noninteractive zero-knowledge proof system for NP with general assumptions. J. Cryptol. **11**, 1–27 (1998)

[Lip12]   Lipmaa, H.: Progression-free sets and sublinear pairing-based non-interactive zero-knowledge arguments. In: Cramer, R. (ed.) TCC 2012. LNCS, vol. 7194, pp. 169–189. Springer, Heidelberg (2012)

[Mic00]   Micali, S.: Computationally sound proofs. SIAM J. Comput. **30**(4), 1253–1298 (2000)

[Ped91]   Pedersen, T.P.: Non-interactive and information-theoretic secure verifiable secret sharing. In: Feigenbaum, J. (ed.) CRYPTO 1991. LNCS, vol. 576, pp. 129–140. Springer, Heidelberg (1992)

[PHGR13]   Parno, B., Howell, J., Gentry, C., Raykova, M.: Pinocchio: nearly practical verifiable computation. In: 2013 IEEE Symposium on Security and Privacy, pp. 238–252, May 2013

JavaScript Sandboxing: Isolating and Restricting Client-Side JavaScript

Steven Van Acker[(✉)] and Andrei Sabelfeld

Chalmers University of Technology, Gothenburg, Sweden
acker@chalmers.se

Abstract. Today's web applications rely on the same-origin policy, the primary security policy of the Web, to isolate their web origin from malicious client-side JavaScript.

When an attacker can somehow breach the same-origin policy and execute JavaScript code inside a web application's origin, he gains full control over all available functionality and data in that web origin.

In the JavaScript sandboxing field, we assume that an attacker has the ability to execute JavaScript code in a web application's origin. The goal of JavaScript sandboxing is to isolate the execution of certain JavaScript code and restrict what functionality and data is available to it.

In this paper we discuss proposed JavaScript sandboxing systems divided into three categories: JavaScript sandboxing through JavaScript subsets and rewriting systems, JavaScript sandboxing using browser modifications and JavaScript sandboxing without browser modifications.

1 Introduction

The Web today is unthinkable without JavaScript. Studies [96] show that close to 90 % of the top 10 million websites of the Web use JavaScript.

JavaScript can turn the Web into a lively, dynamic and interactive end-user experience. For this purpose, today's browsers have an arsenal of powerful JavaScript functionality at their disposal which all becomes available to Web applications running JavaScript. Examples of this powerful functionality include access to audio and video recording devices, real-time communication (RTC) channels than can pierce firewalls, the ability to store data on the client-side, 3D graphics rendering facilities and more.

Giving all this power to unfamiliar web applications is not necessarily a good idea. With great power comes great responsibility, a trait not commonly found in web applications because they often include third-party JavaScript from untrusted sources [70]. In the wrong hands, this powerful JavaScript functionality can be abused to e.g. access and steal sensitive information.

A typical scenario illustrating third-party JavaScript inclusion can be found in online advertising. A recent security-related event in this setting equally illustrates the threat associated with third-party JavaScript inclusions. In July 2015, the website of renowned security expert Troy Hunt experienced [89] a Cross-Site Scripting attack launched through a script used for online advertising.

A. Aldini et al. (Eds.): FOSAD VIII, LNCS 9808, pp. 32–86, 2016.
DOI: 10.1007/978-3-319-43005-8_2

The attack was obvious and visible because the attacker seemingly set out to create a proof-of-concept to display a JavaScript prompt window. However, this attack could have caused a lot more damage while at the same time remain invisible if the attacker has chosen to do so instead.

This scenario is a good case for restricting JavaScript functionality, otherwise known as JavaScript sandboxing. Had the advertisement run in a JavaScript sandbox with restricted functionality, then a successful attack would not be able to abuse the full power of a browser's JavaScript APIs.

In this paper, we discuss the current state-of-the-art research in JavaScript sandboxing on the client-side, and in the browser in particular. JavaScript can be used elsewhere on the client-side, for instance as an embedded scripting in browser extensions [29,66], OpenOffice [9], MongoDB [63], etc. JavaScript can also be used on the server-side, e.g. Node.JS [4], and there are even microcontrollers that understand JavaScript [21,87]. We consider these use cases out of scope and only focus on JavaScript as used in web pages visited by web browsers.

Based on the typical web scenario and attacker model, we divide the JavaScript sandboxing literature in three categories: JavaScript sandboxing through JavaScript subsets and rewriting systems, JavaScript sandboxing using browser modifications and JavaScript sandboxing without browser modifications.

The remainder of this paper is organized as follows. Section 2 draws the context and introduces background material. Section 3 discusses JavaScript sandboxing systems involving JavaScript subsets and rewriting systems. Section 4 discusses browser modifications to achieve JavaScript sandboxing. Section 5 discusses JavaScript sandboxing systems which do not require any browser modifications. Section 6 highlights two well-known JavaScript sandboxing systems and details their usage in the real world. Section 7 concludes this work with a brief discussion of the advantages and disadvantages of the three categories of JavaScript sandboxing systems.

2   Background – Setting the Context

In this section we set the context for the remainder of this paper.

First, we look at a reference browser architecture, the JavaScript language and the different JavaScript APIs available to web developers in Sects. 2.1 to 2.3. We note that a browser is composed of several reusable subsystems such as the JavaScript engine and that the JavaScript engine is disconnected from the rest of the browser, forming a good interception point for enforcing security policies.

Next, we take a brief look at web applications as a combination of web technologies in Sect. 2.4, followed by the same origin policy in Sect. 2.5, a cornerstone of web security, which makes sure that web applications remain separated from each other inside the browser.

A typical web scenario with its actors and interactions, together with the attacker model we use in this paper, is described in Sect. 2.6.

Third party script inclusion is an integral part of web applications today, at the cost of having to trust the third party. This trust is not always deserved, leading to security problems. The threat posed by third party script inclusions is motivated in Sect. 2.7.

Finally, in Sect. 2.8, we describe the concept of JavaScript sandboxing as a means to restrict available functionality inside the JavaScript environment, and three main ways in which this can be accomplished.

2.1   Browser Architecture

Simply put, a web browser is a computer program used to retrieve content from the Web, interact with it and display it on a screen, either directly or through helper applications. More concretely, a web browser is a complex piece of software comprised of multiple subcomponents, each with its own task, that work together to allow a user to visit the Web.

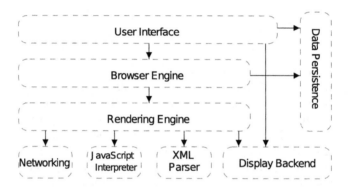

Fig. 1. The eight subsystems of the reference architecture of a web browser, from [31].

The reference architecture of a web browser consists of eight interconnected subsystems [31], shown in Fig. 1:

User Interface. The part of the browser that interacts directly with the user, displaying windows and toolbars.

Browser Engine. Handles *Uniform Resource Identifier* (URI a more generic form of URL) loading, and implements browser actions such as the forward and backward button behavior. The browser engine provides a high-level interface to the rendering engine.

Rendering Engine. The subsystem responsible for displaying content on the screen. It can display HTML and XML, styled with *Cascading Style Sheets* (CSS) and embedding images. It also includes the HTML parser, turning HTML content into the *Document Object Model* (DOM), a structured form more suitable for other components. For the sake of compatibility with older browsers, many HTML parsers also have a *quirks mode* [5] next to a *standards mode*. In standards mode, the HTML parser strictly complies to W3C and IETF standards and rejects any malformed HTML. In quirks mode however, the HTML parser is more lenient and quietly repairs broken HTML instead of rejecting it.

Networking Subsystem. The part of the browser responsible for communicating with the network over protocols such as HTTP, loading content from other web servers, caching data and converting data between different character sets.

JavaScript Interpreter. Also known as the JavaScript engine, this subsystem parses and executes JavaScript code. JavaScript itself is an object-oriented programming language that can evaluate expressions, but does not define ways to influence the rest of the world. To interact with the outside, such as the other browser components, the user or the network, the JavaScript engine must communicate with other subsystems.

XML Parser. Parses XML documents into a DOM structure. This component is different from the HTML parser and is a generic, reusable component. The HTML parser on the other hand, is optimized for performance and tightly coupled with the rendering engine.

Display Backend. This component provides an interface to the underlying operating system to draw windowing primitives and fonts.

Data Persistence. Stores and retrieves data such as browsing history, bookmarks, cookies and browser settings.

The modular subsystems are often reused between different browser vendors. For instance, the Gecko [64] browser engine is used by Mozilla Firefox, Netscape Navigator, Galeon [1] and others. Google Chrome uses the Blink [11] browser engine, also used by Opera [71] and the Android browser [97]. Microsoft Internet Explorer uses the Trident [54] layout engine, also used by the Maxthon [49] browser. Browser components are not only reused by web browsers. Mozilla Firefox's JavaScript engine, SpiderMonkey [80], is also used in the GNOME3 desktop environment [27], and can be used as a standalone JavaScript interpreter. Google Chrome's JavaScript engine, V8 [28], also powers node.js [4], a server-side JavaScript runtime environment.

Many of these subsystems are used by the browser during routine operations such as loading and rendering a webpage. When a user points a browser to a webpage and the browser has downloaded an HTML document, the *rendering pipeline* is started that will eventually display the webpage and allow the user to interact with it.

The rendering pipeline generally consists of 3 steps: parsing, layouting and rendering:

- During the parsing step, the downloaded HTML document is parsed into a data structure known as the *Document Object Model* (DOM) tree. Each node in this tree comprises an HTML element, with links to the parent element and sub-elements.
- In the layouting step, rectangular representations of the nodes in the DOM are arranged according to the styling rules dictated by the webpages and its *Cascading Style Sheets* (CSS) information.

– Finally, in the rendering step, a graphical representation of each HTML element in the DOM is painted in its respective rectangular representation, and finally drawn onto the user's screen.

This rendering pipeline is a gradual process that is re-iterated while a browser loads all the needed resources.

2.2 JavaScript

In 1995, Netscape management told Brendan Eich to create a programming language to run in the web browser that "looked like Java." He created JavaScript in only 10 days [15]. In addition to browser plugins, JavaScript was another novel feature of Netscape Navigator 2.0 that supported Netscape's vision of the Web as a distributed operating system. In contrast with Java, which was considered a heavyweight object-oriented language and used to create Java applets, JavaScript would be Java's "silly little brother" [3], aimed towards non-professional programmers who would not need to learn and compile Java applets.

```
1   var name = prompt("What is your name?");
2   var year = prompt("What year were you born?");

3   var today = new Date();
4   var age = today.getFullYear() - year;

5   alert("Hello "+name+", you are about "+age+" years young");
```

Listing 1.1: Example JavaScript code prompting the user for name and birthyear, calculating age and displaying it in a pop-up.

Listing 1.1 shows a simple example of JavaScript. When executed, the code will prompt for the user's name and birth-year. It will then calculate the user's age based on the current year and display it with a greeting using a pop-up. This JavaScript example makes use of the `prompt()` function, the `Date` object and the `alert()` function.

When an HTML document is about to be loaded, and before the rendering pipeline starts, the browser initializes an instance of the JavaScript engine and ties it uniquely to the webpage about to be loaded.

The webpage's developer can use JavaScript to interact with this rendering pipeline by including JavaScript in several ways. JavaScript can be executed while the pages is loading, using HTML `<script>` tags. These script tags can cause the browser to load external JavaScript and execute them inside the webpage's JavaScript execution environment. Script tags can also contain inline JavaScript, which will equally be loaded and executed. HTML provides a way to register JavaScript event handlers with HTML elements, which will be called when e.g. an image has loaded, or the user hovers the mousepointer over a hyperlink. In addition, JavaScript can register these event handlers itself by querying and manipulating the DOM tree. Events are not only driven by the user, but can also be driven programmatically. For instance, JavaScript has the ability to use a built-in timer to execute a piece of JavaScript at a certain point in the future. Likewise, the `XMLHttpRequest` functionality available in the JavaScript engine allows a web developer to retrieve Internet resources in the background, and execute a specified piece of JavaScript code when they are loaded. Lastly, JavaScript has the ability to execute dynamically generated code through the `eval()` function.

2.3 JavaScript APIs

JavaScript's capabilities inside a web page are limited to the APIs that are offered to it. Typical functionality available to JavaScript in a web page includes manipulating the DOM, navigating the browser and accessing resources on remote servers.

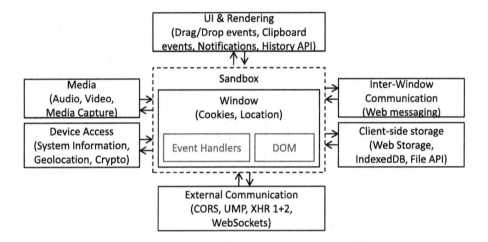

Fig. 2. Synthesized model of the emerging HTML5 APIs, from [91].

In the new HTML 5 and ECMAScript 5 specifications, JavaScript gains access to more and powerful APIs. Figure 2 [17] shows a model of some of these new HTML 5 APIs, which are further explained below.

Inter-frame communication. Facilitates communication between windows (e.g. between mashup components). This includes window navigation, as well as Web Messaging (`postMessage`).

Client-side storage. Enables applications to temporarily or persistently store data. This can be achieved via Web Storage, IndexedDB or the File API.

External communication. Features such as CORS, UMP, XMLHttpRequest level 1 and 2, WebSockets, raw sockets and Web RTC (real-time communication) allow an application to communicate with remote websites.

Device access. Allows the web application to retrieve contextual data (e.g. geolocation) as well as system information such as battery level, CPU information, ambient sensors and high-resolution timers.

Media. Enable a web application to play audio and video fragments, capture audio and video via a microphone or webcam and manage telephone calls through the Web Telephony API.

The UI and rendering. Allow subscription to clipboard and drag-and-drop events, issuing desktop notifications, allow an application to go fullscreen, populating the history via the History API and create new widgets with Web Components API and Shadow DOM.

2.4   Web Applications

A web application combines HTML code, JavaScript and other resources from several web servers, into a functional application that runs in the browser. Unlike typical desktop applications which need to be installed on a computer's hard disk, web applications are accessible through the web browser from anywhere and do not need to be installed.

A key component in today's web application, is JavaScript. JavaScript code in a web application executes in the browser and can communicate with a web server, which typically also executes code for the web application.

Consider a website wishing to display the latest tweets from a Twitter feed. Such a widget can be embedded into a web page, as shown in Fig. 3. Without a client-side programming language such as JavaScript, the web server from which this web page is retrieved, could gather and insert the latest tweets at the moment the web page was requested, and insert them into the web page as HTML-formatted text. When rendered, the visitor would see the latest tweets, but they would not update themselves in the following minutes because the web page is static.

Fig. 3. Example of an embedded live Twitter feed (indicated by the rectangle on the bottom right), from [90].

Another option is to use JavaScript on the client-side. When the web page is requested, the web server can insert JavaScript that regularly requests the latest tweets from the feed and updates the web page to display them. The result is an active web page that always displays the latest information.

This example consists of only one HTML page and requests information from one source. Today's web has many web applications combining a multitude of third-party resources. Examples are Facebook, YouTube, Google Maps and more.

2.5   The Same-Origin Policy

If web applications were allowed complete access to a browser, they would be able to interfere in the operation of other web applications running in the same browser. Given the powerful APIs briefly discussed in the previous section, a web application would be able to access another web application's DOM, local storage and data stored on remote servers.

To prevent this, web applications are executed in their own little universe inside the web browser, without knowledge of each other. The boundaries between these universes are drawn based on the *Same-Origin Policy* (SOP) [92].

When the root HTML document of web application is loaded from a certain URL, the *origin* of that web application is said to be a combination of the scheme, hostname and port-number of that URL. For instance, a web application loaded from https://www.example.com has scheme *https*, hostname *www.example.com* and, in this case implicit, port number *443*. The origin for this web application is thus *(https,www.example.com,443)* or https://www.example.com:443.

The *Same-Origin Policy* (SOP) dictates that any code executing inside this origin only has access to resources from that *same* origin, unless explicitly allowed otherwise by e.g. a Cross-Origin Resource Sharing (CORS) [94] policy. In the previous example, the web application from https://www.example.com:443 cannot retrieve the address book from a webmail application with different origin https://mail.example.com:443 running in the same browser, unless the latter explicitly allows it.

The same-origin policy is part of the foundation of web security and is implemented in every modern browser. In this text we only consider the restrictions imposed by the SOP on the execution of JavaScript.

Insecurely written web applications may allow attackers to breach the same-origin policy by executing their JavaScript code in that web application's origin. Once arbitrary JavaScript code can be injected into a web application, it can take over control and access all available resources in that web application's origin.

Consider a typical webmail application, such as Gmail, allowing an authenticated user to access his emails and contact list. The webmail application offers a user interface in the browser and can send requests to the webmail server to send and retrieve emails, and manipulate the contact list.

An attacker may manage to lure an authenticated user of this webmail application onto a specially crafted website. This website could try to contact the

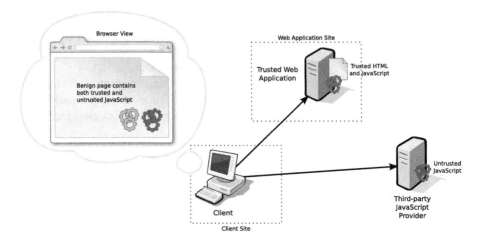

Fig. 4. A typical web application with third-party JavaScript inclusion. The web application running in the browser combines HTML and JavaScript from a trusted source, with JavaScript from an untrusted source.

webmail server to send and retrieve emails and contact information, just as the web application would. However, the webmail application's origin is e.g. https://webmail.com:443, while the attacker's website is https://attacker.com: 443. Because of the SOP, JavaScript running on the attacker's website has no access to resources of the webmail's origin.

Now consider what would happen if the webmail application is written insecurely, so that an attacker can execute JavaScript in its origin: https://webmail. com:443. Because the attacker's code runs inside the same origin as the webmail application, it has access to the same resources and can also read and retrieve emails and contact information. Because of the power of JavaScript, an attacker can do much more. Specially crafted JavaScript can compose spam email messages and send them out using the victim's email account, or it could erase the contact list. It could even download all emails in the mailbox and upload them to another server.

An attacker with the ability to execute JavaScript in a web application's origin can take full control of that web application. In the typical web application scenario, untrusted JavaScript can be executed in two ways: by including it legitimately from a third party, or by having it injected through a Cross-Site Scripting vulnerability in the web application or an installed browser plugin or extension.

2.6   The Typical Web Scenario and Attacker Model

When discussing Web security, it is important to keep in mind a typical web application with third-party JavaScript and the actors involved in it. Figure 4 shows such a typical web application where HTML and JavaScript from a trusted source are combined with JavaScript from an untrusted source. Remember that all JavaScript, trusted or untrusted, running in a web application's origin has access to all available resources.

There are three actors involved in this scenario: The developer of the trusted web application and the server it is hosted on, the developer of the third-party JavaScript and the server it is hosted on, and the client's browser.

Both the client and the trusted web application have a clear motive to keep untrusted JavaScript from accessing the web application's resources. The client will wish to protect his own account and data. The trusted web application has its reputation to consider and will protect a user's account and data as well. Furthermore, the client does not need to steal information from himself and can use any of his browser's functionality without needing to use a remote web application. Likewise, the web application developer owns the origin in which the web application runs. Stealing data from his own users through JavaScript is not necessary.

It may be the case that the client has modified his browser and installed a browser plugin or extension. Such a plugin or extension may be designed to make the interaction with the web application easier or automated, potentially circumventing certain defensive measures put in place by the developer of the web application. In this scenario, the client is still motivated to protect his account and data, but may be exposing himself to additional threats through the installed browser plugins or extensions that form additional attack surface.

The third-party script provider however, does not necessarily share the same desire to protect a user's data. Even with the best of intentions, a third-party script provider may be compromised and serving malicious JavaScript without its knowledge. It may be the case that the script provider has an intrusion-detection system in place that will detect when it is serving malware, but this would be wishful thinking. In the worst case, the third-party script provider is acting maliciously on its own for whatever sinister reason. In any case, the client and trusted web application cannot trust a third-party script provider with their secrets.

The attacker model best associated with this actor is the *gadget attacker* [10]. A gadget attacker is a malicious actor who owns one or more machines on the Internet, but can neither passively not actively intercept network traffic between the client's browser and the trusted web application. Instead, the gadget attacker has the ability to have the trusted web application's developer integrate a gadget chosen by the attacker.

2.7 Third-Party Script Inclusion

Web applications are built from several components that are often included from third-party content providers. JavaScript libraries like jQuery or the Google Maps API are often directly loaded into a web application's JavaScript environment from third-party script providers.

In a large-scale study of the Web in 2012 [70], Nikiforakis et al. found that 88.45 % of the top 10,000 web sites on the Web, include JavaScript from a

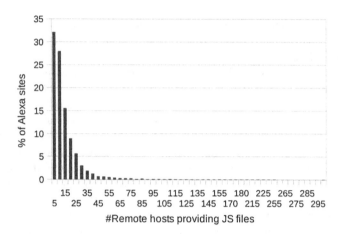

Fig. 5. Relative frequency distribution of the percentage of top Alexa websites and the number of unique remote hosts from which they request JavaScript code, from [70].

third-party script provider. Figure 5 shows the distribution of the number of third-party script providers each web site includes. While about a third include JavaScript from at most 5 remote hosts, there are also web sites that include JavaScript from more than 295 different remote hosts.

Including JavaScript from remote hosts implicitly trusts these hosts not to serve malicious JavaScript. If these third-party script providers are untrustworthy, or if they have been compromised, a web application may end up executing untrusted JavaScript code.

As an example, consider jQuery, a popular multi-purpose JavaScript library used on 60 % of the top million websites on the Web [12]. The host distributing jQuery was compromised in September 2014 [40], giving the attackers the ability to modify the library and possibly infect many websites that include the library directly from http://jquery.com. Fortunately, the attackers did not modify the jQuery library itself, but used the compromised server to spread malware instead. Although the JavaScript library itself was not tampered with, the jQuery compromise indicates the inherent security threat that third-party script inclusions can pose.

2.8   JavaScript Sandbox

The gadget attacker, as defined in Sect. 2.6, has the ability to integrate a malicious gadget into a trusted web application. This allows the attacker to execute any chosen JavaScript code in the JavaScript execution environment of this trusted web application's origin and access its sensitive resources.

Given this attacker model, we cannot stop the attacker from presenting a web application user's browser with chosen JavaScript. In this paper we are not concerned with cross-site scripting or other injection attacks and assume that the attacker already has the ability to execute JavaScript in the JavaScript environment, no matter through which means this was accomplished. In this scenario, it would be helpful to have a mechanism to restrict the available functionality inside the JavaScript environment, according to the least-privilege principle. The impact of executing (potentially malicious) JavaScript in such an environment would then be limited to the available functionality. Such an environment, in which we can isolate JavaScript and restrict its access to certain resources and functionality, is called a JavaScript sandbox.

From the typical web scenario architecture from Sect. 2.6, keeping in mind our attacker model, there are only two possible locations that can be considered to deploy a JavaScript sandboxing mechanism: the trusted web application and the client's browser. The third-party script provider is considered untrustworthy.

The developer of the web application and the server hosting it, are trusted according to the attacker model. This server then offers a possible location to facilitate JavaScript sandboxing. Before serving the untrusted JavaScript from the third-party script provider to the client, the code can be reviewed and optionally rewritten to make sure it does not abuse the web application's available resources.

The client's browser provides a second location to sandbox JavaScript, because it is also considered trusted. With direct access to the JavaScript execution context, a JavaScript sandboxing system located at the client-side has better means to restrict access to resources and functionality.

JavaScript sandboxing can be achieved by restricting the used JavaScript language to a subset that can then be verified to be safe, or even rewrite the JavaScript code into a version which is safe. Such a solution involves a JavaScript subset and a rewriting mechanism which will be discussed in Sect. 3.

Without restricting or rewriting JavaScript code, JavaScript sandboxing can be achieved by modifying the environment in which JavaScript executes. Such a JavaScript sandboxing mechanism can be implemented by modifying the JavaScript engine in the browser and build in machinery to enforce a certain policy. This type of JavaScript sandboxing which uses a browser modification will be discussed in Sect. 4.

Finally, it is also possible to sandbox JavaScript without any language-level restrictions, rewriting or browser modifications, by repurposing JavaScript functionality to isolate and restrict JavaScript. Such JavaScript sandboxing systems which do not require browser modifications, are discussed in Sect. 5.

2.9 Conclusion

This section introduced important Web technologies required to understand the remainder of this text.

Web browsers are used to browse the Web and consist of many different cooperating subsystems, such as the HTML parser and the JavaScript engine. Web applications are a combination of HTML pages, JavaScript code and other resources retrieved from multiple sources running in the browser. Each web application is isolated and protected in its own origin by the same-origin policy.

Web applications often include JavaScript code from third-party script providers, placing often undeserved trust on third parties, who can then execute unrestricted JavaScript code in the web application's origin.

JavaScript sandboxing can limit the functionality available in a JavaScript environment and we consider three categories which we will discuss in the next sections: JavaScript subsets and rewriting systems in Sect. 3, JavaScript sandboxing using browser modifications in Sect. 4 and JavaScript sandboxing without browser modifications in Sect. 5.

3   JavaScript Subsets and Rewriting

JavaScript is a very flexible and expressive programming language which gives web-developers a powerful tool to build web-applications. However, this same powerful tool is also available to attackers wishing to execute malicious JavaScript code in a website visitor's browser.

Moreover, the powerful nature of JavaScript is problematic because it hinders code verification efforts which could prove safety properties for a given piece of JavaScript code.

Example: `eval()`. Consider for instance the JavaScript fragment in Listing 1.2. When executed in a browser, this code will prompt a user to input a line of text. The one-way hashing algorithm MD5 is then used to compute a hash of this line of text. If the hash matches `"3b022ec21226e862450f2155ef836827"`, the MD5 hash for `"alert('hello')"`, then the line of text is passed to the `eval()` function and executed as JavaScript code.

```
1    var cmd = prompt();

2    // MD5 algorithm computes a one-way hash
3    function md5(m) {
4        // ...
5        return m;
6    }

7    // verifies whether the given input is "alert('hello')"
8    if(md5(cmd) == "3b022ec21226e862450f2155ef836827") {
9        eval(cmd);
10   }
```

Listing 1.2: Example JavaScript calling `eval()` on user input, but only if its MD5 hash matches a given hash.

Given that the MD5 hashing algorithm cannot easily be reversed, it is practically impossible for a code verification tool to automatically determine the effect of this code, prior to its execution. The `eval()` function illustrates a feature of JavaScript which makes code verification difficult because of its dynamic nature. For this reason, `eval()` is considered evil [77] and should be used with the greatest care, or not be used at all.

Example: Strange Semantics and Scoping Rules. As another example, the JavaScript fragment in Listing 1.3 illustrates some strange semantic rules in JavaScript, including the `with` construct. This particular example showcases some non-intuitive scoping rules associated with the scope chain. The scope chain consists of an ordered list of JavaScript objects which are consulted when unqualified names are looked up at runtime.

```
1   var o = {f:2, x:4};

2   console.log("before with: f == " + f);
3   console.log("before with: x == " + x);
4   console.log("before with: \"x\" in window == " + ("x" in window));

5   with(o) {
6       function f() { }
7       console.log("inside with: f == " + f);
8       var x = 3;
9       console.log("inside with: x == " + x);
10  }

11  console.log("after with: o.f == " + o.f);
12  console.log("after with: o.x == " + o.x);
13  console.log("after with: f == " + f);
14  console.log("after with: x == " + x);
15  console.log("after with: \"x\" in window == " + ("x" in window));
```

Listing 1.3: Example JavaScript using the `with` construct to place a new object at the front of the scope chain during the evaluation of the construct's body. This example is adapted from Miller et al. [60].

Before continuing, the reader is advised to read the code and try to predict what it will output. The actual output of the code in this example, is listed in Listing 1.4.

```
1   before with: f == function f() { }
2   before with: x == undefined
3   before with: "x" in window == true
4   inside with: f == 2
5   inside with: x == 3
6   after with: o.f == 2
7   after with: o.x == 3
8   after with: f == function f() { }
9   after with: x == undefined
10  after with: "x" in window == true
```

Listing 1.4: Output of example in Listing 1.3.

From the output, it appears that both `f` and `x` are already defined before they are even declared, but `x` has `undefined` as value. Using `with`, the user-defined object `o` is pushed to the front of the scope chain. The new function `f()` is declared, but the subsequent `console.log()` call seemingly is not aware it. Instead, the value of `f` is retrieved from the first object in the scope chain (`o`), resulting in 2. Then, a variable `var x` is declared and assigned 3. The following `console.log()` call is aware of this declaration and outputs the correct value.

Outside the with loop, the object o has changed to reflect the new value of o.x, but did not record any change to o.f.

The strange behavior in this example indicates that variable and function declarations have different semantics in JavaScript. The discrepancy between variable and function declarations can be explained by a process called "variable hoisting." Variable hoisting examines the JavaScript code to be executed and performs all declarations before any code is actually run.

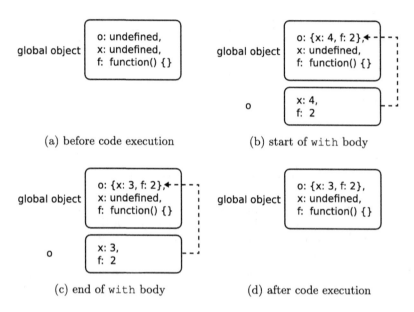

(a) before code execution

(b) start of with body

(c) end of with body

(d) after code execution

Fig. 6. The scope chain during execution of the example in Listing 1.3. In this depiction, the scope chain grows down so that newly pushed objects are at the bottom.

A graphical representation of the scope chain during the execution of this example is shown in Fig. 6 and can be used as a visual aid during the explanation.

Depicted in Fig. 6a is the result of the variable hoisting before any code is run. The function f() and the variable x are declared on the global object. While the variable x has value undefined, the function f() is declared and is assigned its value immediately.

Next, the object o is pushed to the front of the scope chain. The scope chain right after this push and right before the start of the with construct, is shown in Fig. 6b. Any unqualified names are now looked up in the variable o.

The third image shown in Fig. 6c, depicts the state of the scope chain at the end of the with body. Here, the value of the property x of the object o has changed to 3 because of the assignment. Also note that the value of f has not changed because variable hoisting declares and initializes a function in a single step before the code is run, and so outside of the with body.

Finally, in Fig. 6d, the scope chain is restored because the with body ended.

The strange scoping rules and semantics of with are difficult to reason about for uninitiated programmers. Widely-acknowledged as being a "JavaScript wart" [33], it is often recommended to not use the with construct because it may lead to confusing bugs and compatibility issues [68].

JavaScript Subsets: Verification and Rewriting. The goal of JavaScript code verification and rewriting is to inspect JavaScript code before it is executed in a browser, and ensure that it is not harmful.

In the light of the previous examples, it can be desirable to eliminate those constructs from the JavaScript language that hinder code verification efforts or cause confusion in general. At the same time, it is also desirable to maintain as much of the language as possible so that JavaScript is still useful. Such a reduced version of JavaScript, with e.g. eval() and with construct missing, is called a JavaScript subset.

The usage of a JavaScript subset must be accompanied by a mechanism which verifies that a given piece of code adheres to the subset. A deviation from the subset's specification can be handled in two ways: rejection and rewriting.

Rejection is the simpler of both options, treating a deviation from the subset as a hard error and refusing to execute the given piece of code.

Rewriting is a softer alternative, transforming the deviating piece of code into code which conforms to the subset. Such a rewriting phase can also introduce extra instrumentation in the code to ensure that the code behaves in a safe way at runtime.

Interception in a Middlebox. Both the JavaScript subset verification and rewriting steps necessitate the processing of raw third-party JavaScript code before it reaches the client's browser. These steps are to be performed in a *middlebox*, a network device that sits on the network path between a client and a server. Such a middlebox may consist of a physical device unrelated to either client or server, but it may just as well be collocated with either client or server.

From the attacker model discussed in Sect. 2.6, we can eliminate the third-party script provider's site as a possible location to verify and rewrite JavaScript. We are left with two possible locations for these tasks: the site of the trusted web application and the client's site.

A middlebox at the site of the web application, as shown in Fig. 7a, can equally be implemented as part of a separate network device such as a load-balancer, reverse proxy or firewall, or can be integrated to be part of the web-application.

A middlebox at the client's site, as shown in Fig. 7b, can either be a implemented as a proxy performing the required verification and translation steps, or as a browser plugin or extension, implementing the proxy's behavior as part of the browser.

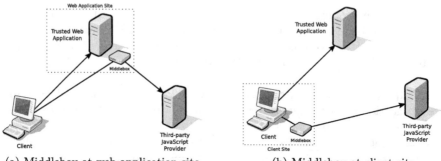

(a) Middlebox at web application site   (b) Middlebox at client site

Fig. 7. Architectural overview of a setup where a middlebox is used for code verification and transformation, at the web application site and at the client site.

ECMAScript 5 Strict Mode. ECMAScript 5 strict mode [65], or JavaScript strict, is a standardized subset of JavaScript with intentionally different semantics than normal JavaScript.

```
1   "use strict";

2   var example = 123;
3   // the following fails because the name is misspelled
4   exmaple = 345;

5   // the following fails because of a duplicate key name
6   var obj = {p:1, p:2};

7   // the following fails because "with" is not allowed
8   with(obj) {
9       alert(p);
10  }
```

Listing 1.5: JavaScript strict mode example.

To use strict mode, a JavaScript developer must only place `"use strict";` at the top of a script of function body, as shown in Listing 1.5. Strict mode will then be enforced for that entire script, or only in the scope of that function. JavaScript strict mode can be mixed with and function together with normal JavaScript.

Strict mode removes silent failures and turns them into hard errors that throw exceptions and halt JavaScript execution. For instance, accidentally creating a global variable by mistyping a variable name, will throw an error. Likewise, overwriting a non-writable global variable like `NaN` or defining an object with a duplicate key, causes strict mode to throw errors.

Strict mode simplifies variable names and allows better JavaScript engine optimization by removing the `with` construct. Through this construct, JavaScript engine optimizations may be confused about the actual memory location of a variable. In addition, strict mode changes the semantics of `eval()` so that it can no longer create variable in the surrounding scope.

Strict mode also introduces some fixes with regard to security. It is no longer possible to access the global object through the `this` keyword, preventing unforeseen runtime leaks. It is also no longer possible to abuse certain variables to walk the stack or access the `caller` from within a function.

Finally, strict mode forbids the use of some keywords that will be used in future ECMAScript versions, such as `private`, `public`, `protected`, `interface`, ...

Research in the area of JavaScript subsets and rewriting systems includes BrowserShield [76], CoreScript [99], ADsafe [16], Facebook JavaScript [88], Caja [60], Jacaranda [36], Microsoft Live Websandbox [58], Jigsaw [53], Gatekeeper [32], Blancura [25], Dojo Secure [42], ... The remainder of this section discusses a selection of work on JavaScript subsets and rewriting systems.

3.1 BrowserShield

Reis et al. have developed BrowserShield, a dynamic instrumentation system for JavaScript. BrowserShield parses and rewrites HTML and JavaScript in a middlebox, rewriting all function calls, property accesses, constructors and control structures to be relayed through specialized methods of the `bshield` object. A client-side JavaScript library then inserts this `bshield` object, which mediates access to DOM methods and properties according to a policy, into the JavaScript execution environment before any scripts run.

BrowserShield aims at preventing the exploitation of browser vulnerabilities, such as MS04-40 [56], a buffer overflow in the Microsoft Internet Explorer browser caused by overly long `src` and `name` attributes in certain HTML elements. To shield the browser from attacks against these vulnerabilities, BrowserShield rewrites both HTML and JavaScript, transforming them to filter out any detected attacks. BrowserShield does not use a JavaScript subset, because it needs to be able to rewrite any HTML and JavaScript found on the Internet to be effective.

```
1    // original JavaScript code
2    eval("...");

3    // rewritten by BrowserShield
4    bshield.invokeFunc(eval, "...");
```

Listing 1.6: Example JavaScript code rewritten by BrowserShield.

Although sandboxing is not the main goal of BrowserShield, its rewriting mechanism provides all the necessary machinery to accomplish this goal by tuning the policy. For instance, BrowserShield could have a policy in place to mediate access to the sensitive `eval()` function. Listing 1.6 shows the output of BrowserShield's rewriting mechanism on a JavaScript example using the eval() function. After the rewriting step, any call to eval() in the original code is relayed through the bshield object, which can mediate access at runtime.

A prototype of BrowserShield was implemented as a Microsoft ISA Server 2004 [55] plugin for evaluation. The plugin in this server-side middlebox is responsible for rewriting HTML and script elements, and injecting the Browser-Shield client-side JavaScript library which implements the bshield object and redirects all JavaScript functionality through it. BrowserShield worked as expected during evaluation. The performance evaluation indicated a maximum slowdown of 136x on micro-benchmarks, and on average 2.7x slowdown on rendering a webpage.

3.2   ADsafe

The ADsafe subset, developed by Douglas Crockford, is a JavaScript subset designed to allow direct placement of advertisements on webpages in a safe way, while enforcing good coding practices. It removes a number of unsafe JavaScript features and does not allow uncontrolled access to unsafe browser components.

Examples of the removed unsafe JavaScript features are: the use of global variables, the use of this, eval(), with, using dangerous object properties like caller and prototype. ADsafe also does not allow the use of the subscript operator, except when it can be verified that the subscript is numerical, e.g. a[i] is not allowed but a[+i] is allowed because +i will always produce a number. In addition, ADsafe removes all sources of non-determinism such as Date and Math.random().

To make use of ADsafe, widgets must be loaded and executed via the ADSAFE.go() method. These widgets must adhere to the ADsafe subset, although there is no verification built into ADsafe. Instead, it is recommended to verify subset adherence in any stage of the deployment pipeline with e.g. JSLint [2], a JavaScript code quality verification tool.

ADsafe does not allow JavaScript code to make use of the DOM directly. Instead, ADsafe makes a dom object available which provides and mediates access to the DOM.

No performance evaluation has been published about ADsafe by its author, who claim that ADsafe "will not make scripts bigger or slower or alter their behavior" [16]. This claim applies if advertisement scripts are written in the ADsafe subset directly, and not translated from full JavaScript.

Research on ADsafe has revealed several problems and vulnerabilities, which allow leaking the document object [83], launch a XSS attack [25], allow the guest to access properties on the host page's global object [75], prototype poisoning [47] and more.

3.3   Facebook JavaScript

Facebook JavaScript (FBJS) is a subset of JavaScript and part of the Facebook Markup Language (FBML) which was used to publish third-party Facebook applications on the Facebook servers. FBJS was designed to allow web application developers as much flexibility as possible while at the same time protecting site integrity and the privacy of Facebook's users.

The FBJS subset excludes some of JavaScript's dangerous constructs such as eval(), with, _parent_, constructor and valueOf(). A preprocessor rewrites FBJS code so that all top-level identifiers in the code are prefixed with an application-specific prefix, thus isolating the code in its own namespace.

```
1    // original code
2    (function() { return this; })();

3    // code rewritten by FBJS
4    (function() { return ref(this); })();
```

Listing 1.7: Example JavaScript code making use of this semantics to return the global object and the code rewritten by FBJS to prevent FBJS code from breaking out of its namespace.

Special care is also taken with e.g. the use of this and object indexing to retrieve properties, making sure that a Facebook application cannot break out of its namespace. The semantics of ithis are dependent on the way and location that it is used. A code fragment such as the one listed in Listing 1.7 can return the global object, allowing FBJS code to break out of its namespace. To remedy this problem, the FBJS rewriter encloses all references to this with the function ref(), e.g. ref(this). This ref() function verifies the way in which it is called at runtime, and prevent FBJS code from breaking out of its namespace. Similarly, the FBJS rewriter also encloses object indices such as property in object["property"] with idx("property") to also prevent that this is bound to the global object.

Research on FBJS has revealed some vulnerabilities [46, 47], which were addressed by the Facebook team.

Maffeis et al. [47] discovered that a specially crafted function can retrieve the current scope object through JavaScript's exception handling mechanism, allowing the ref() and idx() functions to be redefined. This redefinition in turn allows a FBJS code to break out of its namespace and take over the webpage.

After Facebook fixed the previous issues, Maffeis et al. [46] discovered another vulnerability which allows the global object to be returned on some browsers, by tricking the fixed idx() function to return an otherwise hidden property, through a time-of-check-time-of-use vulnerability [62].

3.4 Caja

Google's Caja, short for Capabilities Attenuate JavaScript Authority, is a JavaScript subset and rewriting system using a server-side middlebox. Caja represents an object-capability safe subset of JavaScript, meaning that any code conforming to this subset can only cause effects outside itself if it is given references to other objects. In Caja, objects have no powerful references to other objects by default and can only be granted new references from the outside. The capability of affecting the outside world is thus reflected by holding a reference to an object in that outside world.

The Caja subset removes some dangerous features from the JavaScript language, such as `with` and `eval()`. Furthermore, Caja does not allow variables or properties with names ending in "_" (double-underscore), while at the same time marking variables and properties with names ending in "_" as private.

```
1   window.alert("hello world");
```

Listing 1.8: Example JavaScript code to be cajoled by Caja.

```
1   var tamedwindow = tame(window);
2   var cajoledcode = function(param) {
3       param.alert("hello world");
4   };

5   cajoledcode(tamedwindow);
```

Listing 1.9: Conceptual cajoled code and tamed window.

Caja's rewriting mechanism, known as the "cajoler," examines the guest code to determine any free variables and wraps the guest code into a function without free variables. Listing 1.8 shows some example code and its cajoled form is shown in Listing 1.9 (the `cajoledcode` variable). In addition, Caja adds inline checks to make sure that Caja's invariants are not broken and that no object references are leaked. The output of the cajoler is cajoled code, which is sent to a client's browser.

On the client-side, objects from the host webpage are "tamed" so that they only expose desired properties before being passed to the cajoled guest code. These tamed objects with carefully exposed properties are the only references that cajoled code obtains to the host page. In this way, all accesses to the DOM can be mediated by taming the global object before passing it to cajoled code. Listing 1.9 shows how the `window` object is tamed and passed to the cajoled form of Listing 1.8.

3.5   Discussion

The JavaScript language makes static code verification difficult, because of its dynamic nature (e.g. `eval()`) and strange semantics (e.g. the `with` construct). JavaScript subsets eliminate some of JavaScript's language constructs so that code may be more easily verified. When required, JavaScript rewriting systems can transform the code so that policies can also be enforced at runtime.

This section discussed four JavaScript subsets and rewriting mechanisms: BrowserShield, ADsafe, Facebook JavaScript and Caja. Some of their features are summarized in Table 1.

Table 1. Comparison between prominent JavaScript sandboxing systems using subsets and rewriting systems.

System	Target application	Rewrites	Uses subset	Removed features	Performance	Known weaknesses
BrowserShield	Preventing browser exploitation	Y	N	n/a	max. 136x slowdown on micro-benchmarks, avg. 2.7x slowdown on user experience	
ADsafe	Advertising	N	Y	eval(), with, this, global vars, …	no slowdown	[83] [25] [75] [47]
FBJS	Third-party widgets	Y	Y	eval(), with, …	no data	[47] [46]
Caja	Third-party widgets	Y	Y	eval(), with, …	no data	

It is noteworthy that all three JavaScript subsets remove `with` and `eval()` from the language, which is in line with the standardized JavaScript strict mode subset. The only available performance benchmarks are for BrowserShield, which rewrites code written in full JavaScript, and indicate a heavy performance penalty when rewriting JavaScript in a middlebox. Furthermore, the list of known weaknesses suggest that creating a secure JavaScript subset, although possible, is not an easy task.

JavaScript subsets and code rewriting have been used in real world web applications and have proved to be effective in restricting available functionality to selected pieces of JavaScript code. However, restricting the integration of third-party JavaScript code which conforms to a specific JavaScript subset, puts limitations on third-party JavaScript library developers which they are unlikely to follow without incentive. Even if these developers are willing to limit themselves to a JavaScript subset, they would need to create a version of their code for every subset that they need to conform too. For instance, the jQuery developers would need to create a specific version for use with FBJS, Caja, ADsafe etc. This is an unrealistic expectation.

The standardization of a JavaScript subset, such as e.g. strict mode, helps eliminate this disadvantage for third-party JavaScript providers. But even with a standardized JavaScript subset to aid with code verification, this verification step itself must still happen in a middlebox located at either the server-side or the client-side.

Opting for a middlebox on a server-side has the disadvantage that it changes the architecture of the Internet. From the browser's perspective, JavaScript code would need to be requested from the middlebox instead of directly downloading it from the third-party script provider. Although this poses no problem for generic JavaScript libraries such as jQuery, it does pose a problem for JavaScript code which is generated dynamically depending on the user's credentials, as is the case with e.g. JSONP. In the latter case the third-party script provider might require session information to prove a user's identity, which will not be provided by the browser when requesting said script from a server-side middlebox.

A client-side middlebox on the other hand, does not suffer from this particular problem because it has the option of letting the browser connect to it transparently, e.g. in case of a web proxy. With a client-side middlebox, the web application developers lose control over the rewriting process. Users of the web application should setup the middlebox on the client-side in order to make use of this web application. But requiring users to install a middlebox next to their browser for a single web application, hurts usability and puts a burden on users which they might not like to carry.

From a usability viewpoint, it makes more sense to require only a single middlebox which can be reused for multiple web applications and to integrate this client-side middlebox into the browser somehow.

4 JavaScript Sandboxing Using Browser Modifications

The previous section showed that JavaScript contains several language constructs that cannot easily be verified to be harmless before executing JavaScript code. Instead of verifying the code beforehand, another approach is to control the execution of JavaScript at runtime and monitor the effect of the executing JavaScript to make sure no harm is done.

In a typical modular browser architecture of a browser, as explained in Sect. 2.1, the JavaScript environment is disconnected from other browser components. These other components, such as the DOM, the network layer, the rendering pipeline or HTML parser are not directly accessible to JavaScript code running in the JavaScript environment. Without these components, JavaScript is effectively side-effect free and is unable to affect the outside world.

The connection layer between the JavaScript engine and the different browser components, is an excellent location to mediate access to the powerful functionality that these components can provide. In order to enforce a policy at this location, the browser must be modified with a mechanism that can intercept, modify and block messages between the JavaScript engine and the different components.

```
1  var x = ...;
2  window.setTimeout(x, 1000);
```

Listing 1.10: Example JavaScript calling setTimeout() with unknown input.

Example: Allowing only Function Object Parameters for setTimeout(). Consider the example in Listing 1.10. In this example, the DOM API function setTimeout() is called with a parameter x. The specification for the setTimeout() function in the Web application API standard [98] lists two versions: a version where x must be a Function object, and a version that allows it to be a String. Passing a string to the setTimeout() function is regarded as a bad coding practice and considered as evil as using eval() [41]. Because of the inherent difficulty in verifying JavaScript code before runtime, it can be desirable to enforce a policy at runtime which rejects calls to setTimeout() when a string is passed as an argument.

The setTimeout() function is provided by a browser component which implements timer functionality. To access this function, the JavaScript engine must send a message to this component to invoke the timer functionality, as shown in Fig. 8. At this point, a browser modified with a suitable policy enforcement mechanism can intercept the message, and reject it if the given parameter is not a Function object.

Forms of Browser Modifications. Browser modifications can take many forms, but they can generally be split into three groups: browser plugins, browser extensions and browser core modifications.

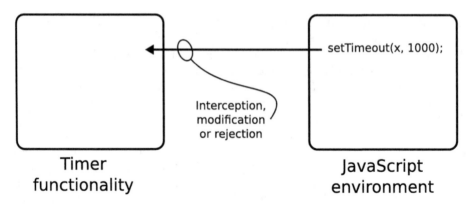

Fig. 8. Executing the `setTimeout()` function will send a message from the JavaScript environment to the component implementing timer functionality, which can be intercepted, modified or rejected by a policy enforcement mechanism in a modified browser.

Browser plugins and browser extensions can add extra functionality to the browser that can be used to enforce a JavaScript sandboxing technique. They are however limited in the modifications they can make in the browser environment.

For more advanced modifications to the browser, such as e.g. the JavaScript engine or the HTML parser, it is typically the case that neither plugins nor extensions are suitable. Therefor, modifying the browser core itself is required.

Research on JavaScript sandboxing through some form of browser modification, includes BEEP [38], ConScript [51], WebJail [91], Contego [45], AdSentry [19], JCShadow [72], Escudo [37], JAMScript [39], ...

4.1 Browser-Enforced Embedded Policies (BEEP)

Jim et al. introduce Browser-Enforced Embedded Policies, a browser modification that introduces a callback mechanism, called every time JavaScript is about to be executed. The callback mechanism provides a hook named `afterParseHook` inside the JavaScript environment, which can be overridden by the web developer.

Every time a piece of JavaScript is to be executed, the browser calls the `afterParseHook` callback to determine whether the piece of JavaScript is allowed to execute or not. To be effective, BEEP must be the first JavaScript code to load in the JavaScript environment, in order to set up the `afterParseHook` callback.

```
1    if (window.JSSecurity) {
2      JSSecurity.afterParseHook =
3        function(code, elt) {
4          if (whitelist[SHA1(code)]) return true;
5          else return false;
6        };
7      whitelist = new Object();
8      whitelist["478zB3KkS+UnP2xz8x62ugOxvd4="] = 1;
9      whitelist["AOOq/aTVjJ7EWQIsGVeKfdg4Gdo="] = 1;
10     ... etc. ...
11   }
```

Listing 1.11: Example whitelist policy implemented in BEEP's `afterParseHook` function, from [38].

The authors experimented with two types of policies: whitelisting and DOM sandboxing.

In the whitelisting policy approach, illustrated in Listing 1.11, the `afterParseHook` callback function receives the script to be executed, and hashes is with the SHA-1 hashing algorithm. This hash is then compared with a list of hashes for allowed scripts. If the hash is found among this whitelist, the `afterParseHook` callback returns `true` and the script is executed.

```
1    <div class="noexecute">
2      <!-- possibly-malicious content starts here -->
3      <script>
4          alert("hello world");
5      </script>
6      <!-- possibly-malicious content ends here -->
7    </div>
```

Listing 1.12: Example HTML with the `noexecute` attribute to be used with BEEP's DOM sandboxing policy.

```
1    <div class="noexecute">
2      <!-- possibly-malicious content starts here -->
3      </div><script>
4          alert("hello world");
5      </script><div>
6      <!-- possibly-malicious content ends here -->
7    </div>
```

Listing 1.13: A node-splitting attack against the example in Listing 1.12. Notice how the enclosing <div> element with `noexecute` attribute is closed by an attacker-injected closing <div> element.

In the DOM sandboxing policy approach, illustrated in Listing 1.12, HTML elements in the web page are clearly marked with a `noexecute` attribute if they can potentially contain untrusted content such as third-party advertising. When a script is about to be executed, the `afterParseHook` callback function receives both the script and the DOM element from which the execution request came. The `afterParseHook` callback function then walks the DOM tree, starting from the given DOM element and following the references to parent nodes. For each DOM node found in this walk, the callback function checks for the presence of a `noexecute` attribute. If such an attribute is found, the `afterParseHook` callback function returns `false`, rejecting script execution.

The authors report two problems with this last approach. First, in an attack to which the authors refer to as "node-splitting," an attacker may write HTML code into the webpage, allowing him to break out of the enclosing DOM element on which a `noexecute` attribute is placed. Shown in Listing 1.13, an attacker could easily break out of the DOM sandboxing policy by closing and opening the enclosing `<div>` tag which has the `noexecute` attribute set, hereby escaping its associated policy of rejecting untrusted scripts. Second, an attacker can introduce an HTML frame, which creates a child document. The `afterParseHook` callback function inside this child document would not be easily able to walk up the parent's DOM tree to check for `noexecute` attributes.

BEEP was implemented in the Konqueror and Safari browsers, and partially in Opera and Firefox. Performance evaluation indicates an average of 8.3 % and 25.7 % overhead on the loadtime of typical webpages for a whitelist policy and DOM sandboxing policy respectively.

4.2   ConScript

Meyerovich et al. present ConScript, a client-side advice implementation for Microsoft Internet Explorer 8. ConScript allows a web developer to wrap a function with an advice function using *around advice*. The advice function is registered in the JavaScript engine as *deep advice* so that it cannot be altered by an attacker.

As with BEEP, ConScript's policy enforcement mechanism must be configured before any untrusted code gains access to the JavaScript execution environment. ConScript introduces a new attribute `policy` to the HTML `<script>` tag, in which a web developer can store a policy to be enforced in the current JavaScript environment. When the web page is loaded, ConScript parses this `policy` attribute and registers the contained policy.

. Unlike shallow advice, which is within reach of attackers and must be secured in order to prevent tampering by an attacker, ConScript registers the advice function as "deep advice" inside the browser core, out of reach of any potential attacker.

```
1    <head>
2      <script policy='
3        let httpOnly: K -> K = function(_ : K) {
4          curse(); throw "HTTP-only cookies"; };
5        around(getField(document, "cookie"), httpOnly);
6        around(setField(document, "cookie"), httpOnly);
7        '>
8      </script>
9    </head>
```

Listing 1.14: Example HttpOnly cookie policy defined on a script element using ConScript, adapted from ConScript [51].

Listing 1.14 shows a ConScript policy being defined in the head of a web page. The policy in this particular example enforces the usage of "HttpOnly" [57] cookies, a version of HTTP cookies which cannot be accessed by JavaScript. To achieve this goal, the policy defines a function HttpOnly which simply throws an exception, and registers this function as "around" advice on the getter and setter of the cookie property of the document object, from which regular cookies are accessible in JavaScript.

Using *around advice* as an advice function allows a policy writer full freedom to block or allow a call to an advised function, possibly basing the decision on arguments passed to the advised function at runtime.

ConScript uses a ML-like subset of JavaScript with labeled types and formal inference rules as its policy language, which can be statically verified for common security holes. To showcase the power of ConScript and its policy language, the authors define 17 example policies addressing a variety of observed bugs and anti-patterns, such as: disallowing inline scripts, restricting XMLHttpRequests to encrypted connections, disallowing cookies to be leaked through hyperlinks, limiting popups and more.

ConScript was implemented in Microsoft Internet Explorer 8 and its performance evaluated. On average, ConScript introduces a slowdown during micro-benchmarks of 3.42x and 1.24x after optimizations. The macro-benchmarks are reported to have negligible overhead.

4.3   WebJail

Van Acker et al. propose WebJail, a JavaScript sandboxing mechanism which uses deep advice functions like ConScript.

In WebJail, HTML iframe elements are used as the basis for a sandbox. A new policy attribute for an iframe element allows a web developer to specify the URL of a WebJail policy, separating concerns between web developers and policy makers.

The authors argue that an expressive policy language such as ConScript's can cause confusion with the integrators who need to write the policy, thus slowing the adoption rate of a sandboxing mechanism. In addition, they warn for a scenario dubbed "inverse sandbox," in which the policy language is so expressive that an attacker may use it to attack a target web application by sandboxing it with a well-crafted policy. For instance, if the policy language is the JavaScript language, an attacker may define a policy on an iframe to intercept any cookie-access and transmit these cookies to an attacker-controlled host. A target web-application could then be loaded into this iframe and would, upon accessing its own cookies, trigger the policy mechanism which leaks the cookies to the attacker.

```
1  {
2    "framecomm": "yes",
3    "extcomm": ["google.com", "youtube.com"],
4    "device": "no"
5  }
```

Listing 1.15: Example WebJail policy allowing inter-frame communication, external communication to Google and YouTube, but disallowing access to the Device API, from [91].

To avoid this scenario, WebJail abstracts away from an overly expressive policy language and defines its own secure composition policy language. Based on an analysis of sensitive JavaScript APIs in the HTML5 specifications, the authors divided the APIs into nine categories. The policy consists of a file written in JSON, describing access rights for each of these categories. Access to a category of sensitive JavaScript APIs in WebJail can be granted or rejected with "yes" or "no", or determined based on a whitelist of allowed parameters. Listing 1.15 shows an example WebJail policy which allows inter-frame communication ("framecomm": "yes"), external communication to Google and YouTube ("extcomm": ["google.com", "youtube.com"]), but disallowing access to the Device API ("device": "no").

WebJail's architecture, depicted in Fig. 9 consists of three layers to process an integrator's policy and turn it into deep advice. The policy layer reads an iframe's policy and combines with the policies of any enclosing iframes. Policy composition is an essential step to ensure that an attacker cannot easily escape the sandbox by creating a child document without a policy defined on it. The advice construction layer processes the composed policy and creates advice functions for all functions in the specified JavaScript APIs. Finally, the deep aspect weaving layer combines the advice functions with the API functions, turning them into deep advice and locking them safely inside the JavaScript engine.

WebJail was implemented in Mozilla Firefox 4.0b10pre for evaluation. The performance evaluation indicated an average of between 6.4 % and 27 % for micro-benchmarks and an average of 6 ms loadtime overhead for macro-benchmarks.

4.4   Contego

Luo et al. design and implement Contego, a capability-based access control system for browsers.

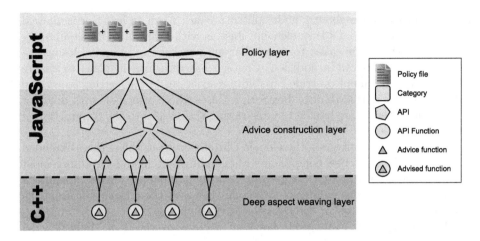

Fig. 9. The WebJail architecture consists of three layers: the policy layer, the advice construction layer and the deep aspect weaving layer, from [91].

In a capability-based access control model, the ability of a principal to perform an action is called a capability. Without the required capability, the principal cannot perform the associated action.

Contego's authors identified a list of capabilities in browsers, among which: performing Ajax requests, using cookies, making HTTP GET requests, clicking on hyperlinks, ... They list three types of actions that can be associated with those capabilities, based on where they originate: HTML-induced actions, JavaScript-induced actions and event-driven actions.

```
1   <div cap="110001111"> ... </div>
2   <!--
3      Capability bitstring:
4         1 AJAX POST request allowed
5         1 AJAX GET request allowed
6         0 Cookie setting not allowed
7         0 Cookie getting not allowed
8         0 Cookie using not allowed
9         1 HTTP GET request allowed
10        1 HTTP POST request allowed
11        1 Hyperlink click allowed
12        1 Button submit click allowed
13  -->
```

Listing 1.16: Example usage of Contego and its capability bitstring, from [45].

Contego allows a web developer to assign capabilities to `<div>` elements in the DOM tree, by assigning a bit-string to the `cap` attribute. Each bit in the bit-string indicates whether a certain capability should be enabled ("1") or disabled ("0") for all DOM elements enclosed by the `<div>` element on which the capabilities apply. The meaning of each bit in the bit-string is shown in Listing 1.16, which also shows an example policy disabling access to cookies.

The authors warn about a node-splitting attack when an attacker is allowed to insert content into a `<div>` element. Just as with BEEP's DOM sandboxing policy, care should be taken to avoid that an attacker can insert a closing tag and escape the policy. In addition, Contego has measures in place to ensure that an attacker cannot override capability restrictions by e.g. setting a new `cap` attribute either in HTML or in JavaScript. Cases where principals with different capabilities interact are handled by restricting the actions to the conjunction of the capability sets.

To implement Contego in the Google Chrome browser, the authors extended the browser with two new components: the binding system and the enforcement system. The binding system assigns and tracks individual principal's capabilities within a webpage. The enforcement system then uses the information from the binding system to allow or deny actions at runtime.

The performance evaluation shows an average overhead of about 3 % on macro-benchmarks.

4.5   AdSentry

Dong et al. propose AdSentry, a confinement solution for JavaScript-based advertisements, which executes the advertisements in a special-purpose JavaScript engine.

An architectural overview of AdSentry is shown in Fig. 10. Next to the regular JavaScript engine, AdSentry implements an additional JavaScript engine, called the shadow JavaScript engine, as a browser plugin. The browser plugin is built on top of the Native Client (NaCl) [30] sandbox, which protects the browser

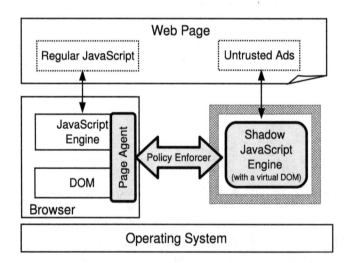

Fig. 10. The AdSentry architecture: advertisements are executed in a shadow JavaScript engine which communicates with the Page Agent via the policy enforcer, from [19].

and the rest of the operating system from drive-by-download attacks occurring inside the sandbox.

Advertisements can either be explicitly marked for use with AdSentry, or they can be automatically detected by AdBlock Plus. When an advertisement is detected in a webpage, AdSentry assigns it a unique identifier and communicates with the shadow JavaScript engine to request that the code be executed there. The shadow JavaScript engine then creates a new JavaScript context with its own global object and virtual DOM and executes the advertisement.

```
1    msg ::= command data
2    command ::= script | callFunc | getProp
3                    | setProp | return
4    data ::= <text>
```

Listing 1.17: Format of the communication protocol used between AdSentry's shadow JavaScript engine and the Page Agent, from [19].

The virtual DOM inside the shadow JavaScript context has no access to the real webpage on which the advertisement is supposed to be rendered. Instead, the methods of the virtual DOM are stubs which trigger the shadow JavaScript engine to communicate with a Page Agent in the real JavaScript engine, requesting access on behalf of the advertisement. The communication between the Page Agent and the shadow JavaScript engine is facilitated with a data exchange protocol, shown in Listing 1.17. This communication channel is also where AdSentry's enforcement mechanism operates, granting or blocking access to the real webpage's DOM according to a user-specified policy. No information is given on how this policy can be specified.

AdSentry was implemented in Google Chrome, and uses a standalone version of SpiderMonkey, Mozilla's JavaScript engine, as the shadow JavaScript engine. The performance evaluation indicates an average overhead of 590x on micro-benchmarks when traversing the boundary between the shadow JavaScript engine and the Page Agent, and an around 3 % to 5 % overall loadtime overhead on macro-benchmarks.

4.6   Discussion

This section discussed five browser modifications that aim to isolate and restrict JavaScript code in the web browser: BEEP, ConScript, WebJail, Contego and AdSentry. Some of their features are summarized in Table 2.

JavaScript sandboxing through a browser modification allows the integration of third-party scripts written in the full JavaScript language. Web applications can be built with a much richer set of JavaScript libraries, since those JavaScript libraries are not confined to a subset of JavaScript.

In addition, a browser modification can control the execution of JavaScript inside the browser, allowing the construction of efficient custom-built machinery to enforce a sandboxing policy, ensuring low overhead.

Table 2. Comparison between prominent JavaScript sandboxing systems using a browser modification.

System	Target application	Isolation unit	Restricts	Policy expressiveness	Deployment	Browser	Performance	Known weaknesses
BEEP	restrict scripts	entire JS environment	execution of JS scripts	full JavaScript to indicate "accept" or "reject"	afterParseHook implementation by integrator	Konqueror, Safari, partially Opera, partially Firefox	8.3 % to 25.7 % macro	node-splitting
ConScript	sandboxing	entire JS environment	??? anything	high: own JS subset	policy attribute on script element	MSIE	1.24x to 3.42x micro, negligible macro	
WebJail	sandboxing	entire JS environment + subframes	access to sensitive APIs	yes/no/whitelist	policy attribute on iframe element	Firefox	6.4% to 27% micro, 6 ms macro	
Contego	restrict capabilities	\<div\> element	capabilities	bitstring	cap attribute on div element	Chrome	3 % macro	
AdSentry	advertisement	shadow JavaScript engine	access to the DOM	???	???	Chrome	590x micro, 3 % to 5 % macro	

However, modified browsers pose a problem with regard to dissemination of the software and compatibility with browsers and browser versions. End-users must take extra steps in order to enjoy the protection of this type of JavaScript sandboxing systems.

Because end-users do not all use the same browser, it becomes impossible to assure that all end-users can keep using their own favorite browser. In the most fortunate case, the developers of this browser core modification may find a way to port their sandboxing system to all browsers. Even if this is the case, a browser core modification is a fork in a browser's code base and must be maintained to keep up with changes in the main code base, which can be a significant time investment.

Likewise, a browser plugin or extension implementing a certain JavaScript sandboxing system, must also be created for all browser vendors and versions, to enable a wide range of users to make use of it. Such a plugin or extension must equally be maintained for future releases of browsers, which can also require a significant time investment.

All in all, modifying a browser through a fork of browser code, a browser plugin or a browser extension in order to implement a JavaScript sandboxing system, is acceptable for a prototype, but proves difficult in a production environment.

An alternative approach is to convince major browser vendors to implement the browser modification as part of their main code base, or even better, pass it through the standardization process so that all browser vendors will implement it. This approach will ensure that the sandboxing technique ends up in a user's favorite browser automatically and that the code base is maintained by the browser vendors themselves.

Unfortunately, getting a proposal accepted by the standardization committees is not a straightforward task, partly because no solution is widely accepted as being "The Solution."

In recent years, the standardization process has yielded new and powerful functionality that could be used to build a JavaScript sandboxing system. Through this approach, a JavaScript sandboxing system would not need any browser modification at all and work out of the box on all browsers that support the latest Web standards.

5 JavaScript Sandboxing Without Browser Modifications

The previous section showed that a sandboxing mechanism implemented as a browser modification, can be used to restrict JavaScript functionality available to untrusted code at runtime. A browser modification is useful for proof-of-concept evaluation of a sandboxing mechanism, but proves problematic in a production environment. Not only must a browser modification be maintained with new releases of the browser on which it is based, but end-users must also be convinced to install the modified browser, plugin or extension.

Given the powerful nature of JavaScript, it is possible to isolate and restrict untrusted JavaScript code at runtime, without the need for a browser modification. This approach is challenging because the enforcement mechanism will execute in the same execution environment as the untrusted code it is trying to restrict. Special care must be taken to ensure that the untrusted code cannot interfere with the enforcement mechanism, and this without any added functionality to protect itself from the untrusted code.

Isolation Unit and Communication Channel. Following the same rationale as in the previous section, a good approach is to create an isolated unit (or sandbox) which is completely cut off from any sensitive functionality, reducing it to a side-effect free execution environment. Figure 11 sketches the relationship between a sandbox and the real JavaScript environment.

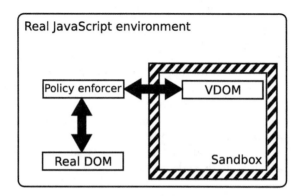

Fig. 11. Relationship between the real JavaScript environment and a sandbox. The sandbox can only interact with a Virtual DOM, which forwards it via the policy enforcer to the real DOM.

Any untrusted code executed in the sandbox, will not be able to affect the outside world, except through a virtual DOM introduced into this sandbox. To access the outside world, the isolated code must make use of the virtual DOM, which will forward the access request over a communication channel to an enforcement mechanism. If the access is allowed, the enforcement mechanism again forwards the access request to the real JavaScript environment.

New and Powerful ECMAScript 5 Functionality. The rise of Web 2.0 resulted in the standardization of ECMAScript 5, which brought new and powerful functionality to mainstream browsers. This new functionality can help with the isolation and restriction of untrusted JavaScript code.

An example of such functionality is the WebWorker API, or WebWorkers [93]. WebWorkers allow web developers to spawn background workers to run in parallel with a web page. These workers are intended to perform long-running computational tasks in the background, while keeping web pages responsive to user interaction.

WebWorkers have a very restricted API available to them, which only allows them to do very basic tasks such as set timers, perform XMLHttpRequests or communicate through `postMessage()`. In particular, WebWorkers have no access to the DOM. Communication between WebWorkers and a web page is achieved through the postMessage API.

Having new ECMAScript 5 functionality in place in browsers today, opens new options for JavaScript sandboxing mechanisms which previously required browser modifications or code verification/transformation in a separate middlebox.

For instance, because WebWorkers restrict JavaScript code from accessing the DOM and other sensitive JavaScript functionality, they can be used as the isolation unit for a JavaScript sandboxing mechanism. TreeHouse, discussed farther in this section, uses WebWorkers as its isolation unit.

Research on JavaScript sandboxing without browser modification includes Self-protecting JavaScript [48,74], AdJail [84], Object Views [50], JSand [6], TreeHouse [35], Privilege-separated JavaScript [7], SafeScript [85], Pivot [52], IceShield [34], SafeJS [14], Two-tier sandbox [73], Virtual Browser [13], ... A selection of this work is discussed in the following sections.

5.1 Self-Protecting JavaScript

Phung et al. propose a solution where DOM API functions are replaced by wrappers which can optionally call the original functions, to which the wrapper has unique access. The wrappers can be used to enforce a policy and, with the ability to store state inside the wrapper function's scope, allow the enforcement of very expressive policies. Access to sensitive DOM properties can also be limited by defining a getter and setter method on them which implements a restricting policy.

```
1   var wrapper = (function (original) {
2       // counter keeps state across
3       // multiple function calls
4       var counter = 0;

5       // create and return the wrapper
6       return function(m) {
7           if(counter < 2) {
8               original(m);
9               counter++;
10          }
11      }
12  })(window.alert);

13  window.alert = wrapper;
```

Listing 1.18: Simplified version of Self-protecting JavaScript's creation of a wrapper around the `alert()` function, allowing it to be called maximum twice.

An example of how a DOM function is replaced with a wrapper, is shown in Listing 1.18. In this example, a wrapper for the function `alert()` is created with a built-in policy to only allow the function to be called twice. A reference to the original native implementation of `alert()` is kept inside the wrapper's scope chain, making it only accessible by the wrapper itself. Finally, the original `alert()` function is replaced by the wrapper.

It is vital that the wrappers are created and put in place of the original DOM functions before any other JavaScript runs inside the JavaScript environment, to achieve full mediation. If any untrusted JavaScript code is run before the wrappers are in place, an attacker may keep copies of the original DOM functions around, thus bypassing any policies that are placed on them later.

The authors warn that references to DOM functions can also be retrieved through the `contentWindow` property of newly created child documents. To prevent this, access to the `contentWindow` property is denied.

A bug in the `delete` operator of older Firefox browsers also allows overwritten DOM functions to be restored to references to their original native implementations, by simply deleting the wrappers.

A performance evaluation of Self-protecting JavaScript revealed a average of 6.33x slowdown on micro-benchmarks, and a 5.37 % average overhead for macro-benchmarks.

Magazinius et al. [48] analyzed Self-protecting JavaScript and uncovered several weaknesses and vulnerabilities that allow the sandboxing mechanism to be bypassed by an attacker.

They note that the original implementation does not remove all references to DOM functions from the JavaScript environment, leaving them open to abuse from attackers. The `alert()` function for instance, has several aliases (such as `window._proto_.alert()`), which must all be replaced with a wrapper for Self-protecting JavaScript to be effective.

Equally, simply denying access to the `contentWindow` property is not sufficient to prevent references to DOM functions from being retrieved from child documents. These references can also be access from child documents through the `frames` property of the `window` object, or from the parent document through the `parent` property of the `window` object.

They also point out that Self-protecting JavaScript is vulnerable to several types of prototype poisoning attacks, allowing an attacker to get access to the original, unwrapped DOM functions as well as the internal state of a policy wrapper.

Lastly, they remind that an attacker could abuse the caller chain during a wrapper's execution, by gaining access to the non-standard `caller` property available in functions, allowing an attacker to gain access to the unwrapped DOM functions.

Finally, Magazinius et al. offer solutions to remedy these vulnerabilities by making sure any functions and objects used inside a wrapper are disconnected from the prototype chain to prevent prototype poisoning, and coercing parameters of functions inside wrappers to their expected types in order to further reduce the attack surface.

5.2 AdJail

Ter Louw et al. propose AdJail, an advertising framework which enforces JavaScript sandboxing on advertisements.

AdJail allows a web developer to restrict what parts of the web page an advertisement has access to, by marking HTML elements in that web page with the `policy` attribute. This `policy` attribute contains the AdJail policy that is in effect for a certain HTML element and its sub-elements.

The AdJail policy language allows the specification of what HTML elements can be read or written to, and whether that access extends to its sub-elements. The web developer can also define a policy to enable or disable images, Flash or iframes, restrict the size of an advertisement to a certain height and width and allow clicked hyperlinks to open web pages in a new window.

By default, an advertisement is positioned in the "default ad zone," an HTML `<div>` element that aids the web developer in positioning the advertisement in the web page. The default policy is set to "deny all."

An overview of AdJail is shown in Fig. 12. The advertisement is executed in a "shadow page," which is a hidden iframe with a different origin, so that it is isolated from the real web page. Those parts of the real web page's DOM that are marked as readable by the advertisement, are replicated inside the shadow page before the advertisement executes.

Changes made by the advertisement inside the shadow page, are detected by hooking into the DOM of the shadow page, and communicated to the real page through a tunnel script. The changes are replicated on the real page if

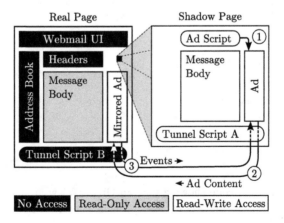

Fig. 12. Overview of AdJail, showing the real page, the shadow page and the tunnel scripts through which they communicate and on which the policy is enforced, from [84].

allowed by the policy. Likewise, events generated by the user on the real page, are communicated to the shadow page so that the advertisement can react to them.

Because AdJail is aimed at sandboxing advertisements, special care must be taken to ensure that the advertisement provider's revenue stream is not tampered with. In particular, AdJail takes special precautions to ensure that content is only downloaded once, to avoid duplicate registration of "ad impressions" on the advertisement network. Furthermore, AdJail leverages techniques used by BLUEPRINT [86] to ensure that an advertisement does not inject scripts into the real webpage.

Performance benchmarks indicate that AdJail has an average overhead of 29.7 % on ad rendering, increasing the rendering time from an average of 374 ms to 532 ms. Further analysis showed that AdJail has an average overhead of 25 % on the entire page loadtime, increasing it from 489 ms to 652 ms.

5.3 Object Views

Meyerovich et al. introduce Object Views, a fine grained access control mechanism over shared JavaScript objects.

An "Object View" is a wrapper around an object that only exposes a subset of the wrapped object's properties to the outside world. The wrapper consists of a proxy between the wrapped object and the outside world, and a policy that determines what properties should be made available through the proxy.

```
1   var wrapper = ...;
2   var obj = { prop: 123, func: function() {
3       alert("hello world");
4       }
5   };

6   defineSetter(wrapper, "prop",
7       function(x) {
8           obj.prop = x;
9       });

10  defineGetter(wrapper, "prop",
11      function() {
12          return obj.prop;
13      });

14  wrapper.func = function() {
15      obj.func(arguments);
16  };

17  alert(wrapper.prop); // displays 123
18  wrapper.prop = 456;  // sets obj.prop to 456
19  wrapper.func()       // displays "hello world"
```

Listing 1.19: Pseudo-code showing how an Object View around an object obj can be used to intercept reading and writing a property, and intercepting a function call, from [50].

Sketched in Listing 1.19, an Object View contains a getter and setter method for each property on the wrapped object, and a proxy function for each function object. Writing a value to a property on an Object View, triggers the setter function which may eventually write the value to the wrapped object's respective property. The getter function works in a similar way for reading properties. Using a property of an Object View as a function and calling it, triggers the proxy function. Object Views are applied recursively to a proxy function's return value.

Creating two Object Views that wrap the same object, poses a problem with regard to reference equality. Although comparing the underlying objects of both object views would result in an equality, this would not be the case for the two wrapping Object Views. This inconsistent view can be prevented by only wrapping an object with an Object View once, and returning that same Object View every time a new Object View for the underlying object is requested.

Object views offer a basis for fine-grained access control through an aspect system. Each getter, setter and proxy function on an Object View can be combined with an "around" advice function, allowing the enforcement of an expressive policy.

Because of its size and complexity, manually wrapping the entire DOM with object views would be a difficult and error-prone process. Instead, the authors advocate a declarative policy system which is translated into advice for the Object Views.

```
1  {
2      "selector": "(//*[@class=âĂŸexampleâĂź]) | (//*[@class=âĂŸexampleâĂź]//*)",
3      "enabled": true,
4      "defaultFieldActions": {read: permit},
5      "fields": {shake: {methCall: permit}}
6  }
```

Listing 1.20: A declarative policy rule specifying that a DOM element of class example and its subtree are read-only. If a method shake() exists, it may be read and invoked as a method.

The declarative policy is specified by a set of rules consisting of an XPath [95] selector to specify a set of DOM nodes and an Enabled flag to indicate that the selected nodes may be accessed. Optionally, each rule can be extended with default and specific rules for each field of a DOM element. An example rule, shown in Listing 1.20, specifies that all DOM elements of class example and its subtree can be accessed (enabled = true) and is by default read-only (defaultFieldActions). A specific rule for a field called shake allows that field to be read and invoked as a method.

The authors discuss using Object Views in two scenarios: a scenario where JavaScript is rewritten[1] to make use of Object Views for same-origin usage, and a scenario where Object Views are used in cross-origin communication between frames.

---

[1] This work could also be listed under Sect. 3, but since the published paper mostly focuses on the cross-origin communication which does not require browser modifications, it is listed in this section instead.

In the latter scenario, each frame provides an Object View around its enclosed document to only expose the view required by the other. Communication between the frames is handled by marshaling requests for the other side to a string and transmitting it with `postMessage()`. Because each Object View has its own built-in policy, the communication channel does not need to enforce a separate policy.

The performance of Object Views was evaluated on a scenario where several objects are wrapped in a view, but where the communication between Object Views is not marshaled and transmitted with `postMessage()`. For this scenario, the average overhead is between 15 % and 236 % on micro-benchmarks.

5.4   JSand

Agten et al. propose JSand, a JavaScript sandboxing mechanism based on Secure ECMAScript (SES).

Secure ECMAScript (SES) is a subset of ECMAScript 5 strict which forms a true object-capability language, guaranteeing that references to objects can only be obtained if they were explicitly passed to an object-capability environment.

Without a reference to the DOM, JavaScript code running in a SES environment cannot affect the outside world. JSand wraps the global object using the Proxy API [20] and passes a reference to this proxied global object to the SES environment. Any access to the global object from inside the SES environment, will traverse the proxy wrapper on which a policy can be enforced.

Without additional care, JavaScript inside the SES environment with access to this proxied global object, can invoke methods that return unwrapped JavaScript objects. Such an oversight can cause a reference to the real JavaScript to leak into the SES environment, making JSand ineffective. To avoid this, JSand wraps return values recursively, according to the Membrane Pattern [61]. In addition, JSand preserves pointer equality between wrappers around the same objects, by storing created wrappers in a cache and returning an existing wrapper if one already exists.

Using the Membrane pattern, any access to the outside world from inside the SES environment, can be intercepted and subjected to a policy enforcement mechanism. The authors do not specify a specific policy implementation, but point out that JSand's architecture allows for expressive fine-grained and stateful policies.

There are two important incompatibilities between the SES subset and ECMAScript 5 code, which makes legacy JavaScript incompatible with JSand.

The first is the mirroring of global variables with properties on the global object and vice versa. When a global variable is created under ECMAScript 5, a property with the same name is created on the global object. Similarly, a property created on the global object results in the creation of a global variable of the same name. This ECMAScript 5 behavior is not present in SES and can cause legacy scripts who depend on that behavior, to break.

Second, because SES is a subset of ECMAScript 5 strict, it does not support the `with` construct, does not bind `this` to the global object in a function call and does not create new variables during `eval()` invocations. Legacy scripts making use of this behavior will also break in SES.

To be backwards compatible with legacy JavaScript that does not conform to SES, JSand applies a client-side JavaScript rewriting step where needed before sandboxing the guest JavaScript code. The UglifyJS [59] JavaScript parser is used to parse JavaScript into an Abstract Syntax Tree (AST). This tree is then inspected and modified for legacy ECMAScript 5 constructs that will break in SES. In particular, JSand rewrites guest code so that the mirroring of global variables and properties of the global object in ECMAScript 5, is replicated explicitly. JSand also finds all occurrences to the `this` keyword and replaces it with an expression that replaces it with `window` if its value is undefined, thus also replicating ECMAScript 5 behavior.

JSand's performance evaluation indicates an average 9x slowdown for function-calls than traverse the membrane wrapper, resulting in an average of 31.2 % overhead in user experience when interacting with a realistic web application. The load-time of a web application is increased on average by 365 % for legacy web applications using ECMAScript 5 code which requires the rewriting step. The authors expect that this rewriting step will not be needed in the future, so that the average load-time overhead will drop to 203 %.

5.5   TreeHouse

Ingram et al. propose TreeHouse, a JavaScript sandboxing mechanism built on WebWorkers. As explained previously, WebWorkers are parallel JavaScript execution environments without a usual DOM, which can only communicate through `postMessage()`.

An overview of TreeHouse's architecture is shown in Fig. 13. TreeHouse loads guest JavaScript code into a WebWorker to isolate it from the rest of a web page. WebWorkers do not have a regular DOM, so TreeHouse installs a broker with a virtual DOM inside the WebWorker that emulates the DOM of a real webpage.

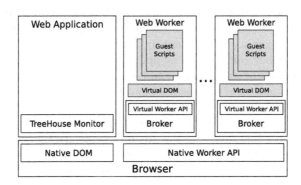

Fig. 13. TreeHouse architectural overview. Sandboxes consist of WebWorkers with a virtual DOM. Access to this virtual DOM is mediated by broker according to a policy. If access is allowed, the request is forwarded to the real page's monitor, from [35].

When this virtual DOM is accessed, the broker first consults the policy to determine whether access is allowed. If access is allowed, the broker then forwards the access request to the real page's "TreeHouse Monitor" using `postMessage()`, which handles the access to the real page's DOM.

TreeHouse offers two deployment options to web developers wishing to use its sandboxing mechanism. One option is to create a sandbox with a policy and load JavaScript in it manually using the TreeHouse API. Another option, is more user-friendly and allows a web developer to specify guest code to be sandboxed, in actual `<script>` elements. These `<script>` elements should have their `type` attribute set to `"text/x-treehouse-javascript"` to prevent them from being executed by the JavaScript engine in the host page. The special script type is also automatically detected by the TreeHouse Monitor, which will create sandboxes and load the script inside them.

```
1   <script src="tetris.js"
2       type="text/x-treehouse-javascript"
3       data-treehouse-sandbox-name="worker1"
4       data-treehouse-sandbox-children="#tetris">
5   </script>
6   <script src="tetris-policy.js"
7       type="text/x-treehouse-javascript"
8       data-treehouse-sandbox-name="worker1"
9       data-treehouse-sandbox-policy>
10  </script>
```

Listing 1.21: TreeHouse integration in a web page. Guest code is loaded into `<script>` tags with type `"text/x-treehouse-javascript"` so that they are automatically sandboxed. The policy is also specified in a `<script>` element marked with a `"data-treehouse-sandbox-policy"` attribute, from [35].

An example use of TreeHouse is shown in Listing 1.21. Here, the first `<script>` element shows how a sandbox is created called `"worker1"`, with access to the DOM element with id `"#tetris"` and its subtree. The `"tetris.js"` script is then loaded inside the sandbox and executed. The second `<script>` tag references the sandbox `"worker1"` and indicates through the `"data-treehouse-sandbox-policy"` attribute that the script `"tetris-policy.js"` should be interpreted as a policy instead of guest JavaScript code.

A TreeHouse policy consists of a mapping between DOM elements and rules. There are three types of rules: a rule can be expressed by a boolean, a function returning a boolean, or a regular expression. If the rule has a boolean value of `true`, access to the associated DOM element is allowed. If the rule is a function, that function is invoked at policy enforcement time by the broker, and access is allowed if the return value is `true`. Finally, if the rule is a regular expression, it refers to a property. If the regular expression matches a property's name, then the guest code is allowed to set a value to that property.

Because WebWorkers are concurrent by design, they present a problem when multiple TreeHouse sandboxes try to access to same DOM element in a real page. Such simultaneous access would cause a race condition and result in undefined behavior. To prevent such a race condition, TreeHouse allows a DOM element to only be accessed by one sandbox.

Another concurrency problem arises when the guest code makes use of a synchronous method such as `window.alert()`. The guest code will expect the JavaScript execution to block, waiting for the end-user to click away the pop-up window. In reality, TreeHouse's communication channel between the host page and the WebWorkers is asynchronous because `postMessage()` is asynchronous. When calling `window.alert()` in the guest code, the broker would send an asynchronous message to the host page, and let code execution in the sandbox resume immediately. This conflicts with the guest code's expected behavior. The authors chose not to handle this case and raise a runtime exception when guest code calls synchronous methods.

The performance benchmarks for TreeHouse show an average slowdown of 15x to 176x for macro-benchmarks, and an average of 7x to 8000x slowdown on micro-benchmarks for method invocations on the DOM.

5.6   SafeScript

Ter Louw et al. propose SafeScript, a client-side JavaScript transformation technique to isolate JavaScript code in namespaces.

SafeScript makes use of Narcissus [67], a JavaScript meta-interpreter, to rewrite JavaScript code on the client-side and instrument the code so that it can interpose on the property resolution mechanism. Narcissus is a full JavaScript interpreter and can correctly handle all of JavaScript's strange semantics, its scoping, prototype chains and thus also the property resolution mechanism.

Through this rewriting step, SafeScript can separate JavaScript code in namespaces by manipulating the property resolution mechanism for each sandboxed script so that it ultimately resolves to its own isolated global object. Because property resolution is under SafeScript's control, it can effectively mediate access to the real DOM when sandboxed JavaScript guest code requests access to it.

```
1   <!-- the transformation tool -->
2   <script src='rewriter.js'></script>
3   <!-- an APIâĂŹs implementation -->
4   <script src='interface0.js'></script>

5   <script>
6   var namespace0 = $_sm[0]();
7   var script0_code = load_script('http://3rd.com/main.js');
8   exec_script(transform(script0_code, namespace0));
9   </script>
```

Listing 1.22: SafeScript used on a webpage. After loading the rewriter and API implementation, a namespace is created and the guest code is loaded. Afterwards, the guest code is transformed so that the property resolution mechanism is locked to the created namespace, and the transformed code is executed, from [85].

Listing 1.22 shows how SafeScript can be used to sandbox a given JavaScript. In this example, the `"rewriter.js"` script contains SafeScript's transformation code and `"interface0.js"` contains an API implementation for a "namespace 0." After creating the namespace with `$_sm[0]()`, the guest code is loaded from a third-party host, transformed so that the property resolution mechanism is locked to "namespace 0", and then executed.

SafeScript ensures that any dynamically generated JavaScript code is also transformed and isolated in a namespace. In order to do so, SafeScript traps methods such as `eval()`, `setTimeout()`, which can inject JavaScript code into the execution environment directly. To capture JavaScript code that is indirectly injected, SafeScript monitors methods such as `document.write()` and properties like `innerHTML`. HTML written through these injection points must first be parsed and have its JavaScript code extracted before it can be transformed by SafeScript.

Despite its many optimizations, SafeScript's performance benchmarks indicate an average slowdown of 6.43x on basic operations such a variable incrementation, because SafeScript rewrites every variable statement. The macrobenchmark reveals an average slowdown of 64x.

5.7   Discussion

This section discussed six JavaScript sandboxing mechanisms that do not require any browser modifications: Self-protecting JavaScript, AdJail, Object Views, JSand, TreeHouse and SafeScript. Some of their features are summarized in Table 3.

Besides Self-protecting JavaScript, which protects all access-routes to the DOM API through enumeration, all solutions isolate untrusted JavaScript in an isolation unit. The isolated JavaScript cannot access the DOM directly, but must communicate with the real web page and request access, which is then mediated by a policy enforcement mechanism.

JavaScript sandboxing systems that do not require browser modifications leverage existing standardized powerful functionality that is available in browsers today. The advantage of this approach is that standardized functionality is, or in the near future will be, available in all browsers and thus the sandbox works out of the box for all Internet users.

Much of the new browser functionality incorporated in the previously discussed JavaScript sandboxing systems, was not designed for sandboxing and may not perform well enough for a seamless user experience.

In the future that may change, because browser vendors optimize their code for speed to compete with other browser vendors. When new browser functionality becomes more popular, it will undoubtedly also be optimized for speed, automatically increasing the performance of the JavaScript sandboxing systems making use of it.

Web standards keep evolving, so that we can expect more advanced browser functionality in the future. This new functionality can then be used to design and implement yet more powerful JavaScript sandboxing systems. Ideally, this new

Table 3. Comparison between prominent JavaScript sandboxing systems not requiring browser modifications.

System	Target application	Isolation unit	Communication	Policy expressiveness	Deployment	Performance	Known weaknesses
Self-protecting JavaScript	sandboxing	JavaScript environment	n/a	high	library	6.33x micro, 5.37 % macro	[48]
AdJail	advertisements	shadow page	postMessage	read/write elements + enable/disable images/other	policy attribute	25 % macro	
Object Views	sandboxing	iframe	postMessage	get/set/call	declarative policy with XPath	15 % to 236 % micro	
JSand	sandboxing	SES environment	Membrane/Proxy API	high	VDOM implementation	9x micro, 203 % to 365 % macro on loadtime, 31.2 % macro on user experience	
TreeHouse	sandboxing	WebWorker	postMessage	high	script elements with custom type	7x to 8000x micro, 15x to 176x macro	
SafeScript	sandboxing	namespace	VDOM implementation	high?	VDOM implementation	6.43x micro, 64x macro	

functionality will also bring APIs dedicated to JavaScript sandboxing, providing purpose-built mechanisms to isolate code in a sandbox and communicate with that sandbox.

When such specialized JavaScript APIs are adopted and implemented, future JavaScript sandboxing mechanisms will no longer need to rely on repurposed functionality, making them simpler and faster.

6   In Practice – Application Examples

Previous sections discussed several JavaScript sandboxing mechanisms that work well in theory. In reality, JavaScript sandboxing solutions have apparently not seen wide-spread adoption.

The reasons for this low adoption rate are not clear. Perhaps JavaScript sandboxing has not attained enough critical mass to be "obviously" needed by web developers. Maybe web developers are waiting for a one-size-fits-all solution, are not confident enough that the JavaScript sandboxing mechanisms work as securely as advertised, or are scared away because the sandboxes are too difficult to deploy.

In this section, we highlight two technologies that have emerged from the JavaScript sandboxing research and have been used in production systems.

6.1   Facebook JavaScript

Facebook Platform launched in May 2007 [24] as a framework to allow Facebook application developers to deeply integrate with Facebook and interact with core Facebook features. Facebook application developers could use Facebook Markup Language (FBML) to customize the look and feel of their applications as rendered on Facebook. This application frontend written in FBML was hosted by Facebook itself and consisted of HTML, CSS and Facebook JavaScript (FBJS), a subset of JavaScript discussed in Sect. 3.

Facebook JavaScript allowed Facebook application developers to include JavaScript in their application, but in a controlled environment. Because applications written in FBML are hosted by Facebook, they execute inside Facebook's Web origin. If Facebook had allowed the applications to make use of a fully functional JavaScript environment, they could have easily exfiltrated Facebook session information and compromise the Facebook accounts and privacy of all users of that Facebook application. Unlike other platforms who isolate with iframes, Facebook has opted to sandbox third-party applications by rewriting HTML, CSS and JavaScript code using a middlebox located on Facebook's site.

Roughly one year after its introduction, in July 2008, FBML was used by about 33,000 applications [8] built by about 400,000 developers [22].

According to some developers, FBML was "increasingly less reliable, which leads to confusion and frustration" and "FBML always seemed like a pretty buggy and unsustainable approach to Facebook coding." Because Facebook restricted applications to FBML, developers felt they had to stray away from standard Web coding practices.

In addition to practicality and usability issues, FBML suffered from several security problems. As discussed in Sect. 3, at least two vulnerabilities [46, 47] were discovered in FBJS, which allowed attackers to break out of FBJS's JavaScript sandbox and thus escape isolation into Facebook's Web origin.

In August 2010, Facebook announced the deprecation of FBML in favor of iframe isolation for its applications [69], stating that this would eliminate the technical difference between developing an application on and off Facebook.

In December 2010, Facebook announced that new FBML applications would still be allowed until Q1 2011 because the implementation of the iframe isolation was not yet finished [79].

In January 2011, Several old and infrequently used FBML tags and API methods were eliminated [26].

In March 2011, Facebook stopped accepting new FBML applications but still allowed existing FBML applications to be updated. Switching to iframes instead of FBML was recommended [23].

In January 2012, Facebook discontinued support for FBML by no longer fixing bugs for FBML. Security and privacy-related bugs were still being addressed.

In June 2012, an "FBML Removal" migration appeared for all apps, enabled by default. This migration tool allowed application developers to disable the migration, extending their usage of FBML for another month.

In July 2012, Facebook also removed the "FBML Removal" migration tool and the FBML endpoints.

In December 2012, Facebook removed the "Static FBML Page app," which could no longer render FBML but still had the ability to display HTML, finalizing the complete removal of FBML from Facebook.

Facebook now isolates applications in iframes, requiring the webpages to be hosted outside of Facebook. The applications can make use of Facebook's Graph API to interact with the social graph.

6.2 Caja

As discussed in Sect. 3, Google's Caja rewrites HTML, CSS and JavaScript on the server-side to secure JavaScript in applications on the client-side. Caja was developed with ECMAScript 3 as a starting point. ES3 is a "very leaky language" [18] with numerous strange scoping rules, making it a nightmare to secure. The lessons learned from working on Caja were applied to the design of ECMAScript 5, making it a version of JavaScript which, as opposed to ES3, is fairly easy to secure through its "strict mode". Contained in ECMAScript 5 is a subset called Secure ECMAScript (SES), which is object-capability safe.

Caja is used, or has been used in several Google products [18, 81, 82] to allow embedding of third-party JavaScript: Google Labs (retired in 2011), iGoogle (retired in 2012), Orkut (retired in 2014), Google Sites, Google Apps Script, Blogspot, . . .

Yahoo used Caja in its Yahoo! Application Platform [78], MySpace for its MySpace Developer Platform [44] and PayPal for PayPal Apps [43]. All three stopped using Caja (although PayPal's case is unconfirmed), but it is unclear why. A popular opinion seems to be that Caja is too restrictive for developers, who expect to be able to use full JavaScript.

Because Caja is an open-source project, it can be freely used and modified by others. Besides the very visible use-cases, Caja can also be used by less prominent websites. Apache Shindig is a container for the OpenSocial specification, which defines a component hosting environment and a set of common APIs for web-based applications. Shindig uses Caja for JavaScript rewriting, which means that less prominent web applications which make use of Shindig may also be using Caja in the background.

To this day, Caja is still actively developed. Used by Google itself and with its developers involved in workgroups on Web standards and the ECMAScript committee, the work on Caja has contributed to the development of the Web and will probably not go away anytime soon.

7   Conclusion

This work gave an overview of the JavaScript sandboxing research field and the different approaches taken to isolate and restrict JavaScript to a chosen set of resources and functionality.

The JavaScript sandboxing research can be divided into three categories: JavaScript subsets and rewriting systems, JavaScript sandboxing through browser modifications and JavaScript sandboxing without browser modifications.

JavaScript subsets and rewriting systems can restrict untrusted JavaScript if it adheres to a JavaScript subset, but a middlebox needs to verify that this is the case, possibly rewriting the code. These middleboxes break the architecture of the Web when implemented on the server-side, and put an extra burden on the user if implemented on the client-side.

Browser modifications are powerful and can sandbox JavaScript efficiently, because of their prime access to the JavaScript execution environment. Unfortunately, the software modifications are difficult to distribute and maintain in the long run unless they are adopted by mainstream browser vendors.

JavaScript sandboxing mechanisms without browser modifications leverage existing browser functionality to isolate and restrict JavaScript. This approach can be slower but requires no redistribution and maintenance of browser code. When implemented correctly, it automatically works on all modern browsers.

Acknowledgments. This work was funded by the European Community under the ProSecuToR and WebSand projects, the Swedish research agencies SSF and VR.

References

1. Galeon. http://galeon.sourceforge.net/
2. JSLint, The JavaScript Code Quality Tool. http://www.jslint.com/
3. Netscape 2.0 reviewed. http://www.antipope.org/charlie/old/journo/netscape.html
4. node.js. http://nodejs.org/
5. QuirksMode - for all your browser quirks. http://www.quirksmode.org/
6. Agten, P., Van Acker, S., Brondsema, Y., Phung, P.H., Desmet, L., Piessens, F.: JSand: complete client-side sandboxing of third-party JavaScript without browser modifications. In: Proceedings of the 28th Annual Computer Security Applications Conference, pp. 1–10. ACM (2012)
7. Akhawe, D., Saxena, P., Song, D.: Privilege separation in HTML5 applications. In: Kohno, T. (ed.) Proceedings of the 21th USENIX Security Symposium, Bellevue, WA, USA, August 8–10, 2012, pp. 429–444. USENIX Association (2012). https://www.usenix.org/conference/usenixsecurity12/technical-sessions/presentation/akhawe
8. Ustinova, A.: Developers compete at Facebook conference, 23 July 2008. http://www.sfgate.com/business/article/Developers-compete-at-Facebook-conference-3203144.php
9. Apache OpenOffice: Writing Office Scripts in JavaScript. https://www.openoffice.org/framework/scripting/release-0.2/javascript-devguide.html
10. Barth, A., Jackson, C., Mitchell, J.C.: Securing frame communication in browsers. Commun. ACM **52**(6), 83–91 (2009). http://doi.acm.org/10.1145/1516046.1516066
11. Blink: Blink. http://www.chromium.org/blink
12. BuiltWith: jQuery Usage Statistics. http://trends.builtwith.com/javascript/jQuery
13. Cao, Y., Li, Z., Rastogi, V., Chen, Y., Wen, X.: Virtual browser: a virtualized browser to sandbox third-party JavaScripts with enhanced security. In: Youm, H.Y., Won, Y. (eds.) 7th ACM Symposium on Information, Compuer and Communications Security, ASIACCS 2012, Seoul, Korea, May 2–4, 2012, pp. 8–9. ACM (2012). http://doi.acm.org/10.1145/2414456.2414460
14. Cassou, D., Ducasse, S., Petton, N.: SafeJS: Hermetic Sandboxing for JavaScript (2013)
15. Charles Severance: JavaScript: Designing a Language in 10 Days. http://www.computer.org/csdl/mags/co/2012/02/mco2012020007.html
16. Crockford, D.: ADsafe - making JavaScript safe for advertising. http://adsafe.org/
17. De Ryck, P., Desmet, L., Philippaerts, P., Piessens, F.: A security analysis of next generation web standards. Technical report. In: Hogben, G., Dekker, M. (eds.) European Network and Information Security Agency (ENISA), July 2011. https://lirias.kuleuven.be/handle/123456789/317385
18. Dio Synodinos: ECMAScript 5, Caja and Retrofitting Security, with Mark S. Miller. http://www.infoq.com/interviews/ecmascript-5-caja-retrofitting-security
19. Dong, X., Tran, M., Liang, Z., Jiang, X.: AdSentry: comprehensive and flexible confinement of javascript-based advertisements. In: Proceedings of the 27th Annual Computer Security Applications Conference, ACSAC 2011, pp. 297–306. ACM, New York (2011). http://doi.acm.org/10.1145/2076732.2076774
20. ECMAScript: Harmony Direct Proxies. http://wiki.ecmascript.org/doku.php?id=harmony:direct_proxies

21. Espruino: Espruino - JavaScript for Microcontrollers. http://www.espruino.com/
22. Facebook: Facebook Expands Power of Platform Across the Web and Around the World, 23 July 2008. http://newsroom.fb.com/news/2008/07/facebook-expands-power-of-platform-across-the-web-and-around-the-world/
23. Facebook: Facebook Platform Migrations (Older). https://developers.facebook.com/docs/apps/migrations/completed-changes
24. Facebook: Facebook Unveils Platform for Developers of Social Applications, 24 May 2007. http://newsroom.fb.com/news/2007/05/facebook-unveils-platform-for-developers-of-social-applications/
25. Finifter, M., Weinberger, J., Barth, A.: Preventing capability leaks in secure javascript subsets. In: Proceedings of the Network and Distributed System Security Symposium, NDSS 2010, San Diego, California, USA, 28th February - 3rd March 2010. The Internet Society (2010). http://www.isoc.org/isoc/conferences/ndss/10/pdf/21.pdf
26. Fran Larkin: Platform Updates: Change Log, Third Party IDs and More, 18 December 2010. https://developers.facebook.com/blog/post/441
27. GNOME: Gjs: JavaScript Bindings for GNOME. https://wiki.gnome.org/action/show/Projects/Gjs?action=show&redirect=Gjs
28. Google: V8 JavaScript Engine. https://code.google.com/p/v8/
29. Google Chrome Developers: Chrome - What are extensions? https://developer.chrome.com/extensions
30. Google Chrome Developers: Native Client. https://developer.chrome.com/native-client
31. Grosskurth, A., Godfrey, M.W.: A case study in architectural analysis: The evolution of the modern web browser. EMSE (2007)
32. Guarnieri, S., Livshits, V.B.: GATEKEEPER: mostly static enforcement of security and reliability policies for javascript code. In: Monrose, F. (ed.) 18th USENIX Security Symposium, Montreal, Canada, August 10–14, 2009, Proceedings, pp. 151–168. USENIX Association (2009). http://www.usenix.org/events/sec09/tech/full_papers/guarnieri.pdf
33. Guha, A., Saftoiu, C., Krishnamurthi, S.: The essence of javascript. In: D'Hondt, T. (ed.) ECOOP 2010. LNCS, vol. 6183, pp. 126–150. Springer, Heidelberg (2010). http://dx.doi.org/10.1007/978-3-642-14107-2_7
34. Heiderich, M., Frosch, T., Holz, T.: ICESHIELD: detection and mitigation of malicious websites with a frozen DOM. In: Sommer, R., Balzarotti, D., Maier, G. (eds.) RAID 2011. LNCS, vol. 6961, pp. 281–300. Springer, Heidelberg (2011). http://dx.doi.org/10.1007/978-3-642-23644-0_15
35. Ingram, L., Walfish, M.: Treehouse: javascript sandboxes to help web developers help themselves. In: Heiser, G., Hsieh, W.C. (eds.) 2012 USENIX Annual Technical Conference, Boston, MA, USA, June 13–15, 2012, pp. 153–164. USENIX Association (2012). https://www.usenix.org/conference/atc12/technical-sessions/presentation/ingram
36. Jacaranda: Jacaranda. http://jacaranda.org
37. Jayaraman, K., Du, W., Rajagopalan, B., Chapin, S.J.: ESCUDO: a fine-grained protection model for web browsers. In: 2010 International Conference on Distributed Computing Systems, ICDCS 2010, Genova, Italy, June 21–25, 2010, pp. 231–240. IEEE Computer Society (2010). http://doi.ieeecomputersociety.org/10.1109/ICDCS.2010.71

38. Jim, T., Swamy, N., Hicks, M.: Defeating script injection attacks with browser-enforced embedded policies. In: WWW 2007: Proceedings of the 16th International Conference on World Wide Web, pp. 601–610. ACM, New York (2007). http://dx.doi.org/10.1145/1242572.1242654

39. Joiner, R., Reps, T.W., Jha, S., Dhawan, M., Ganapathy, V.: Efficient runtime-enforcement techniques for policy weaving. In: Cheung, S., Orso, A., Storey, M.D. (eds.) Proceedings of the 22nd ACM SIGSOFT International Symposium on Foundations of Software Engineering, (FSE-22), Hong Kong, China, November 16–22, 2014, pp. 224–234. ACM (2014). http://doi.acm.org/10.1145/2635868.2635907

40. jQuery: Update on jQuery.com Compromises. http://blog.jquery.com/2014/09/24/update-on-jquery-com-compromises/

41. JSLint Error Explanations: Implied eval is evil. Pass a function instead of a string. http://jslinterrors.com/implied-eval-is-evil-pass-a-function-instead-of-a-string

42. Zyp, K.: Secure Mashups with dojox.secure. http://www.sitepen.com/blog/2008/08/01/secure-mashups-with-dojoxsecure/

43. Dignan, L.: Developing a PayPal App, 20 February 2011. https://web.archive.org/web/20110220013816/https://www.x.com/docs/DOC-3082

44. Dignan, L.: MySpace: Caja JavaScript scrubbing ready for prime time. http://www.zdnet.com/article/myspace-caja-javascript-scrubbing-ready-for-prime-time/

45. Luo, T., Du, W.: Contego: capability-based access control for web browsers - (short paper). In: McCune, J.M., Balacheff, B., Perrig, A., Sadeghi, A.-R., Sasse, A., Beres, Y. (eds.) Trust 2011. LNCS, vol. 6740, pp. 231–238. Springer, Heidelberg (2011). http://dx.doi.org/10.1007/978-3-642-21599-5_17

46. Maffeis, S., Mitchell, J.C., Taly, A.: Isolating javascript with filters, rewriting, and wrappers. In: Backes, M., Ning, P. (eds.) ESORICS 2009. LNCS, vol. 5789, pp. 505–522. Springer, Heidelberg (2009). http://dx.doi.org/10.1007/978-3-642-04444-1_31

47. Maffeis, S., Taly, A.: Language-based isolation of untrusted javascript. In: Proceedings of the 22nd IEEE Computer Security Foundations Symposium, CSF 2009, Port Jefferson, New York, USA, July 8–10, 2009, pp. 77–91. IEEE Computer Society (2009). http://doi.ieeecomputersociety.org/10.1109/CSF.2009.11

48. Magazinius, J., Phung, P.H., Sands, D.: Safe wrappers and sane policies for self protecting javascript. In: Aura, T., Järvinen, K., Nyberg, K. (eds.) NordSec 2010. LNCS, vol. 7127, pp. 239–255. Springer, Heidelberg (2012). http://dx.doi.org/10.1007/978-3-642-27937-9_17

49. Maxthon: Maxthon Cloud Browser. http://www.maxthon.com/

50. Meyerovich, L.A., Felt, A.P., Miller, M.S.: Object views: fine-grained sharing in browsers (2010). http://doi.acm.org/10.1145/1772690.1772764

51. Meyerovich, L.A., Livshits, V.B.: ConScript: specifying and enforcing fine-grained security policies for javascript in the browser. In: 31st IEEE Symposium on Security and Privacy, S&P 2010, 16–19 May 2010, Berleley/Oakland, California, USA, pp. 481–496. IEEE Computer Society (2010). http://doi.ieeecomputersociety.org/10.1109/SP.2010.36

52. Mickens, J.: Pivot: fast, synchronous mashup isolation using generator chains. In: 2014 IEEE Symposium on Security and Privacy, SP 2014, Berkeley, CA, USA, May 18–21, 2014. pp. 261–275. IEEE Computer Society (2014). http://dx.doi.org/10.1109/SP.2014.24

53. Mickens, J., Finifter, M.: Jigsaw: rfficient, low-effort mashup isolation. In: Presented as part of the 3rd USENIX Conference on Web Application Development (WebApps 2012), pp. 13–25. USENIX, Boston (2012). https://www.usenix.org/conference/webapps12/technical-sessions/presentation/mickens

54. Microsoft: Internet Explorer Architecture. http://msdn.microsoft.com/en-us/library/aa741312(v=vs.85).aspx
55. Microsoft: Microsoft Internet Security and Acceleration (ISA) Server 2004. http://technet.microsoft.com/en-us/library/cc302436.aspx
56. Microsoft: Microsoft Security Bulletin MS04-040 - Critical. https://technet.microsoft.com/en-us/library/security/ms04-040.aspx
57. Microsoft: Mitigating Cross-site Scripting With HTTP-only Cookies. http://msdn.microsoft.com/en-us/library/ms533046(VS.85).aspx
58. Microsoft Live Labs: Live Labs Websandbox. http://websandbox.org
59. Mihai Bazon: UglifyJS. https://github.com/mishoo/UglifyJS/
60. Miller, M.S., Samuel, M., Laurie, B., Awad, I., Stay, M.: Caja - safe active content in sanitized JavaScript. Technical report, Google Inc., June 2008
61. Miller, M.S.: Robust composition: towards a unified approach to access control and concurrency control. Ph.D. thesis, Johns Hopkins University, Baltimore, MD, USA (2006). aAI3245526
62. MITRE: CWE-367: Time-of-check Time-of-use (TOCTOU) Race Condition. http://cwe.mitre.org/data/definitions/367.html
63. MongoDB, Inc.: MongoDB. http://www.mongodb.org/
64. Mozilla: Gecko. https://developer.mozilla.org/en-US/docs/Mozilla/Gecko
65. Mozilla: JavaScript Strict Mode Reference. https://developer.mozilla.org/en-US/docs/Web/JavaScript/Reference/Strict_mode
66. Mozilla: MDN - Building an extension. https://developer.mozilla.org/en/docs/Building_an_Extension
67. Mozilla The Narcissus meta-circular JavaScript interpreter. https://github.com/mozilla/narcissus
68. Mozilla: The "with" statement. https://developer.mozilla.org/en-US/docs/Web/JavaScript/Reference/Statements/with
69. Namita Gupta: Facebook Platform Roadmap Update, 19 August 2010. https://developers.facebook.com/blog/post/402
70. Nikiforakis, N., Invernizzi, L., Kapravelos, A., Van Acker, S., Joosen, W., Kruegel, C., Piessens, F., Vigna, G.: You are what you include: large-scale evaluation of remote JavaScript inclusions. In: Yu, T., Danezis, G., Gligor, V.D. (eds.) the ACM Conference on Computer and Communications Security, CCS 2012, Raleigh, NC, USA, October 16–18, 2012, pp. 736–747. ACM (2012). http://doi.acm.org/10.1145/2382196.2382274
71. Opera: Opera Browser. http://www.opera.com
72. Patil, K., Dong, X., Li, X., Liang, Z., Jiang, X.: Towards fine-grained access control in javascript contexts. In: 2011 International Conference on Distributed Computing Systems, ICDCS 2011, Minneapolis, Minnesota, USA, June 20–24, 2011, pp. 720–729. IEEE Computer Society (2011). http://dx.doi.org/10.1109/ICDCS.2011.87
73. Phung, P.H., Desmet, L.: A two-tier sandbox architecture for untrusted JavaScript. In: JSTools 2012, Proceedings of the Workshop on JavaScript Tools, Beijing, 13 June 2012, pp. 1–10 (2012)
74. Phung, P.H., Sands, D., Chudnov, A.: Lightweight self-protecting JavaScript. In: Proceedings of the 4th International Symposium on Information, Computer, and Communications Security, ASIACCS 2009, pp. 47–60. ACM, New York (2009). http://doi.acm.org/10.1145/1533057.1533067
75. Politz, J.G., Eliopoulos, S.A., Guha, A., Krishnamurthi, S.: ADsafety: type-based verification of javascript sandboxing. In: 20th USENIX Security Symposium, San Francisco, CA, USA, August 8–12, 2011, Proceedings. USENIX Association (2011). http://static.usenix.org/events/sec11/tech/full_papers/Politz.pdf

76. Reis, C., Dunagan, J., Wang, H.J., Dubrovsky, O., Esmeir, S.: BrowserShield: vulnerability-driven filtering of dynamic HTML. In: OSDI 2006: Proceedings of the 7th symposium on Operating Systems Design and Implementation, pp. 61–74. USENIX Association, Berkeley (2006). http://citeseerx.ist.psu.edu/viewdoc/summary?doi=10.1.1.85.1661

77. Richards, G., Hammer, C., Burg, B., Vitek, J.: The eval that men do: large-scale study of the use of eval in javascript applications. In: Mezini, M. (ed.) ECOOP 2011. LNCS, vol. 6813, pp. 52–78. Springer, Heidelberg (2011). http://dx.doi.org/10.1007/978-3-642-22655-7_4

78. Sam Pullara: Introducing Y!OS 1.0 - live today! 28 October 2008. https://web.archive.org/web/20081029191209/http://developer.yahoo.net/blog/archives/2008/10/yos_10_launch.html

79. Sandra Liu Huang: Platform Updates: Promotion Policies, Facepile and More, 4 December 2010. https://developers.facebook.com/blog/post/2010/12/03/platform-updates--promotion-policies--facepile-and-more/

80. Mozilla SpiderMonkey. https://developer.mozilla.org/en-US/docs/Mozilla/Projects/SpiderMonkey

81. Stack Exchange (Jasvir Nagra): Why hasn't Caja been popular? http://programmers.stackexchange.com/a/147014

82. Stack Overflow (Kevin Reid): Uses of Google Caja. http://stackoverflow.com/questions/16054597/uses-of-google-caja

83. Taly, A., Erlingsson, U., Mitchell, J.C., Miller, M.S., Nagra, J.: Automated analysis of security-critical javascript APIs. In: IEEE Symposium on Security and Privacy, pp. 363–378 (2011)

84. Ter Louw, M., Ganesh, K.T., Venkatakrishnan, V.N.: Adjail: practical enforcement of confidentiality and integrity policies on web advertisements. In: 19th USENIX Security Symposium, Washington, DC, USA, August 11–13, 2010, Proceedings, pp. 371–388. USENIX Association (2010). http://www.usenix.org/events/sec10/tech/full_papers/TerLouw.pdf

85. Ter Louw, M., Phung, P.H., Krishnamurti, R., Venkatakrishnan, V.N.: SAFE-SCRIPT: javascript transformation for policy enforcement. In: Riis Nielson, H., Gollmann, D. (eds.) NordSec 2013. LNCS, vol. 8208, pp. 67–83. Springer, Heidelberg (2013). http://dx.doi.org/10.1007/978-3-642-41488-6_5

86. Ter Louw, M., Venkatakrishnan, V.N.: Blueprint: Robust prevention of cross-site scripting attacks for existing browsers (2009). http://dx.doi.org/10.1109/SP.2009.33

87. Tessel: Tessel 2. https://tessel.io

88. The FaceBook Team: FBJS. http://wiki.developers.facebook.com/index.php/FBJS

89. Troy Hunt: How I got XSS'd by my ad network. http://www.troyhunt.com/2015/07/how-i-got-xssd-by-my-ad-network.html

90. Twitter: How to embed Twitter timelines on your website. https://blog.twitter.com/2012/embedded-timelines-howto

91. Van Acker, S., De Ryck, P., Desmet, L., Piessens, F., Joosen, W.: WebJail: least-privilege integration of third-party components in web mashups. In: Zakon, R.H., McDermott, J.P., Locasto, M.E. (eds.) Twenty-Seventh Annual Computer Security Applications Conference, ACSAC 2011, Orlando, FL, USA, 5–9 December 2011, pp. 307–316. ACM (2011). http://doi.acm.org/10.1145/2076732.2076775

92. W3C: Same Origin Policy - Web Security. http://www.w3.org/Security/wiki/Same_Origin_Policy

93. W3C: W3C - Web Workers. http://www.w3.org/TR/workers/

94. W3C: W3C Standards and drafts - Cross-Origin Resource Sharing. http://www.w3.org/TR/cors/
95. W3C: XML Path Language (XPath) 2.0. http://www.w3.org/TR/xpath20/
96. W3Techs: Usage of JavaScript for websites. http://w3techs.com/technologies/details/cp-javascript/all/all
97. Webkit Blog - David Carson: Android uses WebKit. https://www.webkit.org/blog/142/android-uses-webkit/
98. WHATWG: HTML Living Standard - Timers. https://html.spec.whatwg.org/multipage/webappapis.html#timers
99. Yu, D., Chander, A., Islam, N., Serikov, I.: JavaScript instrumentation for browser security. In: Proceedings of the 34th Annual ACM SIGPLAN-SIGACT Symposium on Principles of Programming Languages, POPL 2007, pp. 237–249. ACM, New York (2007). http://doi.acm.org/10.1145/1190216.1190252

From Zoos to Safaris—From Closed-World Enforcement to Open-World Assessment of Privacy

Michael Backes[1,2], Pascal Berrang[1], and Praveen Manoharan[1(✉)]

[1] Saarland Informatics Campus, CISPA, Saarland University,
Saarbrücken, Germany
{backes,berrang,manoharan}@cs.uni-saarland.de
[2] Saarland Informatics Campus, MPI-SWS, Saarbrücken, Germany

Abstract. In this paper, we develop a *user-centric privacy framework for quantitatively assessing the exposure* of personal information in open settings. Our formalization addresses key-challenges posed by such open settings, such as the necessity of user- and context-dependent privacy requirements. As a sanity check, we show that hard non-disclosure guarantees are impossible to achieve in open settings.

In the second part, we provide an instantiation of our framework to address the *identity disclosure* problem, leading to the novel notion of d-convergence to assess the linkability of identities across online communities. Since user-generated text content plays a major role in linking identities between Online Social Networks, we further extend this linkability model to assess the effectiveness of countermeasures against linking authors of text content by their writing style.

We experimentally evaluate both of these instantiations by applying them to suitable data sets: we provide a *large-scale evaluation* of the linkability model on a collection of 15 million comments collected from the Online Social Network Reddit, and evaluate the effectiveness of four semantics-retaining countermeasures and their combinations on the *Extended-Brennan-Greenstadt Adversarial Corpus*. Through these evaluations we validate the notion of d-convergence for assessing the linkability of entities in our Reddit data set and explore the practical impact of countermeasures on the importance of standard writing style features on identifying authors.

1 Introduction

The Internet has undergone dramatic changes in the last two decades, evolving from a mere communication network to a global multimedia platform in which billions of users not only actively exchange information, but increasingly conduct sizable parts of their daily lives. While this transformation has brought tremendous benefits to society, it has also created new threats to online privacy that existing technology is failing to keep pace with. Users tend to reveal personal information without considering the widespread, easy accessibility, potential linkage and permanent nature of online data. Many cases reported in the

© Springer International Publishing Switzerland 2016
A. Aldini et al. (Eds.): FOSAD VIII, LNCS 9808, pp. 87–138, 2016.
DOI: 10.1007/978-3-319-43005-8_3

press show the resulting risks, which range from public embarrassment and loss of prospective opportunities (e.g., when applying for jobs or insurance), to personal safety and property risks (e.g., when sexual offenders or burglars learn users' whereabouts online). The resulting privacy awareness and privacy concerns of Internet users have been further amplified by the advent of the Big-Data paradigm and the aligned business models of personalized tracking and monetizing personal information in an unprecedented manner.

Developing a suitable methodology to reason about the privacy of users in such a large-scale, open web setting, as well as corresponding tool support in the next step, requires at its core a formal privacy model that lives up to the now increasingly dynamic dissemination of unstructured, heterogeneous user content on the Internet: While users traditionally shared information mostly using public profiles with static information about themselves, nowadays they disseminate personal information in an unstructured, highly dynamic manner, through content they create and share (such as blog entries, user comments, a "Like" on Facebook), or through the people they befriend or follow. Furthermore, ubiquitously available background knowledge about a dedicated user needs to be appropriately reflected within the model and its reasoning tasks, as it can decrease a user's privacy by inferring further sensitive information. As an example, Machine Learning and other Information Retrieval techniques provide comprehensive approaches for profiling a user's actions across multiple Online Social Networks, up to a unique identification of a given user's profiles for each such network.

Prior research on privacy has traditionally focused on closed database settings – characterized by a complete view on structured data and a clear distinction of key- and sensitive attributes – and has aimed for strong privacy guarantees using global data sanitization. These approaches, however, are inherently inadequate if such closed settings are replaced by open settings as described above, where unstructured and heterogeneous data is being disseminated, where individuals have a partial view of the available information, and where global data sanitization is impossible and hence strong guarantees have to be replaced by probabilistic privacy assessments.

As of now, *even the basic methodology is missing* for offering users technical means to comprehensively assess the privacy risks incurred by their data dissemination, and their daily online activities in general. Existing privacy models such as k-anonymity [54], l-diversity [40], t-closeness [39] and the currently most popular notion of Differential Privacy [22] follow a database-centric approach that is inadequate to meet the requirements outlined above. We refer the reader to Sect. 3.3 for further discussions on existing privacy models.

1.1   Contribution

In this paper, we present a rigorous methodology for quantitatively assessing the exposure of personal information in open settings. Concretely, the paper makes the following three tangible contributions: (1) a formal framework for reasoning about the disclosure of personal information in open settings, (2) an instantiation of the framework for reasoning about the identity disclosure problem, and (3) an evaluation of the framework on a collection of 15 million comments collected from the Online Social Network Reddit.

A Formal Framework for Privacy in Open Settings. We propose a novel framework for addressing the essential challenges of privacy in open settings, such as providing a data model that is suited for dealing with unstructured dissemination of heterogeneous information through various different sources and a flexible definition of user-specific privacy requirements that allow for the specification of context-dependent privacy goals. In contrast to most existing approaches, our framework strives to assess the degree of exposure individuals face, in contrast to trying to enforce an individual's privacy requirements. Moreover, our framework technically does not differentiate between non-sensitive and sensitive attributes a-priori, but rather starts from the assumption that all data is equally important and can lead to privacy risks. More specifically, our model captures the fact that the sensitivity of attributes is highly user- and context-dependent by deriving information sensitivity from each user's privacy requirements. As a sanity check we prove that hard non-disclosure guarantees cannot be provided for the open setting in general, providing incentive for novel approaches for assessing privacy risks in the open settings.

Reasoning about Identity Disclosure in Open Settings. We then instantiate our general privacy framework for the specific use case of identity disclosure. Our framework defines and assesses identity disclosure (i.e., identifiability and linkability of identities) by utilizing entity similarity, i.e., an entity is private in a collection of entities if it is sufficiently similar to its peers. At the technical core of our model is the new notion of d-convergence, which quantifies the similarity of entities within a larger group of entities. It hence provides the formal grounds to assess the ability of any single entity to blend into the crowd, i.e., to hide amongst peers. The d-convergence model is furthermore capable of assessing identity disclosure risks specifically for single entities. To this end, we extend the notion of d-convergence to the novel notion of (k, d)-anonymity, which allows for entity-centric identity disclosure risk assessments by requiring d-convergence in the local neighborhood of a given entity. Intuitively, this new notion provides a generalization of k-anonymity that is not bound to matching identities based on pre-defined key-identifiers.

Empirical Evaluation on Reddit. Third, we perform an instantiation of our identity disclosure model for the important use case of analyzing user-generated text content in order to characterize specific user profiles. We use unigram frequencies extracted from user-generated content as user attributes, and we subsequently demonstrate that the resulting unigram model can indeed be used for quantifying the degree of anonymity of – and ultimately, for differentiating – individual entities. For the sake of exposition, we apply this unigram model to a collection of 15 million comments collected from the Online Social Network Reddit. The computations were performed on two Dell PowerEdge R820 with 64 virtual cores each at 2.60 GHz over the course of six weeks. Our evaluation shows that (k, d)-anonymity suitably assesses an identity's anonymity and provides deeper insights into the data set's structure.

Assessing the Effectiveness of Countermeasures Against Authorship Recognition. Fourth, by extending the linkability model model introduced in the second step, we develop a novel measure for assessing the importance of stylometric features for the identifiability of authors. We adapt and extend the user models introduced in the general framework to fit our use case of authorship recognition, effectively defining a model for writing style that allows us to capture a comprehensive list of stylometric features, as introduced by Abbasi and Chen [3]. Overall, we develop a model of the authorship recognition problem that allows us to formally reason about authorship recognition in the open setting of the Internet.

By using these writing-style models, we then derive how we can identify important stylometric features that significantly contribute to the identification of the correct author from the context in which text is published. We employ standard regression and classification techniques to determine the importance of each type of stylometric feature. From this importance assessment we then further derive the *gain* measure for the effectiveness of countermeasures against authorship identification by measuring how well they reduce the importance of stylometric features.

Countermeasure Evaluation. Finally, we apply this measure to assess the effectiveness of four automatic countermeasures, namely synonym substitution, spell checking, special character modification and adding/removing misspellings. In this evaluation, we follow a general and comprehensive methodology that structures the evaluation process and is easily extensible for future evaluation.

We perform our experiments on the Extended-Brennan-Greenstadt Adversarial Corpus consisting of texts written by 45 different authors. Each author contributed at least 6500 words to the corpus [11].

1.2 Outline

We begin by discussing related work in Sect. 2 and explain why existing privacy notions are inadequate for reasoning about privacy in open web settings in Sect. 3. We then define our privacy framework in Sect. 4 and instantiate it for reasoning about identity disclosure in Sect. 5. In Sect. 6 we perform a basic evaluation of the identity disclosure model on the Reddit Online Social Network. We extend the identity disclosure model to a model for assessing the effectiveness of countermeasures against authorship recognition in Sect. 7, which we then also evaluate on Reddit in Sect. 8. We summarize our findings Sect. 9.

2   Related Work

In this section, we give an overview over other relevant related work that has not yet been considered in the previous subsection.

Privacy in Closed-World Settings. The notion of privacy has been exhaustively discussed for specific settings such as statistical databases, as well as for more general settings. Since we already discussed the notions of k-anonymity [54], l-diversity [40] t-closeness [39] and Differential Privacy [22] in Sect. 3.3 in great detail, we will now discuss further such notions.

A major point of criticism of Differential Privacy, but also the other existing privacy notions, found in the literature [9,35] is the (often unclear) trade-off between utility and privacy that is incurred by applying database sanitation techniques to achieve privacy. Several works have shown that protection against attribute disclosure cannot be provided in settings that consider an adversary with arbitrary auxiliary information [21,23,24]. We later show, as sanity check, that in our formalization of privacy in open settings, general non-disclosure guarantees are indeed impossible to achieve. By providing the necessary formal groundwork in this paper, we hope to stimulate research on *assessing* privacy risks in open settings, against explicitly spelled-out adversary models.

Kasiviswanathan and Smith [34] define the notion of ϵ-semantic privacy to capture general non-disclosure guarantees. We define our adversary model in a similar fashion as in their formalization and we use ϵ-semantic privacy to show that general non-disclosure guarantees cannot be meaningfully provided in open settings.

Several extensions of the above privacy notions have been proposed in the literature to provide privacy guarantees in use cases that differ from traditional database privacy [7,15,16,30,59,61]. These works aim at suitably transforming different settings into a database-like setting that can be analyzed using differential privacy. Such a transformation, however, often abstracts away from essential components of these settings, and as a result achieve impractical privacy guarantees. As explained in Sect. 3.3, the open web setting is particularly ill-suited for such transformations.

Specifically for the use case in Online Social Networks (in short, OSNs), many works [16,30,37,59,61] apply the existing database privacy notions for reasoning about attribute disclosure in OSN data. These works generally impose a specific structure on OSN data, such as a social link graph, and reason about the disclosure of private attributes through this structure. Zhaleva et al. [59] show that mixed public and private profiles do not necessarily protect the private part of a profile since they can be inferred from the public part. Heatherly et al. [30] show how machine learning techniques can be used to infer private information from publicly available information. Kosinksi et al. [37] moreover show that machine learning techniques can indeed be used to predict personality traits of users and their online behavior. Zhou et al. [61] apply the notions of k-anonymity and l-diversity to data protection in OSNs and discuss the complexity of finding private subsets. Their approach does however suffer from the same problems these techniques have in traditional statistical data disclosure, where an adversary with auxiliary information can easily infer information about any specific user. Chen et al. [16] provide a variation of differential privacy which allows for privacy and protection against edge-disclosure attacks in the correlated setting of OSNs. The setting, however, remains static, and it is assumed that the data can be globally sanitized in order to provide protection against attribute disclosure. Again, as discussed in Sect. 3.3, this does not apply to the open web setting with its highly unstructured dissemination of data.

Privacy in Online Social Networks. A growing body of research shows that commonly used machine learning and information retrieval techniques can be used to match a user's profiles across different OSNs [13,19] or to identify the unique profile of a given user [8,17,53]. Scerri et al., in particular, present the digital.me framework [51,52] which attempts to unify a user's social sphere across different OSNs by, e.g., matching the profiles of the same user across these OSNs. While their approach is limited to the closed environment they consider, their work provides interesting insights into identity disclosure in more open settings.

Several works in the literature (e.g., [38,41]) have focused on the protection of so-called Personally Identifiable Information (PII) introduced in privacy and data-protection legislation [2], which constitute a fixed set of entity attributes that even in isolation supposedly lead to the unique identification of entities. Narayanan and Shmatikov, however, show that the differentiation between key attributes that identify entities, and sensitive attributes that need to be protected, is not appropriate for privacy in pervasive online settings such as the Internet [47,48]. Technical methods for identifying and matching entities do not rely on the socially perceived sensitivity of attributes for matching, but rather any combination of attributes can lead to successful correlation of corresponding profiles. Our privacy model treats every type of entity attribute as equally important for privacy and allows for the identification of context-dependent, sensitive attributes.

Authorship Recognition. The field of linguistic stylometry is a is a widely explored topic in the literature [3,36,43,57]. This starts from pre-computer approaches to identifying text-authors based on simple text features such as word-length [43] to the, nowadays, machine-learning centered approaches that try to include a plethora of statistical features to correctly identify the author of a given text [3,36,57].

Stylometry has successfully been utilized in various areas: as an assisting tool in historical research [31,49], allowing for the correct attribution of text with previously unknown origin, or providing evidence in criminal investigations [12,14].

With the rise of the Internet as a large-scale communication platform for end-users, however, stylometry now also poses a significant threat to user privacy. As shown by Narayanan et al. [46], it is entirely feasible to identify the authors of, e.g., blog-posts on a scale as large as the Internet. Afroz et al. [5] also show that authors of private messages in underground forums can effectively be de-anonymized by stylometry.

Adversarial Stylometry. Several works have shown that hiding an author's identity is indeed possible by means of obfuscation and imitation [10,42].

In particular, Brennan *et al.* [10] show that, for text corpora with at least 6500 words per author, applying methods such as asking the authors to rewrite their texts or doubly translating with machine translation can indeed reduce the accuracy of state-of-the-art stylometric methods. They also provide an implementation of their ideas in Anonymouth [6], a semi-automatic tool, assisting users in anonymizing their writing style by identifying critical text features and asking them to rewrite corresponding text passages. This work, however, only provides results for text corpora with large amounts of text per author and is based on the same dataset as ours.

Authorship obfuscation can also be detected, as shown by various work in the literature [4,33,50]. However, these works again require text corpora with large amounts of text per author. It would be interesting to see the effectiveness of these obfuscation-detection methods in the online setting with much less text per author.

3   Privacy in Open Settings

Before we delve into the technical parts of this paper, we give an informal overview over privacy in the Internet of the future. To this end, we first provide an example that illustrates some of the aspects of privacy in the Internet, and then in detail discuss the challenges of privacy in the Internet and why existing privacy notions are not applicable to this setting.

3.1   Example

Consider the following example: Employer Alice receives an application by potential employee Bob which contains personal information about Bob. Before she makes the decision on the employment of Bob, however, she searches the internet and tries to learn even more about her potential employee. A prime source of information are, for example, Online Social Networks (OSNs) which Alice can browse through. If she manages to identify Bob's profile in such an OSN she can then learn more about Bob by examining the publicly available information of this profile.

In order to correctly identify Bob's profile in an OSN, Alice takes the following approach: based on the information found in Bob's application, she constructs a model θ_B that contains all attributes, such as name, education or job history, extracted from Bob's application. She then compares this model θ_B to the profiles $P_1, \ldots, P_n$ found in the OSNs and ranks them by similarity to the model θ_B. Profiles that show sufficient similarity to the model θ_B are then chosen by Alice as belonging to Bob. After identifying the (for Alice) correctly matching profiles $P_1^*, \ldots, P_i^*$ of Bob, Alice can finally merge their models $\theta_1^*, \ldots, \theta_i^*$ with θ_B to increase her knowledge about Bob.

Bob now faces the problem that Alice could learn information about him that he does not want her to learn. He basically has two options: he either does not share this critical information at all, or makes sure that his profile is not identifiable as his. In OSNs such as Facebook, where users are required to identify themselves, Bob can only use the first option. In anonymous or pseudonymous OSNs such as Reddit or Twitter, however, he can make use of the second option. He then has to make sure that he does not share enough information on his pseudonymous profiles that would allow Alice to link his pseudonymous profile to him personally.

Privacy in the open web is mostly concerned with the second option: we cannot protect an entity ϵ against sharing personal information through a profile which is already uniquely identified with the entity ϵ. We can, however, estimate how well an pseudonymous account of ϵ can be linked to ϵ, and through this link, learn personal information about ϵ. As the example above shows, we can essentially measure privacy in terms of similarity of an entity ϵ in a collection of entities $\mathcal{E}$.

The identifiability of ϵ then substantially depends on the attributes ϵ exhibits in the context of $\mathcal{E}$ and does not necessarily follow the concept of personally identifiable information (PII) as known in the more common understanding of privacy and in privacy and data-protection legislation [2]: here, privacy protection only goes as far as protecting this so-called personally identifiable information, which often is either not exactly defined, or restricted to an a-priori-defined set of attributes such as name, Social Security number, etc. We, along with other authors in the literature [47,48], find however that the set of critical attributes that need to be protected differ from entity to entity, and from community to community. For example, in a community in which all entities have the name "Bob", exposing your name does not expose any information about yourself. In a different community, however, where everyone has a different name, exposing your name exposes a lot of information about yourself.

In terms of the privacy taxonomy formulated by Zheleva and Getoor [60], the problem we face corresponds to the identity disclosure problem, where one tries to identify whether and how an identity is represented in an OSN. We think that this is one of the main concerns of users of frequently used OSNs, in particular those that allow for pseudonymous interactions: users are able to freely express their opinions in these environments, assuming that their opinions cannot be connected to their real identity. However, any piece of information they share in their interactions can leak personal information that can lead to identity disclosure, defeating the purpose of such pseudonymous services.

To successfully reason about the potential disclosure of sensitive information in such open settings, we first have to consider various challenges that have not been considered in traditional privacy research. After presenting these challenges, we discuss the implications of these challenges on some of the existing privacy notions, before we consider other relevant related work in the field.

3.2   Challenges of Privacy in Open Settings

In this subsection, we introduce the challenges induced by talking about privacy in open settings:

(C1) Modeling Heterogeneous Information. We require an information model that allows for modeling various types of information and that reflects the heterogeneous information shared throughout the Internet. This models needs to adequately represent personal information that can be inferred from various sources, such as static profile information or from user-generated content, and should allow statistical assessments about the user, as is usually provided by knowledge inference engines. We propose a solution to this challenge in Sect. 4.1.

(C2) User-Specified Privacy Requirements. We have to be able to formalize user-specified privacy requirements. This formalization should use the previously mentioned information model to be able to cope with heterogeneous information, and specify which information should be protected from being publicly disseminated. We present a formalization of user privacy requirements in Sect. 4.4.

(C3) Information Sensitivity. In open settings, information sensitivity is a function of user expectations and context: we therefore need to provide new definitions for sensitive information that takes user privacy requirements into account. We present context- and user-specific definitions of information sensitivity in Sect. 4.5.

(C4) Adversarial Knowledge Estimation. To adequately reason about disclosure risks in open settings we also require a parameterized adversary model that we can instantiate with various assumptions on the adversary's knowledge: this knowledge should include the information disseminated by the user, as well as background knowledge to infer additional information about the user. In Sect. 4, we define our adversary model based on statistical inference.

In the following sections, we provide a rigorous formalization for these requirements, leading to a formal framework for privacy in open settings. We will instantiate this framework in Sect. 5.3 to reason about the identity disclosure in particular.

We begin by discussing why existing privacy notions are not suited for reasoning about privacy in open settings. Afterwards, we provide an overview over further related work.

3.3   Inadequacy of Existing Models

Common existing privacy notions such as k-anonymity [54], l-diversity [40], t-closeness [39] and the currently most popular notion of Differential Privacy [22] provide the technical means for privacy-friendly data-publishing in a closed-world setting: They target scenarios in which all data is available from the beginning, from a single data source, remains static and is globally sanitized in order to provide rigorous privacy guarantees. In what follows, we describe how these notions fail to adequately address the challenges of privacy in open settings discussed above.

(a) *Absence of Structure and Classification of Data.* All the aforementioned privacy models require an a-priori structure and classification of the data under consideration. Any information gathered about an individual thus has to be embedded in this structure, or it cannot be seamlessly integrated in these models.

(b) *No Differentiation of Attributes.* All of these models except for Differential Privacy require an additional differentiation between key attributes that identify an individual record, and sensitive attributes that a users seeks to protect. This again contradicts the absence of an a-priori, static structure in our setting. Moreover, as pointed out above and in the literature [48], such a differentiation cannot be made a-priori in general, and it would be highly context-sensitive in the open web setting.

(c) *Ubiquitously Available Background Knowledge.* All of these models, except for Differential Privacy, do not take into account adversaries that utilize ubiquitously available background knowledge about a target user to infer additional sensitive information. A common example of background knowledge is openly available statistical information that allows the adversary to infer additional information about an identity.

(d) *Privacy for Individual Users.* All these models provide privacy for the whole dataset, which clearly implies privacy of every single user. One of the major challenges in open settings such as the Internet, however, is that accessing and sanitizing all available data is impossible. This leads to the requirement to design a local privacy notion that provides a lower privacy bound for every individual user, even if we only have partial access to the available data.

The notion of Differential Privacy only fails to address some of the aforementioned requirements (parts *a* and *d*), but it comes with the additional assumption that the adversary knows almost everything about the data set in question (everything except for the information in one database entry). This assumption enables Differential Privacy to avoid differentiation between key attributes and sensitive attributes. This strong adversarial model, however, implies that privacy guarantees are only achievable if the considered data is globally perturbed [21,23,24], which is not possible in open web settings.

The conceptual reason for the inadequacy of existing models for reasoning about privacy in open web settings is mostly their design goal: Privacy models have thus far mainly been concerned with the problem of attribute disclosure within a single data source: protection against identity disclosure was then attempted by preventing the disclosure of any (sensitive) attributes of a user to the public. In contrast to static settings such as private data publishing, where we can decide which information will be disclosed to the adversary, protection against any attribute disclosure in open settings creates a very different set of challenges which we will address in the following sections.

4 A Framework for Privacy in Open Settings

In this section, we first develop a user model that is suited for dealing with the information dissemination behavior commonly observed on the Internet. We then formalize our adversary model and show, as a sanity check, that hard privacy guarantees cannot be achieved in open settings. We conclude by defining privacy goals in open settings through user-specified privacy requirements from which we then derive a new definition of information sensitivity suited to open settings.

4.1 Modeling Information in Open Settings

We first define the notion of entity models and restricted entity models. These models capture the behavior of these entities and in particular describe which attributes an entity exhibits publicly.

Definition 1 (Entity Model). *Let $\mathcal{A}$ be the set of all attributes. The* entity model θ_ϵ *of an entity ϵ provides for all attributes $\alpha \in \mathcal{A}$ an attribute value $\theta_\epsilon(\alpha) \in \mathsf{dom}(\alpha) \cup \{\mathsf{NULL}\}$ where $\mathsf{dom}(\alpha)$ is the domain over which the attribute α_i is defined.*

The domain $\mathsf{dom}(\theta)$ of an entity model θ is the set of all attributes $\alpha \in \mathcal{A}$ with value $\theta(\alpha) \neq \mathsf{NULL}$.

An entity model thus corresponds to the information an entity can publicly disseminate. With the specific null value NULL we can also capture those cases where the entity does not have any value for that specific attribute.

In case the adversary has access to the full entity model, a set of entity models basically corresponds to a database with each attribute $\alpha \in \mathcal{A}$ as its columns. In the open setting, however, an entity typically does not disseminate all attribute values, but instead only a small part of them. We capture this with the notion of restricted entity models.

Definition 2 (Restricted Entity Model). *The* restricted entity model $\theta_\epsilon^{\mathcal{A}'}$ *is the entity model of ϵ restricted to the non empty attribute set $\mathcal{A}' \neq \emptyset$, i.e.,*

$$\theta_\epsilon^{\mathcal{A}'}(\alpha) = \begin{cases} \theta_\epsilon(\alpha), & \text{if } \alpha \in \mathcal{A}' \\ \mathsf{NULL}, & \text{otherwise} \end{cases}$$

In the online setting, each of the entities above corresponds to an online profile. A user u usually uses more than one online service, each with different profiles $P_1^u, \ldots, P_l^u$. We thus define a user model as the collection of the entity models describing each of these profiles.

Definition 3 (User Model / Profile Model). *The* user model $\theta_u = \{\theta_{P_1^u},$ $\ldots, \theta_{P_l^u}\}$ *of a user u is a set of the entity models $\theta_{P_1^u}, \ldots, \theta_{P_1^u}$, which we also call* profile models.

With a user model that separates the information disseminated under different profiles, we will be able to formulate privacy requirements for each of these profiles separately. We will investigate this in Sect. 4.4.

4.2 Adversary Model

In the following we formalize the adversary we consider for privacy in open settings. In our formalization, we follow the definitions of a semantic, Bayesian adversary introduced by Kasiviswanathan and Smith [34].

For any profile P, we are interested in what the adversary Adv learns about P observing publicly available information from P. We formalize this learning process through *beliefs* on the models of each profile.

Definition 4 (Belief). *Let $\mathcal{P}$ be the set of all profiles and let $\mathcal{D}_\mathcal{A}$ be the set of all distributions over profile models. A* belief $b = \{b_P | P \in \mathcal{P}\}$ *is a set of distributions $b_P \in \mathcal{D}_\mathcal{A}$.*

We can now define our privacy adversary in open settings using the notion of belief above.

Definition 5 (Adversary). *An adversary Adv is a pair of* prior *belief b and* world knowledge κ, *i.e.*, Adv $= (b, \kappa)$.

The adversary Adv's prior belief b represents his belief in each profile's profile model before makes any observations. This prior belief can, in particular, also include background knowledge about each profile P. The world knowledge κ of the adversary represents a set of inference rules that allow him to infer additional attribute values about each profile from his observations.

We next define the publicly observations based on which the adversary learns additional information about each profile.

Definition 6 (Publication Function). *A publication function G is a randomized function that maps each profile model θ_P to a restricted profile model $G(\theta_P) = \theta_P^{\mathcal{A}'}$ such that there is at least one attribute $\alpha \in \mathcal{A}'$ with $\theta_P(\alpha) = G(\theta_P)(\alpha)$.*

The publication function G reflects which attributes are disseminated publicly by the user through his profile P. G can, in particular, also include local sanitization where some attribute values are perturbed. However, we do require that at least one attribute value remains correct to capture utility requirements faced in open settings.

A public observation now is the collection of all restricted profile models generated by a publication function.

Definition 7 (Public Observation). *Let $\mathcal{P}$ be the set of all profiles, and let G be a publication function. The* public observation $\mathcal{O}$ *is the set of all restricted profile models generated by G, i.e., $\mathcal{O} = \{G(\theta_P) | P \in \mathcal{P}\}$.*

The public observation $\mathcal{O}$ essentially captures all publicly disseminated attribute values that can be observed by the adversary. Given such an observation $\mathcal{O}$, we can now determine what the adversary Adv learns about each profile by determining his *a-posteriori belief.*

Definition 8 (A-Posteriori Belief). *Let $\mathcal{P}$ be the set of all profiles. Given an adversary* $\mathsf{Adv} = (b, \kappa)$ *and a public observation $\mathcal{O}$, the adversary's a-posteriori belief* $\bar{b} = \{\bar{b}_P \in \mathcal{D}_A | P \in \mathcal{P}\}$ *is determined by applying the Bayesian inference rule, i.e.,*

$$\bar{b}_P[\theta | \mathcal{O}, \kappa] = \frac{Pr[\mathcal{O}|\kappa, \theta] \cdot b_P[\theta]}{\sum_{\theta'} Pr[\mathcal{O}|\kappa, \theta'] \cdot b_P[\theta']}.$$

Here, the conditional probability $Pr[\mathcal{O}|\kappa, \theta]$ describes the likelihood that the observational $\mathcal{O}$ is created by the specific entity model θ.

We will utilize the a-posteriori belief of the adversary to reason about the violation of the user specified privacy requirements in Sect. 4.4.

4.3   Inapplicability of Statistical Privacy Notions

In the following, we formally show that traditional non-disclosure guarantees, e.g., in the style of Differential Privacy, are not possible in open settings.

Kasiviswanathan and Smith [34] provide a general definition of non-disclosure they call ϵ-privacy. In their definition, they compare the adversary Adv's a-posteriori beliefs after observing the transcript t generated from a database sanitazitaion mechanism $\mathcal{F}$ applied on two adjacent databases with n rows: first on the database x, leading to the belief $\bar{b}_0[.|t]$, and secondly on the database x_{-i}, where a value in the ith row in x is replaced by a default value, leading to the belief $\bar{b}_i[.|t]$.

Definition 9 (ϵ-semantic Privacy [34]). *Let $\epsilon \in [0,1]$. A randomized algorithm $\mathcal{F}$ is ϵ-semantically private if for all belief distributions b on D^n, for all possible transcripts, and for all $i = 1 \ldots n$:*

$$\mathsf{SD}(\bar{b}_0[.|t], \bar{b}_i[.|t]) \le \epsilon.$$

Here, SD is the total variation distance of two probability distributions.

Definition 10. *Let X and Y be two probability distributions over the sample space D. The total variation distance SD of X and Y is*

$$\mathsf{SD}(X, Y) = \mathsf{max}_{S \subset D} \left[Pr[X \in S] - Pr[Y \in S] \right].$$

Kasiviswanathan and Smith [34] show that ϵ-differential privacy is essentially equivalent to ϵ-semantic privacy.

In our formalization of privacy in open settings, varying a single database entry corresponds to changing the value of a single attribute α in the profile model θ_P of a profile P to a default value. We denote this modified entity model with θ_P^α, and the thereby produced a-posteriori belief by $\bar{b}_P^\alpha$. A profile P would then be ϵ-semantically private if for any modified profile model θ_P^α, the a-posteriori belief of adversary Adv does not change by more than ϵ.

Definition 11 (ϵ-semantic Privacy in Open Settings). *Let $\epsilon \in [0,1]$.*
A profile P is ϵ-semantically private in open settings if for any attribute α,

$$\mathsf{SD}(\overline{b}_P[.|\mathcal{O}], \overline{b}_P^\alpha[.|\mathcal{O}]) \leq \epsilon$$

where $\overline{b}_P$ and $\overline{b}_P^\alpha$ are the a-posteriori beliefs of the adversary after observing the public output of θ_P and θ_P^α respectively.

As expected, we can show that ϵ-semantic privacy can only hold for $\epsilon = 1$ in open settings.

Theorem 1. *For any profile model θ_P and any attribute α, there is an adversary* Adv *such that*

$$\mathsf{SD}(\overline{b}[.|\mathcal{O}], \overline{b}^\alpha[.|\mathcal{O}]) \geq 1.$$

Proof. Let Adv have a uniform prior belief, i.e., all possible profile models have the same probability, and empty world knowledge κ. Let α be the one attribute that remains the same after applying the publication function G. Let x be the original value of this attribute α and let x^* be the default value that replaces x.

Observing the restricted profile model $\theta_P[\mathcal{A}']$ without any additional world knowledge will lead to an a-posteriori belief, where the probability of the entity model θ with $\theta[\mathcal{A}'] = \theta_P[\mathcal{A}']$ and NULL everywhere else, is set to 1.

Conversely, the modified setting will result in an a-posteriori belief that sets the probability for the entity model θ^* to one, where θ^* is constructed for the modified setting as θ above. Thus $\overline{b}[\theta|\mathcal{O}] = 1$, whereas $\overline{b}^\alpha[\theta|\mathcal{O}] = 0$, and hence $\mathsf{SD}(\overline{b}[.|\mathcal{O}], \overline{b}^\alpha[.|\mathcal{O}]) = 1$. □

Intuitively, the adversary can easily distinguish differing profile models because (a) he can directly observe the profiles publicly available information, (b) he chooses which attributes he considers for his inference and (c) only restricted, local sanitization is available to the profile. Since these are elementary properties of privacy in open settings, we can conclude that hard security guarantees in the style of differential privacy are impossible to achieve in open settings.

However, we can provide an assessment of the disclosure risks by explicitly fixing the a-priori knowledge and the attribute set considered by the adversary. While we no longer all-quantify over all possible adversaries, and therefore lose the full generality of traditional non-disclosure guarantees, we might still provide meaningful privacy assessments in practice. We further discuss this approach in Sect. 4.5, and follow this approach in our instantiation of the general model for assessing the likelihood of identity disclosure in Sect. 5.

4.4   User-Specified Privacy Requirements

In the following we introduce user-specified privacy requirements that allow us to formulate privacy goals that are user- and context-dependent. These can then lead to restricted privacy assessments instead of general privacy guarantees that we have shown to be impossible in open setting in the previous section.

We define a user's privacy requirements on a per-profile basis, stating which attribute values should not be inferred by adversary after seeing a public observations $\mathcal{O}$.

Definition 12 (Privacy Policy). *A privacy policy $\mathcal{R}$ is a set of privacy requirements $r = (P, \{\alpha_i = x_i\})$ which require that profile P should never expose the attribute values x_i for the attributes $\alpha_i \in \mathcal{A}$.*

By setting privacy requirements in a per-profile basis we capture an important property of information dissemination in open settings: users utilize different profiles for different context (e.g., different online services) assuming these profiles remain separate and specific information is only disseminated under specific circumstances.

Given the definition of privacy policies, we now define the violation of a policy by considering the adversary's a-posterior belief $\bar{b}$, as introduced in Sect. 4.2.

Definition 13 (Privacy Policy Satisfaction / Violation). *Let $\mathsf{Adv} = (b, \kappa)$ be an adversary with a-posteriori belief $\bar{b}$, and let $\theta[\alpha = x]$ be the set of all entity models that have the value x for the attribute α. A profile P_i^u σ-satisfies a user's privacy requirement $r_j^u = (P, \{\alpha_i = x_i\})$, written $P_i^u \models_\sigma r_j^u$, if*

- $P = P_i^u$
- $\forall \alpha_i : \sum_{\theta \in \theta[\alpha_i = x_i]} \bar{b}_P[\theta | \mathcal{O}, \kappa] \leq \sigma$

and σ-violates the user's privacy requirement otherwise.

A user model θ_u σ-satisfies a user u's privacy policy $\mathcal{R}_u$, written $\theta_u \models_\sigma \mathcal{R}_u$, if all profile models $\theta_{P_i^u}$ σ-satisfy their corresponding privacy requirements, and σ-violates the privacy policy otherwise.

The above attributes can also take the form of "P belongs to the same user as P'", effectively restricting which profiles should be linked to each other. We will investigate this profile linkability problem specifically in Sect. 5.

4.5 Sensitive Information

In contrast to the closed-world setting, with its predefined set of sensitive attributes that automatically defines the privacy requirements, a suitable definition of information sensitivity in the open setting is still missing. In the following, we derive the notion of sensitive information from the user privacy requirements we defined in Sect. 4.4.

Definition 14 (Sensitive Attributes). *A set of attributes $\mathcal{A}^*$ is sensitive for a user u in the context of her profile P_i^u if u's privacy policy $\mathcal{R}_u$ contains a privacy requirement $r = (P_i^u, \mathcal{A}' = X)$ where $\mathcal{A}^* \subseteq \mathcal{A}'$.*

Here, we use the notation $\mathcal{A} = X$ as vector representation for $\forall \alpha_i \in \mathcal{A} : \alpha_i = x_i$.

Sensitive attributes, as defined above, are not the only type of attributes that are worth to protect: In practice, an adversary can additionally infer sensitive attributes from other attributes through statistical inference using a-priori knowledge. We call such attributes that allow for the inference of sensitive attributes *critical attributes*.

Definition 15 (Critical Attributes). *Given a set of attributes $\mathcal{A}^*$, let P be a profile with $\mathsf{dom}(\theta_P) \supseteq \mathcal{A}$, and let P' be the profile with the restricted profile model $\theta_{P'} = \theta_P^{\mathcal{A}'}$, where $\mathcal{A}' = \mathsf{dom}(\theta_P) \setminus \mathcal{A}^*$.*

The set of attributes $\mathcal{A}^*$ is σ-critical for the user u that owns the profile P and an adversary with prior belief b_P and world knowledge κ, if u's privacy policy $\mathcal{R}_u$ contains a privacy requirement r such that P σ-violates r but P' does not.

Critical information require the same amount of protection as sensitive information, the difference however being that critical information is only protected for the sake of protecting sensitive information.

As a direct consequence of the definition above, sensitive attributes are also critical.

Corollary 1. *Let $\mathcal{A}$ be a set of sensitive attributes. Then $\mathcal{A}$ is also 0-critical.*

Another consequence we can draw is that privacy requirements will always be satisfied if no critical attributes are disseminated.

Corollary 2. *Let $\mathcal{O}$ be a public observations that does not include any critical attributes for a user u and an adversary Adv. Then u's privacy policy $\mathcal{R}_u$ is σ-satisfied against Adv.*

The corollary above implies that, while we cannot provide general non-disclosure guarantees in open settings, we can provide privacy assessments for specific privacy requirements, given an accurate estimate of the adversary's prior beliefs.

While privacy assessments alone are not satisfactory from a computer security perspective, where we usually require hard security guarantees quantified over all possible adversaries, the fact remains that we are faced with privacy issues in open settings that are to this day unanswered for due to the impossibility of hard guarantees in such settings. Pragmatically thinking, we are convinced that we should move from impossible hard guarantees to more practical privacy assessments instead. This makes particularly sense in settings where users are not victims of targeted attacks, but instead fear attribute disclosure to data-collecting third parties.

5   Linkability in Open Settings

In the following we instantiate the general privacy model introduced in the last section to reason about the likelihood that two profiles of the same user are linked by the adversary in open settings. We introduce the novel notion of (k, d)-anonymity with which we assess anonymity and linkability based on the similarity of profiles within an online community.

To simplify the notation we introduce in this section, we will, in the following, talk about matching *entities* ϵ and ϵ' the adversary wants to link, instead of profiles P_1 and P_2 that belong to the same user u. All definitions introduced in the general framework above naturally carry over to entities as well.

5.1   Model Instantiation for Linkability

In the linkability problem, we are interested in assessing the likelihood that two matching entities ϵ and ϵ' can be linked, potentially across different online platforms. The corresponding privacy requirements, as introduced in Sect. 4.4, are $r_1 = (\epsilon, \alpha_L)$ and $r_2 = (\epsilon', \alpha_L)$, where α_L is the attribute that ϵ and ϵ' belong to the same user. Consequently, we say that these entities are unlinkable if they satisfy the aforementioned privacy requirements.

Definition 16 (Unlinkability). *Two entities ϵ and ϵ' are σ-unlinkable if $\{\theta_\epsilon, \theta_{\epsilon'}\} \models_\sigma \{r_1, r_2\}$.*

5.2   Anonymity

To assess the identity disclosure risk of an entity ϵ within a collection of entities $\mathcal{E}$, we use the following intuition: ϵ is anonymous in $\mathcal{E}$ if there is a subset $\mathcal{E}' \subseteq \mathcal{E}$ to which ϵ is very similar. The collection $\mathcal{E}'$ then is an anonymous subset of $\mathcal{E}$ for ϵ.

To assess the similarity of entities within a collection of entities, we will use a distance measure dist on the entity models of these entities. We will require that this measure provides all properties of a metric.

A collection of entities in which the distance of all entities to ϵ is small (i.e., $\leq$ a constant d) is called d-convergent for ϵ.

Definition 17. *A collection of entities $\mathcal{E}$ is d-convergent for ϵ if $\mathsf{dist}(\theta_\epsilon, \theta_{\epsilon'}) \leq d$ for all $\epsilon' \in \mathcal{E}$.*

Convergence measures the similarity of a collection of individuals. Anonymity is achieved if an entity can find a collection of entities that are all similar to this entity. This leads us to the definition of (k, d)-anonymity, which requires a subset of similar entities of size k.

Definition 18. *An entity ϵ is (k, d)-anonymous in a collection of entities $\mathcal{E}$ if there exists a subset of entities $\mathcal{E}' \subseteq \mathcal{E}$ with the properties that $\epsilon \in \mathcal{E}$, that $|\mathcal{E}'| \geq k$ and that $\mathcal{E}'$ is d-convergent.*

An important feature of this anonymity definition is that it provides anonymity guarantees that can be derived from a subset of all available data, but continue to hold once we consider a larger part of the dataset.

Corollary 3. *If an entity is (k, d)-anonymous in a collection of entities $\mathcal{E}$, then it is also (k, d)-anonymous in the collection of entities $\mathcal{E}' \supset \mathcal{E}$.*

Intuitively, (k, d)-anonymity is a generalization of the classical notions of k-anonymity to open settings without pre-defined quasi-identifiers. We schematically illustrate such anonymous subsets in Fig. 1.

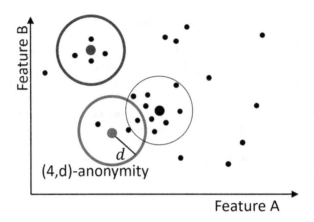

Fig. 1. Anonymity in crowdsourcing systems. (Color figure online)

5.3 Entity Matching

We define the notion of *matching* identities. As before, we use the distance measure dist to assess the similarity of two entities.

Definition 19. *An entity ϵ c-matches an entity ϵ' if* $\mathsf{dist}(\theta_\epsilon, \theta_{\epsilon'}) \leq c$.

Similarly, we can also define the notion of one entity matching a collection of entities.

Definition 20. *A collection of entities $\mathcal{E}$ c-matches an entity ϵ' if all entities $\epsilon \in \mathcal{E}$ c-match ϵ'.*

Assuming the adversary only has access to the similarity of entities, the best he can do is comparing the distance of all entities $\epsilon \in \mathcal{E}$ to ϵ' and make a probabilistic choice proportional to their relative distance values.

Now, if the matching identity ϵ^* is d-convergent in $\mathcal{E}$ the, all entities in $\mathcal{E}$ will have a comparatively similar distance to ϵ'.

Lemma 1. *Let $\mathcal{E}$ be d-convergent for ϵ^*. If ϵ^* c-matches ϵ', then $\mathcal{E}$ $(c + d)$-matches ϵ'.*

Proof. Since $\mathcal{E}$ is d-convergent for ϵ^*, $\forall \epsilon' \in \mathcal{E} : \mathsf{dist}(\epsilon^*, \epsilon') \leq d$. Using the triangle inequality, and the fact that ϵ^* c-matches the entity ϵ', we can bound the distance of all entities $\epsilon \in \mathcal{E}$ to ϵ' by $\forall \epsilon'' \in \mathcal{E} : \mathsf{dist}(\epsilon, \epsilon') \leq c + d$. Hence $\mathcal{E}$ $(c+d)$-matches the entity ϵ'.   □

Hence, the matching entity ϵ^* does not c-match ϵ' for a small value of c, the adversary Adv he will have a number of possibly matching entities that are similarly likely to match ϵ'.

We get the same result if not the whole collection $\mathcal{E}$ is convergent, but if there exists a subset of convergent entities that allows the target to remain anonymous.

Corollary 4. *Let ϵ' be (k, d)-anonymous in $\mathcal{E}$. If ϵ' c-matches an entity ϵ then there is a subset $\mathcal{E}' \subseteq \mathcal{E}$ of size at least k which $(c + d)$-matches ϵ.*

5.4 Identity Disclosure

We assume that the adversary uses the similarity of the candidate entities to his target entity ϵ' to make his decision. The likelihood that the adversary chooses a specific entity ϵ^* then is the relative magnitude of $\mathsf{dist}(\epsilon^*, \epsilon)$, i.e.

$$Pr[\mathsf{Adv} \text{ chooses } \epsilon^*] = 1 - \frac{\mathsf{dist}(\epsilon^*, \epsilon')}{\sum_{\epsilon \in \mathcal{E}} \mathsf{dist}(\epsilon, \epsilon')}.$$

We can now bound the likelihood with which a specific entity ϵ^* would be chosen by the adversary if ϵ^* is (k, d)-anonymous.

Theorem 2. *Let the matching entity ϵ^* of the entity ϵ' in the collection $\mathcal{E} = \{\epsilon_1, \ldots, \epsilon_n\}$ be (k, d)-anonymous in $\mathcal{E}$. Furthermore let ϵ^* c-match ϵ'. Then an adversary $\mathsf{Adv} = (b, \emptyset)$ with uniform prior belief b and with empty world knowledge that only observes the similarity of entities links the entity ϵ^* to ϵ' with a likelihood of at most $t \leq 1 - \frac{c}{c+(k-1)(c+d)}$.*

Proof. Let $\mathcal{E}^*$ be the (k, d) anonymous subset of ϵ^* in $\mathcal{E}$. Let t^* be the likelihood of identifying ϵ^* from $\mathcal{E}^*$. Then clearly $t < t^*$ since we remove all possible, but wrong candidates in $\mathcal{E} \setminus \mathcal{E}^*$.

Since ϵ^* c-matches ϵ', by Lemma 1, we can upper bound the distance of each entity in $\mathcal{E}^*$ to ϵ', i.e.,

$$\forall \epsilon \in \mathcal{E}^* : \mathsf{dist}(\epsilon, \epsilon') \leq c + d$$

We can now bound t^* as follows:

$$t^* = Pr[\mathsf{Adv} \text{ chooses } \epsilon]$$

$$= 1 - \frac{c}{c + (k - 1)(\sum_{\epsilon \in \mathcal{E}^* \setminus \{\epsilon^*\}} \mathsf{dist}(\epsilon, \epsilon'))} \leq 1 - \frac{c}{c + (k - 1)(c + d)}$$

$\square$

Theorem 2 shows that, as long as entities remain anonymous in a suitably large anonymous subset of a collection of entities, an adversary will have difficulty identifying them with high likelihood. Recalling our unlinkability definition from the beginning of the section, this result also implies that ϵ^* is σ-unlinkable for $\sigma = t$.

Corollary 5. *Let the matching entity ϵ^* of the entity ϵ' in the collection $\mathcal{E} = \{\epsilon_1, \ldots, \epsilon_n\}$ be (k, d)-anonymous in $\mathcal{E}$. Then ϵ^* and ϵ' are σ-unlinkable for $\sigma = 1 - \frac{c}{c+(k-1)(c+d)}$ against an adversary $\mathsf{Adv} = (b, \emptyset)$ with uniform prior belief and empty world knowledge that only observes entity similarity.*

In Sect. 6.5 we present experiments that evaluate the anonymity and linkability of individuals in the Online Social Network Reddit, and measure how well they can be identified from among their peers.

5.5   Limitations

The quality of the assessment provided by the d-convergence model largely depends on adversarial prior belief we assume: in our results above, we assume an adversary without any prior knowledge. In practice, however, the adversary might have access to prior beliefs that can help him in his decision making. Therefore, turning such assessments into meaningful estimates in practice requires a careful estimation of prior knowledge by, e.g., producing a more accurate profile model: the problem of comprehensive profile building for entities in an open setting is an open question that has been examined somewhat in the literature [8,13,17,19,53], but on the whole still leaves a lot of space for future work.

This concludes the formal definitions of our d-convergence model. In the next sections, we instantiate it for identity disclosure risk analyses based on user-generated text-content and apply this instantiation to the OSN Reddit.

6   Linkability Evaluation on Reddit

While the main focus of this paper is to present the actual privacy model as such, the following experiments are meant to provide first insights into the application of our framework, without taking overly complex adversarial capabilities into account. The evaluation can easily be extended to a more refined model of an adversary without conceptual difficulties.

We first articulate the goals of this evaluation, and then, secondly, describe the data collection process, followed by defining the instantiation of the general framework we use for our evaluation in the third step. Fourth, we introduce the necessary processing steps on our dataset, before we finally discuss the results of our evaluation.

6.1   Goals

In our evaluation, we aim at validating our model by conducting two basic experiments. First, we want to empirically show that, our model instantiation yields a suitable abstraction of real users for reasoning about their privacy. To this end, profiles of the same user should be more similar to each other (less distant) than profiles from different users.

Second, we want to empirically show that a larger anonymous subset makes it more difficult for an adversary to correctly link the profile. Thereby, we inspect whether anonymous subsets provide a practical estimate of a profile's anonymity.

Given profiles with anonymous subsets of similar size, we determine the percentage of profiles which the adversary can match within the top k results, i.e., given a source profile, the adversary computes the top k most similar (less distant) profiles in the other subreddit. We denote this percentage by *precision@k* and correlate it to the size of the anonymous subsets.

We fix the convergence of the anonymous subsets to be equal to the matching distance between two corresponding profiles. Our intuition is that, this way, the anonymous subset captures most of the profiles an adversary could potentially consider matching.

6.2 Data-Collection

For the empirical evaluation of our privacy model, we use the online social network Reddit [1] that was founded in 2005 and constitutes one of the largest discussion and information sharing platforms in use today. On Reddit, users share and discuss topics in a vast array of topical subreddits that collect all topics belonging to one general area; e.g. there are subreddits for world news, tv series, sports, food, gaming and many others. Each subreddit contains so-called submissions, i.e., user-generated content that can be commented on by other users.

To have a ground truth for our evaluation, we require profiles of the same user same user across different OSNs to be linked. Fortunately, Reddit's structure provides an inherent mechanism to deal with this requirement. Instead of considering Reddit as a single OSN, we treat each subreddit as its own OSN. Since users are identified through the same pseudonym in all of those subreddits, they remain linkable across the subreddits' boundaries. Hence our analysis has the required ground truth. The adversary we simulate, however, is only provided with the information available in the context of each subreddit and thus can only try to match profiles across subreddits. Ground truth in the end allows us to verify the correctness of his match.

To build up our dataset, we built a crawler using Reddit's API to collect comments. Recall that subreddits contain submissions that, in turn, are commented by the users. For our crawler, we focused on the large amount of comments because they contain a lot of text and thus are best suitable for computing the unigram models.

Our crawler operates in two steps that are repeatedly executed over time. During the whole crawling process, it maintains a list of already processed users. In the first step, our crawler collects a list of the overall newest comments on Reddit from Reddit's API and inserts these comments into our dataset. In the second step, for each author of these comments who has not been processed yet, the crawler also collects and inserts her latest 1,000 comments into our dataset. Then, it updates the list of processed users. The number of 1,000 comments per user, is a restriction of Reddit's API.

In total, during the whole September 2014, we collected more than 40 million comments from over 44,000 subreddits. The comments were written by about 81,000 different users which results in more than 2.75 million different profiles.

The whole dataset is stored in an anonymized form in a MySQL database and is available upon request.

6.3 Model Instantiation

On Reddit, users only interact with each other by by posting comments to text of link submissions. Reddit therefore does not allow us to exploit features found in other social networks, such as friend links or other static data about each user. On the other hand, this provides us with the opportunity to evaluate the linkability model introduced in Sect. 5 based dynamic, user-generated content, in this case user-generated text content.

Since we only consider text content, we instantiate the general model from the previous sections with an unigram model, where each attribute is a word unigram, an its value is the frequency with which the unigram appears in the profiles comments. Such unigram models have succesfully been used in the past to characterize the information within text content and to correlate users across different online platforms [28,45].

Definition 21 (Unigram Model). *Let $\mathcal{V}$ be a finite vocabulary. The unigram model $\theta_P = p_i$ of a profile is a set of frequencies $p_i \in [0,\dots,1]$ with which each unigram $w_i \in \mathcal{V}$ appears in the profile P. Each frequency p_i is determined by*

$$p_i = \frac{\mathrm{count}(w_i, P)}{\sum_{w \in \mathcal{V}} \mathrm{count}(w, P)}$$

Since the unigram model essentially constitutes a probability distribution, we instantiate our distance metric dist with the Jensen-Shannon divergence [25]. The Jensen-Shannon divergence is a symmetric extension of the Kullback-Leiber divergence has been shown to be successful in many related information retrieval scenarios.

Definition 22. *Let P and Q be two statistical models over a discrete space Ω. The Jensen-Shannon divergence is defined by*

$$D_{\mathsf{JS}} = \frac{1}{2} D_{\mathsf{KL}}(P||M) + \frac{1}{2} D_{\mathsf{KL}}(Q||M)$$

where D_{KL} is the Kullback-Leibler divergence

$$D_{\mathsf{KL}}(P||Q) = \sum_{w \in \Omega} log\left(\frac{P(\omega)}{Q(\omega)}\right) P(\omega)$$

and M is the averaged distribution $M = \frac{1}{2}(P + Q)$.

In the following, we will use the square-root of the Jensen-Shannon divergence, constituting a metric, as our distance measure, i.e., dist $= \sqrt{D_{\mathsf{JS}}}$.

6.4 Data-Processing

The evaluation on our dataset is divided into sequentially performed computation steps, which include the normalization of all comments, the computation of unigram models for each profile, a filtering of our dataset to keep the evaluation tractable, the computation of profile distances and the computation of (k, d)-anonymous subsets.

Normalizing Comments. Unstructured, heterogeneous data, as in our case, may contain a variety of valuable information about a user's behavior, e.g., including formatting and punctuation. Although we could transform these into attributes, we do not consider them here for the sake of simplicity.

In order to get a clean representation to apply the unigram model on, we apply various normalization steps, including transformation to lower case, the removal of Reddit formatting and punctuation except for smilies. Moreover, we apply a encoding specific normalization, replace URLs by their hostnames and shorten repeated characters in words like `cooool` to a maximum of three. Finally, we also filter out a list of 597 stopwords from the comments. Therefore, we perform six different preprocessing steps on the data, which we describe in more detail in the following.

1. **Convert to lower case letters:** In our statistical language models, we do not want to differentiate between capitalized and lowercased occurrences of words. Therefore, we convert the whole comment into lower case.
2. **Remove Reddit formatting:** Reddit allows users to use a wide range of formatting modifiers that we divide into two basic categories: formatting modifiers that influence the typography and the layout of the comment, and formatting modifiers that include external resources into a comment. The first kind of modifier, named layout modifiers, is stripped off the comment, while leaving the plain text. The second kind of modifier, called embedding modifiers, is removed from the comment completely.

   One example for a layout modifier is the asterisk: When placing an asterisk both in front and behind some text, e.g., `*text*`, this text will be displayed in italics, e.g., *text*. Our implementation removes these enclosing asterisks, because they are not valuable for computing statistical language models for n-grams and only affect the layout. Similarly, we also remove other layout modifiers such as table layouts, list layouts and URL formatting in a way that only the important information remains.

   A simple example for embedding modifiers are inline code blocks: Users can embed arbitrary code snippets into their comments using the ` modifier. Since these code blocks do not belong to the natural language part of the comment and only embed a kind of external resource, we remove them completely. In addition to code blocks, the category of embedding modifiers also includes quotes of other comments.
3. **Remove stacked diacritics:** In our dataset, we have seen that diacritics are often misused. Since Reddit uses Unicode as its character encoding, users can create their own characters by arbitrarily stacking diacritics on top of them. To avoid this kind of unwanted characters, we first normalize the comment by utilizing the unicode character composition, which tries to combine each letter and its diacritics into a single precombined character. Secondly, we remove all remaining diacritic symbols from the comment. While this process preserves most of the normal use of diacritics, it is able to remove all unwanted diacritics.

4. **Replace URLs by their hostname:** Generally, a URL is very specific and a user often does not include the exact same URL in different comments. However, it is much more common that a user includes different URLs that all belong to the same hostname, e.g., www.mypage.com. Since our statistical language models should represent the expected behavior of a user in terms of used words (including URLs), we restrict all URLs to their hostnames.

5. **Remove punctuation:** Most of the punctuation belongs to the sentence structure and, thus, should not a part of our statistical language models. Therefore, we remove all punctuation except for the punctuation inside URLs and smilies. We do not remove the smilies, because people are using them in a similar role as words to enrich their sentences: Every person has her own subset of smilies that she typically uses. To keep the smilies in the comment, we maintain a list of 153 different smilies that will not be removed from the comment.

6. **Remove duplicated characters:** In the internet, people often duplicate characters in a word to add emotional nuances to their writing, e.g., `cooooo-oooool`. But sometimes the number of reduplicated characters varies, even if the same emotion should be expressed. Thus, we reduce the number of duplicated characters to a maximum of 3, e.g., `coool`. In practice, this truncation allows us to differentiate between the standard use of a word and the emotional variation of it, while it does not depend on the actual number of duplicated characters.

Computing Unigram Models. From the normalized data, we compute the unigram frequencies for each comment. Recall that our dataset consists of many subreddits that each form their own OSN. Thus, we aggregate the corresponding unigram frequencies per profile, per subreddit, and for Reddit as a whole. Using this data, we compute the word unigram frequencies for each comment as described in Sect. 6.3.

Since a subreddit collects submissions and comments to a single topic, we expect the unigrams to reflect its topic specific language. Indeed, the 20 most frequently used unigrams of a subreddit demonstrate that the language adapts to the topic. As an example, we show the top 20 unigrams (excluding stopwords) of Reddit and two sample subreddits *Lost* and *TipOfMyTongue* in Table 1. As expected, there are subreddit specific unigrams that occur more often in the context of one subreddit than in the context of any other subreddit. For example, the subreddit *Lost* deals with a TV series that is about the survivors of a plane crash and its aftermath on an island. Unsurprisingly, the word *island* is the top unigram in this subreddit. In contrast, the subreddit *TipOfMyTongue* deals with the failure to remember a word from memory and, thus, has the word *remember* in the list of its top three unigrams.

Filtering the Dataset. To reduce the required amount of computations we restrict ourselves to *interesting profiles*. We define an interesting profile as one that contains at least 100 comments and that belongs to a subreddit with at

Table 1. Top 20 unigrams of Reddit and two sample subreddits Lost and TipOfMy-Tongue.

Top	Reddit		Subreddit: Lost		Subreddit: TipOfMyTongue	
	Unigram	Frequency	Unigram	Frequency	Unigram	Frequency
1	people	4,127,820	island	832	www.youtube.com	3663
2	time	2,814,841	show	750	song	1,542
3	good	2,710,665	lost	653	remember	1,261
4	gt	2,444,240	time	580	en.wikipedia.org	1,100
5	game	1,958,850	people	527	sounds	1,007
6	pretty	1,422,640	locke	494	solved	924
7	2	1,413,118	season	431	movie	918
8	lot	1,385,167	jacob	429	find	829
9	work	1,352,292	mib	372	:)	786
10	1	1,184,029	jack	310	game	725
11	3	1,124,503	episode	280	time	678
12	great	1,070,299	ben	255	thinking	633
13	point	1,063,239	good	250	good	633
14	play	1,060,985	monster	237	www.imdb.com	584
15	years	1,032,270	lot	220	video	583
16	bad	1,008,607	gt	182	pretty	570
17	day	989,180	character	165	youtu.be	569
18	love	988,567	walt	163	mark	548
19	find	987,171	man	162	edit	540
20	shit	976,928	dharma	162	post	519

least 100 profiles. Additionally, we dropped the three largest subreddits from our dataset to speed up the computation.

In conclusion, this filtering results in 58,091 different profiles that belong to 37,935 different users in 1,930 different subreddits.

Distances Within and Across Subreddits. Next, we compute the pairwise distance within and across subreddits using our model instantiation. Excluding the distance of profiles to themselves, the minimal, maximal and average distance of two profiles within subreddits in our dataset are approximately 0.12, 1 and 0.79 respectively. Across subreddits, the minimal, maximal and average distance of two profiles are approximately 0.1, 1 and 0.85 respectively.

Anonymous Subsets. Utilizing the distances within subreddits, we can determine the anonymous subsets for each profile in a subreddit. More precisely, we compute the anonymous subset for each pair of profiles from the same user.

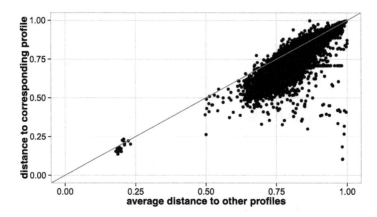

Fig. 2. The average distance between a profile in subreddit s and all profiles in s' versus the matching distance between the profile and its correspondence in s'. (Color figure online)

We set the convergence d to the matching distance between both profiles and determine the size of the resulting anonymous subset.

6.5   Evaluation and Discussion

In this subsection, we inspect and interpret the results of our experiments with regard to our aforementioned goals. Therefore, we first start by giving evidence that our approach indeed provides a suitable abstraction of real users for reasoning about their privacy.

To this end, we compare the distance of matching profiles to the average distance of non-matching profiles. In particular, for each pair of profiles from the same user in subreddits s and s', we plot the average distance from the profile in s to the non-matching profiles in s' in relation to the distance to the matching profile in s' in Fig. 2. The red line denotes the function $y = x$ and divides the figure into two parts: if a point lies below the line through the origin, the corresponding profiles match better than the average of the remaining profiles. Since the vast majority of datapoints is located below the line, we can conclude that profiles of the same user match better than profiles of different users.

Our second goal aimed at showing that anonymous subsets indeed can be used to reason about the users' privacy. Therefore, we investigate the chances of an adversary to find a profile of the same user within the top k matches and relate its chance to the size of the profile's anonymous subset. More precisely, given multiple target profiles with similar anonymous subset sizes, we determine the, so called, precision@k, i.e., the ratio of target profiles that occur in the top k ranked matches (by ascending distance from the source profiles). We relate this precision@k to the anonymous subset sizes with a convergence d set to the

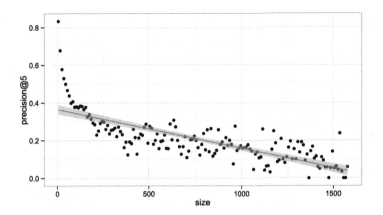

Fig. 3. The anonymous subset size correlated to the precision an adversary has if considering the top 5 profiles as matching. (Color figure online)

distance between the source and target profiles, and we group the anonymous subset sizes in bins of size 10.

In our evaluation, we considered $k \in \{1, 5, 10, 20\}$, which all yield very similar results. Exemplarily, we correlate the aforementioned measures for $k = 5$ in Fig. 3, clearly showing that an increasing anonymous subset size correlates with an increasing uncertainty – i.e., decreasing precision – for the adversary.

7   Assessing the Effectiveness of Countermeasures Against Authorship Recognition

In this section, we explore another application of the linkability model we introduced in Sect. 5: we develop a method to assess the effectiveness of various countermeasures against authorship recognition, i.e. the process of linking text content that were authored by the same user based on stylometric features exhibited by the content.

7.1   Theoretical Foundation

We first develop the formal foundation for our evaluation of authorship recognition countermeasures. We derive our definitions from those in the previous sections and adapt them to capture information about writing style.

Threat Model. In our threat model, we assume multiple collections of entities $\mathcal{E}_i$, also called *communities*. An entity $\epsilon \in \mathcal{E}_i$ is characterized by its writing style and corresponds to a pseudonymous author of a collection of texts. Two entities ϵ_1 and ϵ_2 are called matching, if both belong to the same author.

The adversary's goal is now to identify matching entities across several communities by analyzing their writing style. Figure 4 (see Sect. 7.1) shows two exemplary communities including the links between matching entities.

For the application of countermeasures, we assume that a community $\mathcal{E}$ already exists, together with all text passages published by the entities in $\mathcal{E}$, and a test author applies a countermeasure on his text passage before it is published into $\mathcal{E}$. We simulate this by simply choosing a subset of test authors from $\mathcal{E}$ for which we evaluate the countermeasures.

Statistical Models of Writing-Style. For authorship attribution, we extend the definition of entity models from Definition 1 in Sect. 4 to include different types of attributes that each will represent one feature type of the writing style feature set (e.g., as presented in [3]).

Definition 23 (Attribute Types). *An attribute type class $\mathcal{T}$ is a collection of attribute types $\tau \in \mathcal{T}$. We denote with $\mathcal{A}_\tau$ the set of all attributes $\alpha \in \mathcal{A}_\tau$ that realize the attribute type τ.*

Intuitively, an attribute type corresponds to a feature or class of features, e.g., the sentence length or word unigrams. A possible realization for the sentence length would be 5, whereas *house* is a possible realization for a word unigram. Statistical models now associate with each attribute and attribute type a probability, or relevance estimation, of this attribute for the specific entity.

Definition 24 (Extended Statistical Model). *The entity model $\theta_\epsilon = (\theta_\epsilon^{\tau_1}, \ldots, \theta_\epsilon^{\tau_n})$ of an entity ϵ consists of the statistical models of its attribute types $\tau_i \in \mathcal{T}, 1 \leq i \leq n$.*

Each statistical model $\theta_\epsilon^{\tau_i}$ determines the probability $Pr[\alpha \mid \theta_\epsilon^{\tau_i}]$ that the entity ϵ exhibits the attribute $\alpha \in \mathcal{A}_{\tau_i}$.

In the easiest case, the probability of exhibiting a specific attribute (i.e., a specific feature realization) will be proportional to its frequency in a user's text. Additionally, in our experimental evaluation, we also explore the possibility to set the probability proportional to the popular *term frequency inverse document frequency* to better capture the relevance of an attribute in a user's text given the context in which it is published.

Entity Similarity. In the following, we will use these entity models together with a similarity measure on these models to evaluate the similarity of entities with regard to their writing style. We follow the intuition that a higher similarity between two entities in different communities implies a higher likelihood that they both correspond to the same author.

Since we characterize each author in terms of statistical models, determining their similarity boils down to measuring the similarity of probability distributions. As proposed in Sect. 6.3, we utilize the Jensen-Shannon divergence [25] to determine the similarity of our statistical models. The Jensen-Shannon divergence is a symmetric variant of the popular Kullback-Leibler divergence, and fulfills all properties of a metric distance measure.

We extend this similarity measure to fit our notion of statistical models with attribute types, resulting in a linear combination of the similarities of each attribute type.

Definition 25 (Similarity of Entities). *Given two entities* $\epsilon_1, \epsilon_2 \in \mathcal{E}$, *the similarity of* ϵ_1 *and* ϵ_2 *is the linear combination of the similarities of their statistical models. Let* $\mathbf{sim}(\theta_{\epsilon_1}, \theta_{\epsilon_2}) = (\mathrm{sim}(\theta_{\epsilon_1}^{\tau_1}, \theta_{\epsilon_2}^{\tau_1}), \dots, \mathrm{sim}(\theta_{\epsilon_1}^{\tau_n}, \theta_{\epsilon_2}^{\tau_n}))$ *and* $\boldsymbol{\lambda} = (\lambda_{\tau_1}, \dots, \lambda_{\tau_n})$. *Then,*

$$\mathrm{sim}(\theta_{\epsilon_1}, \theta_{\epsilon_2}) = \boldsymbol{\lambda} \cdot \mathbf{sim}(\theta_{\epsilon_1}, \theta_{\epsilon_2}) + \rho,$$

where ρ *denotes an optional constant.*

When applying this theory to an actual dataset, $\boldsymbol{\lambda}$ and ρ can be learned using established regression and classification techniques.

Average Entity in a Collection. Next, we further extend statistical models to a collection of entities $\mathcal{E}$, which gives us the probability that a randomly chosen entity from the collection exhibits an attribute. While the former part of this section introduced the formal ground for attributing authorship by similarities, the definitions in this and the next paragraph will be used for powering some of our countermeasures.

Definition 26 (Stat. Models for Collections). *Given a set of attribute types* $\mathcal{T}$, *the statistical model* $\theta_{\mathcal{E}}$ *of a collection of entities* $\mathcal{E}$ *is defined as* $(\theta_{\mathcal{E}}^{\tau_1}, \dots, \theta_{\mathcal{E}}^{\tau_n})$, *where each* $\theta_{\mathcal{E}}^{\tau_i}$ *determines the probability* $Pr[\alpha \mid \theta_{\mathcal{E}}^{\tau_i}]$ *that an entity* $\epsilon \in \mathcal{E}$, *chosen uniformly at random, exhibits an attribute* $\alpha \in \mathcal{A}_{\tau_i}$.

We can compute each statistical model $\theta_{\mathcal{E}}^{\tau_i}$ *of a collection* $\mathcal{E}$ *by*

$$Pr[\alpha \mid \theta_{\mathcal{E}}^{\tau_i}] = \frac{\sum_{\epsilon \in \mathcal{E}} Pr[\alpha \mid \theta_{\epsilon}^{\tau_i}]}{|\mathcal{E}|}$$

for each attribute $\alpha \in \mathcal{A}_{\tau_i}$.

The statistical model for a collection corresponds to the average entity in that collection.

(k, d)-anonymity. As described in Sect. 5.2 (cf. Definition 18), we assess anonymity of an entity by identifying *anonymous* subsets within a community that allow an entity to hide amongst her peers: The (k, d)-anonymous subset of an entity $\epsilon \in \mathcal{E}$ is a subset of entities $\mathcal{A} \subseteq \mathcal{E}$ of size k, each of which are at least d-similar to ϵ. For a fixed value of k, the anonymous subset's convergence is a good indicator for *how* close the nearest k entities are. We will utilize these anonymous subsets to improve the automatic countermeasures we propose in Sect. 7.2 by not changing the text towards the average author from the whole community, but rather an existing author within an anonymous subset of the community.

Countermeasure Formalization. Finally, we formally define countermeasures in the context of statistical models and then define our novel notion of gain provided by a countermeasure.

Definition 27 (Countermeasure). *A* countermeasure C *is a function that changes the statistical model* θ_ϵ *to* $C(\theta_\epsilon)$.

The optimal weights $\lambda = \lambda_{\tau_1}, \ldots, \lambda_{\tau_n}$ obtained from the regression or trained classifier can be used to determine the importance of each attribute type for the stylometric similarity. Since their values might also be negative, the actual importance is defined as $(\lambda_{\tau_i})^2$, similar to an approach by Guyon *et al.* [29].

Definition 28 (Feature Importance). *Given* λ *and an attribute type* τ, τ*'s importance is defined as* $(\lambda_\tau)^2$. *The vector* $\mathbf{I}$ *is defined as the element-wise multiplication* $\lambda \odot \lambda$ *and contains each attribute type's importance.*

In an ideal, private world no attribute type reliably contributes to the matching of corresponding authors, and hence no attribute type is particularly important. We capture this ideal scenario through ideal importances $\hat{\mathbf{I}}$ that we aim to achieve through the application of countermeasures. In our case, if no attribute type is particularly important, we set $\hat{\mathbf{I}} = \mathbf{0}$. Motivated by this intuition, we define a countermeasure's gain as the improvement towards the ideal scenario.

Definition 29 (Gain). *Let* $\mathbf{I}$ *be attribute type importances before the application of a countermeasure and* $\mathbf{I}'$ *be attribute type importances after the application. Then the* improvement potential *towards the ideal scenario* $\hat{\mathbf{I}}$ *is defined as* $\mathbf{I} - \hat{\mathbf{I}}$.

A countermeasure C*'s gain* gain_C^τ *with respect to a specific attribute type* τ *is the actual improvement towards the ideal scenario, while the countermeasure's overall gain* gain_C *is defined as the sum over the gains for all attribute types.*

$$\mathsf{gain}_C^\tau = |\mathbf{I}_\tau - \hat{\mathbf{I}}_\tau| - |\mathbf{I}'_\tau - \hat{\mathbf{I}}_\tau|$$

$$\mathsf{gain}_C = \sum_{\tau \in \mathcal{T}} \mathsf{gain}_C^\tau$$

In the case that the ideal importances are 0, *this simplifies to* $\mathsf{gain}_C^\tau = \mathbf{I}_\tau - \mathbf{I}'_\tau$.

Comparison to Other Measures. We compare our approach of computing the gain of countermeasures to other approaches that can be used to capture the effectiveness of countermeasures. Namely, we consider both (1) classifier-dependent measures such as precision, recall, accuracy, and (2) the classifier-independent measure of information gain.

By comparing such measures before and after the countermeasure's application, a similar measure to our **gain** is achieved. In contrast to our approach, however, both of the above approaches lead to drawbacks we will elaborate in the following.

Classifier-Dependent Measures. In general, a comparison of precision, recall and accuracy before and after a countermeasure's application only gives a global view on the effectiveness of a countermeasure, i.e., the global loss in those measures after the countermeasure's application. Such an approach fails in giving precise results on a feature-class level, since the underlying measures describe the total outcome of the classification.

Classifier-Independent Measures. While information gain is capable of both, providing a feature-level assessment of importance as well as being classifier-independent, it still fails to match our needs: Intuitively, a feature's information gain is higher if it is more discriminating. However, in its computation, information gain does not take into account which authors are actually matching.

Narayanan *et al.* [46] define information gain as $IG(F_i) = H(B) - H(B \mid F_i) = H(B) + H(F_i) - H(B, F_i)$ where H is the Shannon entropy, B is the random variable corresponding to a set identifier (in their case, the blog number), and F_i is the random variable corresponding to feature i. Adopting this definition let us define the notions of a feature's information gain for authors $IG_A(F_i)$ and for entities $IG_\epsilon(F_i)$.

Unfortunately, knowing which features distinguish authors is not necessarily the same as knowing which features help matching authors. For example, consider the two communities in Fig. 4, where matching entities are highlighted in the same color and are connected by a line. In this scenario, $IG_A(F_i)$ tells us to which extent F_i helps distinguishing the authors in general. However, without considering the boundaries between both communities, it is possible that F_i is only well discriminating in C_1, but not in C_2, and is in particular not very helpful in matching from C_1 to C_2.

Using $IG_\epsilon(F_i)$ instead respects the boundaries of the communities, but in fact does not help us in matching the entities across both communities, since $IG_\epsilon(F_i)$ only tells us which features can be used to distinguish between all entities within one community. The same feature might very well be completely useless in discriminating entities in the other community.

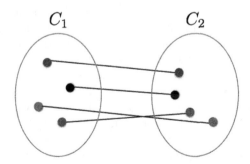

Fig. 4. Two different communities with matching authors. (Color figure online)

Gain. In contrast to the previous methods, gain is directly defined in terms of the optimal matching and values each feature class in their importance for achieving this matching. In the rest of the paper, we will not only show the validity of our approach by correlating the countermeasures' gain to classifier-dependent performance measures, but we will also demonstrate the usefulness of our methodology in a detailed analysis of several countermeasures.

7.2   Experimental SetUp

This section provides an overview over our experimental setup. In particular, we provide a detailed explanation of our dataset, the stylometric features we consider and the countermeasures we evaluate, including a description of each countermeasures' implementation.

Dataset. For our experimental evaluation, we leverage the Extended-Brennan-Greenstadt corpus [10,11], which provides a decent collection of writing samples from 45 different authors. The corpus contains writing samples of at least 6500 words for each author, which are split into approximately 500-word passages. Each writing sample is from a formal source, e.g., school essays, reports or other types of professional or academic correspondence, which was manually validated by the creators of the corpus.

We do not use the (1) *obfuscation* and (2) *imitiation* part of the corpus, in which the authors were requested to write passages on a specific topic while (1) trying to hide their writing style and (2) trying to imitate the writing style of another author, namely Cormac McCarthy. The methodology we develop is intended for evaluating the effect of countermeasures changing a given text, while both the obfuscation and imitation part of the corpus are already obfuscated texts that do not correspond to the original writing samples.

In order to evaluate authorship attribution between different communities, we artifically distribute all text passages of an author into three distinct communities. This way, our dataset consists of 3 communities, each containing 233 text passages of 45 authors (between 4 to 8 text passages per author in one community).

Feature Set. For our evaluation, we take the Writeprints extended feature set [3] as a basis that we further extend with additional features. However, we remove *word trigrams* to make our evaluation computationally more tractable. In total, we include 33 different stylometric features into our model, some of which we adjust to fit the structure of our dataset.

In correspondence with the model presented in Sect. 7.1, a feature class, such as, e.g., letter bigrams, corresponds to an attribute type, whereas each instance of a feature, e.g., the actual letter bigram "aa", corresponds to an attribute within this attribute type. During the evaluation, we store the frequency of each attribute and construct the statistical model from this observation. The quantity of a feature class describes the maximum number of features in that feature class, which we observed in our unmodified dataset. As mentioned in

Table 2. List of features.

Category	Identifier	Description	Quantity	λ	_spell	_syn	_mis	_spch
Character-Based	F1	count of letters (e.g., a, b, c)	44	−0.00936	✓	✓	✓	✓
	F2	letter bigrams (e.g., aa, ab, ac)	634	0.00133	✓	✓	✓	✓
	F3	letter trigrams (e.g., aaa, aab, aac)	5048	−0.00304	✓	✓	✓	✓
	F4	digits (e.g., 1, 2, 3)	10	0.00161				
	F5	digit bigrams (e.g., 01, 11, 12)	100	0.00379				
	F6	digit trigrams (e.g., 011, 111, 112)	1000	0.00138				
	F7	frequency of punctuation determined by unicode punctuation categories	27	0.01102	✓		✓	
	F8	frequency of punctuation as in Writeprints (?!,.'\";:)	8	0.00688	✓		✓	
	F9	frequency of special characters determined unicode symbol character categories (except for modifier symbols)	6	−0.01028	✓			✓
	F10	frequency of special characters as in Writeprints (~@#$%^&*-_=+><[]{}/|)	19	−0.00906	✓			✓
	F11	number of characters per text passage	432	−0.00114	✓	✓	✓	✓
POS-Tagger-Based	F12	gunning fog index (rounded to nearest whole number)	23	0.00421	✓	✓	✓	✓
	F13	flesch reading ease (rounded to nearest tenth)	10	0.00042	✓	✓	✓	✓
	F14	flesch kincaid grade level (rounded to nearest whole number)	48	−0.00108	✓	✓	✓	✓
	F15	frequency of POS tags (e.g., NN, VB)	44	0.009	✓	✓	✓	✓
	F16	frequency of POS tag bigrams (e.g., NN VB)	1171	−0.03563	✓	✓	✓	✓
	F17	frequency of POS tag trigrams (e.g., NN VB NN)	12,507	0.00387	✓	✓	✓	✓
	F18	number of characters per sentence	388	0.00471	✓	✓	✓	✓
	F19	number of words per sentence	110	−0.00939	✓	✓	✓	✓
	F20	ratio of adjectives and adverbs compared to the total number of words	13	0.00149	✓	✓	✓	✓
	F21	ratio of comparatives and superlatives compared to all adjectives	16	0.00214	✓	✓	✓	✓
	F22	ratio of nouns to all words	22	0.00311	✓	✓	✓	✓
	F23	ratio of verbs to all words	14	0.00145	✓	✓	✓	✓
	F24	ratio of verbs in past tense to all verbs	69	0.00448	✓	✓	✓	✓
	F25	ratio of verbs in the third person present to all verbs	49	−0.00101	✓	✓	✓	✓
	F26	ratio of verbs in the first or second person to all verbs	76	0.00108	✓	✓	✓	✓
Word-Based	F27	hapax legomena	21,126	−0.04912	✓	✓	✓	✓
	F28	misspelled words (e.g., abandonned, abudance)	37	−0.00042	✓		✓	
	F29	frequency of function words (e.g., I, for, of)	451	0.00502	✓	✓	✓	
	F30	word unigrams (e.g., lemon, tree)	21,723	0.12246	✓	✓	✓	✓
	F31	word bigrams (e.g., lemon tree)	172,764	0.04693	✓	✓	✓	✓
	F32	number of words per text passage	64	0.00153	✓			✓
	F33	number of characters per word	30	−0.0058	✓	✓	✓	✓

Sect. 7.1, we also evaluate the use of *term frequency inverse document frequency* instead of frequency to instantiate our statistical models in Sect. 8.

A full list of the feature classes and their quantities can be found in Table 2. We will use the identifiers F1 to F33 for each feature class introduced in this table throughout the rest of the paper. The table's last five columns will be formally introduced throughout the next sections.

In general, we group our features into three different categories depending on the actual implementation:

1. *Character-based* feature classes, for which we represent an author's text-passage as a list of characters and compute the corresponding attribute frequencies on that list.
2. *POS-tagger-based* feature classes rely on the output of the Stanford POS tagger [55,56] used with a twitter model [20] in order to use enhanced information about the current sentence and word in a text passage (e.g., a word's POS tag).
3. *Word-based* feature classes leverage a Java break iterator to efficiently iterate over the words of an authors text passages.

Additional resources from which we construct feature classes include a syllable counter that first tries to determine a word's syllable count from the dictionary CMUDict [18] by counting the number of vowels in the pronunciation. In case of failure, it determines an approximate syllable count based on an algorithm written by Greg Fast [26], counting the number of vowel groups in the word and adjusting the number for certain special cases. Moreover, we use a list of 512 function words as well as a list of common misspellings taken from Wikipedia [58] and the Anonymouth framework [42] to construct feature classes (e.g., F28 and F29).

Countermeasures. In this section, we discuss the countermeasures whose impact we aim to evaluate. We detail their implementation and also argue why these countermeasures preserve the semantics of the text. Finally, we present a list of features affected by each countermeasure.

Generally, we distinguish between two types of countermeasures: *simple countermeasures* and *optimizing countermeasures*. Simple countermeasures apply the first possible action to a given text, independent of its context, whereas optimizing countermeasures rank each available action and apply the most promising one. We first introduce all countermeasures in general before we discuss their optimizing variants in Sect. 7.2.

In total, our experiments incorporate four different countermeasures, which we will not only apply individually, but also in meaningful combinations. For referencing purposes, we name our countermeasures and present the affected features per countermeasure in Table 2 (some of which can be affected indirectly by, e.g., causing the POS tagger to fail).

Spell Checking (_spell). Since we are interested in assessing the impact of a standard text rewriting tool on the anonymity of text authors, we start with the arguably most common such tool: a spell checker. Spell checkers constitute a simple, but widely used example for tools that modify a text.

Our implementation of this countermeasure employs the open source Java spell checker LanguageTool [32] that is even able to detect grammar problems. Each text-passage that gets fed into this countermeasure will be corrected by the spell checker, always choosing the first suggestion. Due to the usual field of application of spell checkers, we consider this countermeasure to be mostly semantics-retaining.

Synonym Substitution (_syn). Our technically most sophisticated counter-measure replaces words by synonyms. Considering the highly flexible and changing nature of language, this task introduces several challenges:

1. Most often in natural language, words do not occur in its root form but rather in an inflected grammatical form. Thus, it is essential to get the canonical root form of a word.
2. Given such a root form, we have to maintain a dictionary of synonyms for each word. The dictionary should contain synonyms for at least nouns, verbs and adjectives – possibly also adverbs.
3. We need to be able to examine the inflection of the original word in order to replace it by a synonym in exactly the same grammatical form.
4. Finally, if we know the desired form, we have to inflect the synonym.

Fortunately, 1. and 2. can both be handled by leveraging WordNet [27,44], which is a large lexical database providing so called synsets for nouns, verbs, adjectives and adverbs. It can also be queried using non-root forms, which renders the first challenge irrelevant.

Since English as a language is only weakly inflected, a few hints for 3. suffice to generate the correct inflection of the synonym. More concretely, the output of the Stanford POS Tagger [55,56] used with a twitter model [20] is enough to infer the lexical category as well as attributes like tense, plural and person that allow us to determine the correct grammatical form.

Finally, we use simplenlg, a natural language generation API for Java, to realize the correct form of our synonym.

Repeating this for all potential synonyms, we select the optimal replacement according to our optimization strategy. Consequently, this countermeasure is optimizing. Also, substituting words by synonyms should preserve the initial semantics of a text.

Adding/Removing Misspellings (_mis). Another optimizing countermeasure that we implement makes use of misspellings, e.g., for cases where the misspelled word is more common than its correct form. Thus, this countermeasure first looks up the correct or misspelled variants of a word from a dictionary and then evaluates which form to use.

To accomplish this task, we adapt a list of common misspellings from Wikipedia [58] and generate a dictionary, providing a set of possibly misspelled and corrected substitutions for every word in the list. Although a misspelled word can potentially create confusion, this kind of substitutions should not drastically change the semantics of a text, because the correct word is nearly always recognizable from the context.

Special Characters Modification (_spch). Our last countermeasure seeks for the replacement of potentially identifying special characters. Since special characters (excluding punctuation) generally occur only infrequently in natural language, their usage is more likely to be unique and, consequently, can lead to an easy author identification. In order to counter this problem, we created a list of the most common special characters in our dataset and mapped them to their textual meanings. One example for such a mapping is © ↔ copyright ↔ (C), where each of the three alternatives could be substituted by another if the optimization yields a higher result.

Obviously, if the special characters are used with their usual meaning, this countermeasure preserves the semantics of a text.

Combinations. Instead of only evaluating the presented countermeasures individually, we also examine the impact of multiple countermeasures applied in a sequential manner. However, we exclude any combination that involves both _spell and _mis as the two countermeasures are very similar to each other and potentially could cancel each other out. To further narrow down the number of possible combinations, we also only apply countermeasures in a meaningful order. For example, it makes sense to apply spell checking first, because it is not optimizing and thus could influence the result of previous countermeasures in a negative way. Synonym substitution should also precede the addition/removal of misspellings, since our synonym substitution will not be capable of substituting misspelled words. Only _spch is essentially independent of the other countermeasures and therefore could be placed at any point in the ordering.

In conclusion, we end up with seven different combinations of our countermeasures: _spell_syn, _spell_spch, _syn_mis, _syn_spch, _mis_spch, _spell_syn_spch and _syn_mis_spch.

Optimizing Countermeasures. For optimizing countermeasures, we try to make the affected entity more similar to a pre-chosen target entity. We consider two different methods for choosing a suitable target, and introduce them in the following.

Optimizing to the Average: The first method simply chooses the average entity of the community as the target, thus trying to align the current entity's feature distribution with the community's overall feature distribution (cf. Definition 26).

Optimizing using Anonymous Subsets. The second method makes use of the (k, d)-anonymous subsets to find a (possibly) more suitable target entity: intuitively, this method tries to find an (actually existing) entity close by that has

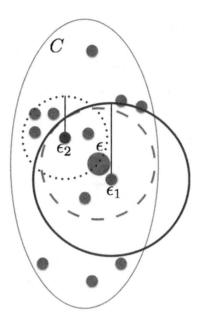

Fig. 5. Optimizing countermeasure using anonymous subsets. (Color figure online)

many other entities within its near environment. Figure 5 illustrates the following, more formal definition of this method: First, we compute the entity ϵ's (k, d)-anonymous subset $\mathcal{A}_\epsilon$ for a given k, such that d is minimal (indicated by the purple, dashed circle). Then, we compute the (k, d')-anonymous subset for every $\epsilon' \in \mathcal{A}_\epsilon$ for the same k and choose that entity ϵ' as the target, which has the smallest d. In our illustration, ϵ_2's anonymous subset (the red, dotted circle) has the smallest convergence and, thus, would be chosen as the countermeasure's target for ϵ.

Given a target ϵ', consider a optimizing countermeasure $\mathcal{C}$ that could replace the current word *house* by its synonym *domicile*. Then, $\mathcal{C}$ would first estimate the similarity to the target for both actions – *keeping house* and *replacing it by domicile* – and choose that action that provides the highest similarity (no matter if ϵ' is the average entity or an actually existing entity like ϵ_2).

7.3   Methodology

On a higher level, our evaluation consists of four parts, which are depicted in Fig. 6:

(1) *A-Priori Weight Determination*: Both, authorship attribution as well as assessing the effectiveness of our countermeasures, require training a classifier to obtain the weights $\boldsymbol{\lambda}$ and the intercept ρ to determine the similarity of entities (cf. Definition 25). Thus, we first determine optimal weights $\lambda_{\mathsf{F1}}, \ldots, \lambda_{\mathsf{F33}}$ for our dataset by extracting the features from each text passage and computing

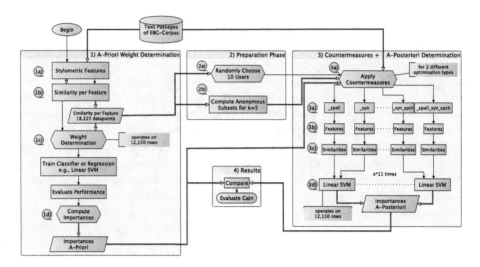

Fig. 6. This flowchart represents our actual set-up and methodology.

the similarity per feature. Ideally, we then compare the weights returned by multiple different optimization techniques to obtain the best performing set of weights. In the context of this paper, however, we simply consider the weights produced by training a linear support vector machine (SVM) using 10-fold cross validation, as exemplified in [3], with the features F1 to F33, since this approach has proven to be well-performing for the task of author-attribution.

(2) *Preparation Phase*: We assume that from the set of all authors, only one actually deploys countermeasures at any given time: this simulates the scenario where the community, together with all related text passages, already exists, and a chosen test author wants to privately publish a new text passage into this community. To capture this scenario, we select a set of test authors for which we evaluate the application of countermeasures before the text passage is published.

For our optimizing countermeasures, we pre-compute the (k, d)-anonymous subsets for the target selection performed by these countermeasures. A detailed description of this part is presented in Sect. 7.3.

(3) *Application of Countermeasures and A-Posteriori Weight Determination*: In this part, we generate the test authors' text-passages after the application of the countermeasures introduced in Sect. 7.2. We then calculate the new feature distributions and the resulting similarities for every countermeasure application to derive the a-posteriori weights λ' as well as the intercept ρ'. A detailed description of this part is presented in Sect. 7.3.

(4) *Results*: This last part finally computes the gain for each countermeasure given the a-priori and a-posteriori weights and will be discussed in Sect. 8.

Figure 6 depicts the overall methodology behind our experiments to the point of each single computation step. While the gray boxes represent the structure given above, we also numbered each step for reference purposes.

A-Priori Weight Determination

Step (1a,b). The goal of the first part is to determine the weights $\lambda_{F1}, \ldots, \lambda_{F33}$ as well as the intercept ρ as required in Definitions 25 and 28. To this end, we first determine the feature frequencies *(1a)* and compute the resulting similarities per feature *(1b)*.

The similarities are not only computed between entities across communities, but also between entities within the same community. While only the first kind of similarities is needed for the training (resulting in 12,150 pairs of entities) and the authorship attribution, the second kind of similarities is needed for the determination of (k, d)-anonymous subsets within the communities.

Step (1c). Next, we apply regression or classification algorithms to determine the weights $\lambda_{F1}, \ldots, \lambda_{F33}$ and the intercept ρ in such a way that matching entities, i.e. entities that belong to the same author, receive a high similarity score, whereas non-matching entities receive a low one.

Conceptually, we could apply various methods, such as simple linear regression, regularized linear regression etc., compare their output and choose the best performing weights. Due to space restrictions, however, we directly choose the classification via linear support vector machines (SVMs) using 10-fold cross validation, since SVMs have already shown promising results in previous work on authorship attribution [3,10]. The resulting weights for each feature are depicted in the fifth column of Table 2 and are directly obtained from the decision function $D(\boldsymbol{x}) = \boldsymbol{\lambda} \cdot \boldsymbol{x} + \rho$ of linear SVMs.

Step (1d): In this final a-priori steps we then take the output of the classifier above and determine the importance (cf. Definition 28) of each feature class in discriminating the different authors' writing styles. We will later compare this a-prior importance value of each feature with their importance determined after applying a countermeasure to determine the countermeasure's gain (cf. Definition 29).

Preparation Phase. The purpose of the preparation phase is to generate a list of test authors and to prepare further data necessary for the countermeasures to be applied.

Step (2a). The set of test authors is randomly chosen from the whole range of available authors in our dataset. We choose a representative set of least 20 % of the available authors as test authors, which resulted in 10 authors for our test set.

Step (2b). For applying optimizing countermeasures using the (k, d)-anonymous subset technique, we also have to compute the anonymous subsets within each community. For this task, we fixed $k = 5$, which corresponds to

Table 3. Total gains and matching accuracy at top k.

Countermeasure	Gain	Top 1	Top 5	Top 10	Top 15	Top 20
Before countermeasures	-	0.9821	0.98613	0.96025	0.93395	0.9065
_spell_syn	0.00948	0.98062	0.98062	0.95556	0.92893	0.90189
_spell_syn_spch	0.00934	0.98053	0.98029	0.95498	0.92844	0.90156
_syn	0.00879	0.98053	0.98119	0.9558	0.92951	0.90247
_syn_spch	0.00876	0.98045	0.98095	0.95572	0.92901	0.90214
_syn_mis	0.00363	0.98053	0.98078	0.95564	0.92885	0.9023
_syn_mis_spch	0.00357	0.98045	0.98053	0.95539	0.92847	0.90206
_spell_spch	0.00069	0.982181	0.98638	0.960576	0.93403	0.90658
_spell	0.00062	0.98193	0.98564	0.95967	0.93337	0.90593
_spch	−0.00042	0.98235	0.98695	0.96107	0.93453	0.90716
_mis	−0.0018	0.98202	0.98613	0.96058	0.93362	0.90593
_mis_spch	−0.00227	0.98226	0.9863	0.96132	0.93428	0.90658

approximately 10 % of the entities in a community in our dataset. This way, the $(5, d)$-anonymous subset tells us how similar the closest 10 % of the community is at least.

Application of Countermeasures and A-Posteriori Weight Determination. This section deals with the actual application of the countermeasures on our dataset *(3a)* and the a-posteriori weight and importance determination *(3b–3d)*.

Step (3a). We apply each countermeasure $\mathcal{C}$ separately to the original text-passages m_i of our test authors, yielding modified text-passages $\mathcal{C}(m_i)$ for every countermeasure. Afterwards, we yield further modified messages by following the countermeasure combinations presented in Sect. 7.2, each modified message recorded separately.

Step (3b,c). The next step on the way towards the countermeasures' gains is the computation of the new feature distributions and, thereafter, the corresponding similarities. This time, we only need to compute the similarities across communities, resulting in a total of 12,150 pairs of entities together with their corresponding similarity, forming the base for the following a-posteriori weight determination.

Step (3d). For the a-posteriori weight determination, we follow the same approach as in step *(1c)*: For every application of countermeasures, we compute the optimal weights λ and the intercept ρ, and therefrom derive the corresponding importance for each feature class.

8   Evaluation of Countermeasures

Before reviewing the actual results of our countermeasures, we first examine the use of the *term frequency inverse document frequency* (tf-idf) for our statistical models and analyze the impact of the optimization strategy of our countermeasures.

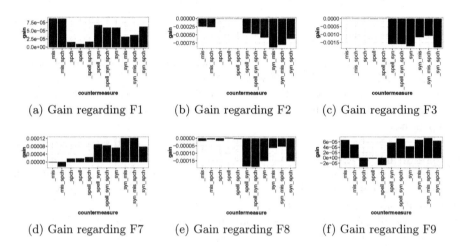

(a) Gain regarding F1   (b) Gain regarding F2   (c) Gain regarding F3

(d) Gain regarding F7   (e) Gain regarding F8   (f) Gain regarding F9

Fig. 7. Gain regarding different feature classes plotted for each countermeasure.

TF-IDF. At least regarding our dataset, the use of the tf-idf for our statistical models does not substantially improve the matching accuracy. When considering only that entity with the highest similarity to a given target entity as matching, the number of true positives increases only by 1 when using tf-idf. When considering the top 15 as matching, the accuracy with the usage of tf-idf is even worse than without. In total, as the use of tf-idf would only increase the complexity of our methodology without providing substantial benefit, we decided to rely on the features' frequencies only and did not consider tf-idf any further in our evaluation.

Optimizing Countermeasures. When comparing both optimization strategies for our countermeasures, optimization to the average and optimization using anonymous subsets, the second one provided the better results for our evaluation. In some cases the optimization to the average results in larger changes to the accuracy (with a maximum change of 0.00634 for _syn_mis in the top 20 accuracy), because the artificial target might be very dissimilar to the entity applying the countermeasure and, thus, more likely results in substantial changes to the features.

However, it frequently happens that the averaged entity of a community is not the best target for our countermeasures: Consider a community with only three entities, two of which are far away from each other. Then placing the third entity in the middle of the others yields a higher identifiability compared to placing it beneath one of the others. In the latter case, two entities are nearly indistinguishable, while in the first case all entities are clearly distinguishable. We therefore focus on the optimization using anonymous subsets in our discussion.

8.1   Observations

We now present the results obtained by following the methodology presented in the last section. In Figs. 7 and 8 we illustrate the gain for some of the feature classes individually (cf. Definition 29). A global comparison of all countermeasures and their gains with respect to each feature can be found in Fig. 9 in the Apppendix.

Some of the observed gains are negative: in these cases, the countermeasure caused an increase in the importance of the corresponding feature class. For example, applying countermeasure _mis (Misspellings) results in a significant increase of feature F30's (word unigrams) weight, i.e., making it more significant in the authorship recognition task.

The overall gain scored by each countermeasure is illustrated in Table 3: the gains are given in absolute values, summing all feature specific gains. Moreover, we show also the matching accuracy when considering the top k entities regarding their similarity to our target entity as matching. Note that we trained our classifier on the whole data set using 10-fold cross validation. We therefore get a very high accuracy rating, and the countermeasures have a rather low absolute gain overall. We only use the presented values for a relative comparison of the gains achieved by each countermeasure. A practical, absolute assessment would require us to make additional assumptions on how an adversary trains his classifier, and the presented results can be seen as a worst-case estimation at best.

Interestingly, most of our countermeasures have a positive total gain, with the only exceptions being _mis, _spch and _mis_spch. While _mis seems to generally replace almost all words by their misspelling and thereby facilitates the matching of those entities, _spch performs better, but nevertheless is not optimal in its decisions. In contrast, the best countermeasures are those involving _syn and _spell: Although _spell alone does not seem powerful enough to change a lot (also due to the small amount of spelling mistakes in our dataset), its combination with _syn seems to help the synonym replacement, which is able to shift the weights into the desired direction.

We can also see that, in almost all cases, a higher total gain also implies a decreased matching accuracy. Figure 8f depicts this relation exemplary for the top 1 accuracy.

Furthermore, Fig. 9 in the appendix clearly shows that only those weights change for which we expect a modification by our countermeasures (if the weights do not change, the gain is 0 according to our definition). A more detailed and in depth explanation for some of the feature classes will be presented in the next subsection.

8.2   Discussion

We now discuss the results observed in the last section and provide in depth explanations for the gains achieved for the most interesting feature classes. Notice, however, that we use different scales on the y-axes in the Figs. 7 and 8 for better readability. For a more comprehensive comparison of each counter-measure's gain per feature class please refer to Fig. 9.

Letter Unigrams, Bigrams and Trigrams. While all of our countermeasures have a very small positive gain for letter unigrams (F1), this is certainly not true for letter bigrams (F2) and trigrams (F3), which both have negative gains for most countermeasures and especially those involving _syn. To further investigate this, we start by looking at the letter bigrams (F2) for the _syn countermeasure and trace back the reason for the negative gain:

Letter Bigrams. One frequent action by our synonym replacer is to replace adjectives by participles (e.g., *afraid → frightened*), which results in an increased

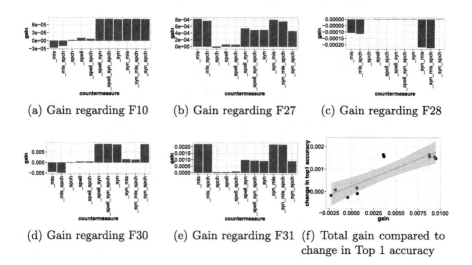

(a) Gain regarding F10   (b) Gain regarding F27   (c) Gain regarding F28

(d) Gain regarding F30   (e) Gain regarding F31   (f) Total gain compared to change in Top 1 accuracy

Fig. 8. Gain regarding different feature classes plotted for each countermeasure and comparison of total gain.

use of the bigram *ed* for our test authors. In fact, the frequency of *ed* increased by approximately 100 usages for every test author.

Another frequent action by the synonym replacer is caused by the natural language generation tool having problems with some adjectives and adverbs: often, it replaces *most* by *mostest* and thereby increases the use of *es* in a similar magnitude as of *ed*.

Letter Trigrams. Next, we also explore _syn's changes with respect to letter trigrams (F3). Here, the most interesting change is the increased frequency of *ive*, which is caused by frequent replacements of *have* with *give* and forms of *to be* with *live*.

Letter Unigrams. In general, all of the aforementioned changes in fact facilitate the matching of our test authors and thus provide a negative gain. However, although the changes also affect the letter unigrams, we can observe a small positive gain for this feature class. While we especially notice an increased usage of *e*, this letter is frequent in our dataset anyway (and in English in general) and thus does not contribute to a facilitated matching as much as the combinations in letter bigrams and trigrams.

Punctuation and Special Characters. Since the gains are very different among all four feature classes (F7-F10), we directly discuss their results individually. However, it is important to note that the gain of both special character feature classes is nearly zero when compared with others in Fig. 9.

Unicode Punctuation. The unicode punctuation feature class (F7) reveals an interesting phenomenon: while the _mis countermeasure provides almost no gain and the _syn countermeasure provides a positive gain, the combination of both countermeasures further increases the positive gain.

A careful examination shows that the _mis countermeasure only changes this feature very little by introducing misspelled variants with ' in it, e.g., *countries* → *countrie's*. The _syn countermeasure primarily replaces words like *double* with compound words as *two-fold*, changing the feature distribution more substantially. In combination, the application of the _mis countermeasure after _syn yields much more added ' than without the combination and, thus, is able to further improve the gain.

Writeprints Punctuation. Regarding the writeprints punctuation feature class (F8), all of our countermeasures provide either a gain close to 0 or a negative gain. While the gain close to 0 can be observed for those feature classes, which have no real impact on the punctuation, the negative gain clearly is caused by the _syn feature class as it is present in all those countermeasures.

The reason for the negative impact of the _syn countermeasure is that it introduces new punctuation for our test authors when replacing *a(n)* by *one's*. Since our dataset contains more formal writing, this punctuation character has not been used very frequently (159 times for our test authors) before the countermeasure's application, such that the increased usage (341 times for our test authors) helps in identifying them.

Unicode Special Characters. Interestingly, the gain of our dedicated _spch countermeasure is negative regarding the Unicode special characters (F9), while other countermeasures can achieve a positive gain here. When inspecting the reason for that, however, it becomes clear that for example the _syn countermeasure does not change the unicode special characters at all and the very small gain is only caused by the SVM. This shows that it is very hard to reason about gains close to 0 and it is better to focus on the substantial gains.

Nevertheless, it is worth noting that our _spch countermeasure succeeds in removing special characters from the test author's writing, but thereby facilitates the identification of other authors.

Writeprints Special Characters. Finally, we also take a look at the Writeprints special characters (F10), for which the gains have approximately the same small magnitude compared to the Unicode Special Characters. Again, we can observe the phenomenon that very small gains can be caused by the SVM without changes in the actual features in case of the _mis countermeasure.

The most notable, but nevertheless small change in the actual features is due to the _syn countermeasure, which increases the frequency of - because of compound words like *two-fold* (cf. Unicode Punctuation).

Hapax Legomena. Hapax Legomena (F27) are of difficult nature, as the same action can increase or decrease their frequency only depending on the surrounding text. Fortunately, both _mis and _syn countermeasures achieve a positive gain for this feature class.

Our _mis countermeasure mainly creates new hapax legomena by replacing all occurrences except for one by a misspelled variant, e.g., for words like *from* (→ *fomr*), who often appear as hapax legomena in other text passages. Unfortunately, it cannot eliminate hapax legomena, because replacing such a word by a misspelled variant only yields a new, uniquely appearing word.

The _syn countermeasure often eliminates hapax legomena by replacing those with compound words whose components are more frequent within the text, e.g., *are* → *make up*.

This way, both optimizing countermeasures are able to harden the matching in our dataset, at least concerning the hapax legomena.

Misspelled Words. Since we have a dedicated countermeasure for misspelled words (F28), we also explore the very small, but negative gain caused by our _mis countermeasure.

Clearly, misspelled words were nearly unimportant for the matching before the countermeasures' applications (there were only 853 words identified as misspelled in the whole dataset). However, after the application of the _mis countermeasure, 13,212 misspellings can be found in the dataset, naturally resulting in a larger importance during the matching.

Word Unigrams and Bigrams. The last two features, which we will examine in more detail, are word unigrams (F30) and word bigrams (F31). Especially word unigrams appear to be the most important feature class in our dataset, so that we will conclude its analysis with possible reasons for the countermeasures total gains.

Word Unigrams. When examining the gains of our countermeasures regarding word unigrams (F30), it becomes visible that _syn and _mis have the most impact on our test authors. While _syn provides a positive gain, mainly by blending into the vocabulary and word frequencies of other authors, _mis provides only a negative gain, because it introduces a lot of misspelled words, thereby facilitating the matching. Moreover, as already mentioned for the hapax legomena, the _mis countermeasure often replaces all occurrences except for one by a misspelling, which on the one hand influences the hapax legomena in a positive way, but on the other hand has a negative impact on the word unigrams.

Word Bigrams. Similar to word unigrams, here, the _syn countermeasure also is able to adapt word bigram (F31) frequencies of our test authors to those that are present in our dataset anyway. Interestingly, the _mis countermeasure produces a positive gain for word bigrams, although the gain for word unigrams was negative. While, in contrast to the other feature classes, we did not find a compelling reason for that during our examination, we believe that this happens because of the strong correlation between word unigrams and bigrams: As the importance of word unigrams increases, the importance of word bigrams decreases.

9   Conclusion and Future Work

We presented a user-centric privacy framework for reasoning about privacy in open web settings. In our formalization, we address the essential challenges of privacy in open settings: we defined a comprehensive data model that can deal with the unstructured dissemination of heterogeneous information, and we derived the sensitivity of information from user-specified and context-sensitive privacy requirements. We showed that, in this formalization of privacy in open settings, hard security guarantees in the sense of Differential Privacy are impossible to achieve. We then instantiated the general framework to reason about the identity disclosure problem. The technical core of our identity disclosure model is the new notion of (k, d)-anonymity that assesses the anonymity of entities based on their similarity to other entities within the same community. We applied this instantiation to a dataset of 15 million user-generated text entries collected from the Online Social Network Reddit and showed that our framework is suited for the assessment of linkablity threats in Online Social Networks.

In a second step, we extended the linkability model we derived from general privacy framework, and provided the foundations for comprehensively assessing the effectiveness of countermeasures against authorship recognition. Central to this formalization is the notion of *gain* with which we quantify how well a countermeasure achieves reduces the significance of identifying writing style features. We evaluate this formalization on the Extended-Brennan-Greenstadt corpus [10,11]. In our evaluation we follow a comprehensive experimental methodology we also introduce in this work, structuring the evaluation process and allowing for an easy extension. We then evaluate four different countermeasures, one simple and three optimizing, and their combinations and discuss the reduction regarding feature importance they achieved.

As far as future work is concerned, many directions are highly promising. First, our general framework only provides a static view on privacy in open settings. Information dissemination on the Internet, however, is, in particular, characterized by its highly dynamic nature. Extending the model presented in this paper with a suitable transition system to capture user actions might lead to powerful system for monitoring privacy risks in dynamically changing, open settings. Second, information presented in Online Social Networks is often highly time-sensitive, e.g., shared information is often only valid for a certain period of time, and personal facts can change over time. Explicitly including timing information in our entity model will hence further increase the accuracy of the entity models derived from empirical evidence. Finally, our privacy model is well-suited for the evaluation of protection mechanisms for very specific privacy requirements, and new such mechanisms with provable guarantees against restricted adversaries can be developed. On the long run, we pursue the vision of providing the formal foundations for comprehensive, trustworthy privacy assessments and, ultimately, for developing user-friendly privacy assessment tools.

A   Countermeasure Gain

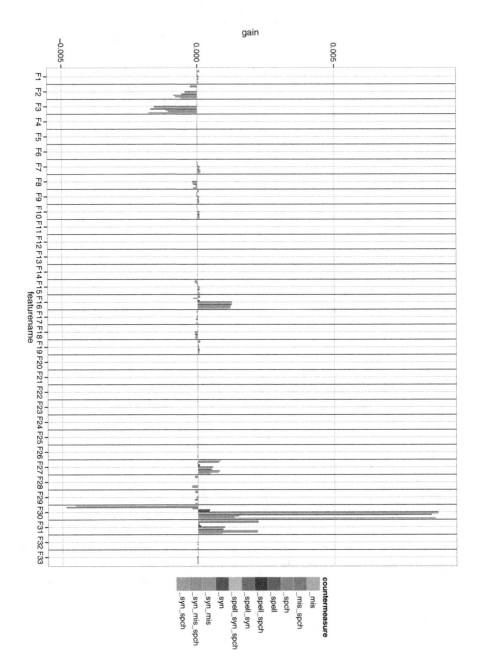

Fig. 9. All gains in a global comparison.

References

1. The online social network reddit. http://www.reddit.com. Accessed Sept 2015
2. Directive 95/46/EC of the European Parliament and of the Council on the Protection of Individuals with Regard to the Processing of Personal Data and on the Free Movement of Such Data (1996)
3. Abbasi, A., Chen, H.: Writeprints: a stylometric approach to identity-level identification and similarity detection in cyberspace. ACM Trans. Inf. Syst. (TOIS) **26**(2), 1–29 (2008)
4. Afroz, S., Brennan, M., Greenstadt, R.: Detecting hoaxes, frauds, and deception in writing style online. In: Proceedings of the 33rd IEEE Symposium on Security and Privacy (S&P), pp. 461–475 (2012)
5. Afroz, S., Islam, A.C., Stolerman, A., Greenstadt, R., McCoy, D.: Doppelgänger finder: taking stylometry to the underground. In: Proceedings of the 35th IEEE Symposium on Security and Privacy(S&P), pp. 212–226 (2014)
6. Anonymouth. https://www.cs.drexel.edu/~pv42/thebiz/
7. Backes, M., Kate, A., Manoharan, P., Meiser, S., Mohammadi, E.: AnoA: a framework for analyzing anonymous communication protocols. In: Proceedings of the 26th IEEE Computer Security Foundations Symposium (CSF), pp. 163–178 (2013)
8. Balduzzi, M., Platzer, C., Holz, T., Kirda, E., Balzarotti, D., Kruegel, C.: Abusing social networks for automated user profiling. In: Jha, S., Sommer, R., Kreibich, C. (eds.) RAID 2010. LNCS, vol. 6307, pp. 422–441. Springer, Heidelberg (2010)
9. Bambauer, J., Muralidhar, K., Sarathy, R.: Fool's gold! An illustrated critique of differential privacy. Vanderbilt J. Entertainment Technol. Law **16**(4), 701–755 (2014)
10. Brennan, M.R., Afroz, S., Greenstadt, R., Stylometry, A.: Circumventing authorship recognition to preserve privacy and anonymity. ACM Trans. Inf. Syst. Secur. (TISSEC) **15**(3), 12:1–12:22 (2012)
11. Brennan, M.R., Greenstadt, R.: Practical attacks against authorship recognition techniques. In: Proceedings of the 21st Annual Conference on Innovative Applications of Artificial Intelligence (IAAI) (2009)
12. Bromby, M.: Security against crime: technologies for detecting and preventing crime. Int. Rev. Law **20**(1–2), 1–6 (2007)
13. Calì, A., Calvanese, D., Colucci, S., Di Noia, T., Donini, F.M.: A logic-based approach for matching user profiles. In: Negoita, M.G., Howlett, R.J., Jain, L.C. (eds.) KES 2004. LNCS (LNAI), vol. 3215, pp. 187–195. Springer, Heidelberg (2004)
14. Chaski, C.E.: Who's at the keyboard? Authorship attribution in digital evidence investigations. Int. J. Digit. Evid. **4**(1), 1–13 (2005)
15. Chatzikokolakis, K., Andrés, M.E., Bordenabe, N.E., Palamidessi, C.: Broadening the scope of differential privacy using metrics. In: De Cristofaro, E., Wright, M. (eds.) PETS 2013. LNCS, vol. 7981, pp. 82–102. Springer, Heidelberg (2013)
16. Chen, R., Fung, B.C.M., Philip, S.Y., Desai, B.C.: Correlated network data publication via differential privacy. VLDB J. **23**(4), 653–676 (2014)
17. Chen, T., Kaafar, M.A., Friedman, A., Boreli, R.: Is more always merrier? A deep dive into online social footprints. In: Proceedings of the 2012 ACM Workshop on Online Social Networks (WOSN), pp. 67–72 (2012)
18. The cmu pronouncing dictionary (version 0.7b). http://www.speech.cs.cmu.edu/cgi-bin/cmudict. Accessed Feb 2015
19. Cortis, K., Scerri, S., Rivera, I., Handschuh, S.: Discovering semantic equivalence of people behind online profiles. In: Proceedings of the 5th International Workshop on Resource Discovery (RED), pp. 104–118 (2012)

20. Derczynski, L., Ritter, A., Clark, S., Bontcheva, K.: Twitter part-of-speech tagging for all: overcoming sparse and noisy data. In: Proceedings of RANLP, pp. 198–206 (2013)
21. Dinur, I., Nissim, K.: Revealing information while preserving privacy. In: Proceedings of the 22nd ACM SIGMOD-SIGACT-SIGART Symposium on Principles of Database Systems (PODS), pp. 202–210 (2003)
22. Dwork, C.: Differential privacy: a survey of results. In: Proceedings of the 5th International Conference on Theory and Applications of Models of Computation, pp. 1–19 (2008)
23. Dwork, C., Kenthapadi, K., McSherry, F., Mironov, I., Naor, M.: Our data, ourselves: privacy via distributed noise generation. In: Vaudenay, S. (ed.) EURO-CRYPT 2006. LNCS, vol. 4004, pp. 486–503. Springer, Heidelberg (2006)
24. Dwork, C., Naor, M.: On the difficulties of disclosure prevention in statistical databases or the case for differential privacy. J. Priv. Confidentiality **2**(1), 8 (2008)
25. Endres, D.M., Schindelin, J.E.: A new metric for probability distributions. IEEE Trans. Inf. Theor. **49**(7), 1858–1860 (2003)
26. Fast, G.: Syllable counter. http://search.cpan.org/~gregfast/Lingua-EN-Syllable-0.251/Syllable.pm. Accessed Feb 2015
27. Fellbaum, C.: WordNet: An Electronic Lexical Database. MIT Press, Massachusetts (1998)
28. Goga, O., Lei, H., Parthasarathi, S.H.K., Friedland, G., Sommer, R., Teixeira, R.: Exploiting innocuous activity for correlating users across sites. In: WWW (2013)
29. Guyon, I., Weston, J., Barnhill, S., Vapnik, V.: Gene selection for cancer classification using support vector machines. Mach. Learn. **46**(1–3), 389–422 (2002)
30. Heatherly, R., Kantarcioglu, M., Thuraisingham, B.: Preventing private information inference attacks on social networks. IEEE Trans. Knowl. Data Eng. **25**(8), 1849–1862 (2013)
31. Holmes, D.I.: The evolution of stylometry in humanities scholarship. Literary Linguist. Comput. **13**(3), 111–117 (1998)
32. Languagetool spell checker. https://languagetool.org. Accessed Feb 2015
33. Juola, P.: Detecting stylistic deception. In: Proceedings of the 2012 EACL Workshop on Computational Approaches to Deception Detection, pp. 91–96 (2012)
34. Kasivisiwanathan, S.P., Smith, A.: On the 'Semantics' of differential privacy: a Bayesian formulation. J. Priv. Confidentiality **6**(1), 1–16 (2014)
35. Kifer, D., Machanavajjhala, A.: No free lunch in data privacy. In: Proceedings of the 2011 ACM SIGMOD International Conference on Management of Data, pp. 193–204 (2011)
36. Koppel, M., Schler, J., Argamon, S.: Computational methods in authorship attribution. J. Am. Soc. Inf. Sci. Technol. **60**(1), 9–26 (2009)
37. Kosinski, M., Bachrach, Y., Kohli, P., Stillwell, D., Graepel, T.: Manifestations of user personality in website choice and behaviour on online social networks. Mach. Learn. **95**(3), 357–380 (2014)
38. Krishnamurthy, B., Wills, C.E.: On the leakage of personally identifiable information via online social networks. In: Proceedings of the 2nd ACM Workshop on Online Social Networks (WSON), pp. 7–12 (2009)
39. Li, N., Li, T.: t-closeness: privacy beyond k-anonymity and l-diversity. In: Proceedings of the 23rd International Conference on Data Engineering (ICDE) 2007
40. Machanavajjhala, A., Kifer, D., Gehrke, J., Venkitasubramaniam, M.: l-diversity: privacy beyond k-anonymity. ACM Trans. Knowl. Discov. Data **1**(1), 3 (2007)

41. McCallister, E., Grance, T., Scarfone, K.A.: Sp 800–122. Guide to Protecting the Confidentiality of Personally Identifiable Information (PII). Technical report (2010)

42. McDonald, A.W.E., Afroz, S., Caliskan, A., Stolerman, A., Greenstadt, R.: Use fewer instances of the letter "i": toward writing style anonymization. In: Fischer-Hübner, S., Wright, M. (eds.) PETS 2012. LNCS, vol. 7384, pp. 299–318. Springer, Heidelberg (2012)

43. Mendenhall, T.C.: The characteristic curves of composition. Science 9, 237–249 (1887)

44. Miller, G.A.: WordNet: a lexical database for english. Commun. ACM 38(11), 39–41 (1995)

45. Almishari, M., Tsudik, G.: Exploring linkability of user reviews. In: Foresti, S., Yung, M., Martinelli, F. (eds.) ESORICS 2012. LNCS, vol. 7459, pp. 307–324. Springer, Heidelberg (2012)

46. Narayanan, A., Paskov, H., Gong, N.Z., Bethencourt, J., Stefanov, E., Shin, E.C.R., Song, D.: On the feasibility of internet-scale author identification. In: Proceedings of the 33rd IEEE Symposium on Security and Privacy (S&P), pp. 300–314 (2012)

47. Narayanan, A., Shmatikov, V.: Myths, fallacies of "Personally Identifiable Information". Commun. ACM 53(6), 24–26 (2010)

48. Narayanan, A., Shmatikov, V.: De-anonymizing social networks. In: Proceedings of the 30th IEEE Symposium on Security and Privacy (S&P), pp. 173–187 (2009)

49. Oakes, M.P.: Ant colony optimisation for stylometry: the federalist papers. In: Proceedings of the 5th International Conference on Recent Advances in Soft Computing, pp. 86–91 (2004)

50. Pearl, L., Steyvers, M.: Detecting authorship deception: a supervised machine learning approach using author writeprints. Literary Linguist. Comput. 27(2), 183–196 (2012)

51. Scerri, S., Cortis, K., Rivera, I., Handschuh, S.: Knowledge discovery in distributed social web sharing activities. In: Proceedings of the 3rd International Workshop on Modeling Social Media: Collective Intelligence in Social Media (MSM) (2012)

52. Scerri, S., Gimenez, R., Herman, F., Bourimi, M., Thiel, S.: digital.me-towards an integrated Personal Information Sphere. In: Federated Social Web Summit Europe (2011)

53. Sharma, N.K., Ghosh, S., Benevenuto, F., Ganguly, N., Gummadi, K.: Inferring who-is-who in the twitter social network. In: Proceedings of the 2012 ACM Workshop on Workshop on Online Social Networks (WSON), pp. 55–60 (2012)

54. Sweeney, L.: k-anonymity: a model for protecting privacy. Int. J. Uncertain. Fuzziness Knowl. Based Syst. 10(5), 557–570 (2002)

55. Toutanova, K., Klein, D., Manning, C.D., Singer, Y.: Feature-rich part-of-speech tagging with a cyclic dependency network. In: Proceedings of the 2003 Conference of the North American Chapter of the Association for Computational Linguistics on Human Language Technology, pp. 173–180 (2003)

56. Toutanova, K., Manning, C.D.: Enriching the knowledge sources used in a maximum entropy part-of-speech tagger. In: Proceedings of the 2000 Joint SIGDAT conference on Empirical Methods in Natural Language Processing and Very Large Corpora, pp. 63–70 (2000)

57. Uzuner, Ö., Katz, B.: A comparative study of language models for book and author recognition. In: Dale, R., Wong, K.-F., Su, J., Kwong, O.Y. (eds.) IJCNLP 2005. LNCS (LNAI), vol. 3651, pp. 969–980. Springer, Heidelberg (2005)

58. Wikipedia. Lists of common misspellings/for machines. http://en.wikipedia.org/w/index.php?title=Wikipedia:Lists_of_common_misspellings/For_machines&oldid=640791958. Accessed Feb 2015

59. Zheleva, E., Getoor, L.: To join or not to join: the illusion of privacy in social networks with mixed public and private user profiles. In: Proceedings of the 18th International Conference on World Wide Web (WWW), pp. 531–540 (2009)

60. Zheleva, E., Getoor, L.: Privacy in social networks: a survey. In: Aggarwal, C.C. (ed.) Social Network Data Analytics, pp. 277–306. Springer, New York (2011)

61. Zhou, B., Pei, J.: The k-anonymity and l-diversity approaches for privacy preservation in social networks against neighborhood attacks. Knowl. Inf. Syst. **28**(1), 47–77 (2011)

Distributed Authorization in Vanadium

Ankur Taly[✉] and Asim Shankar

Google Inc., Mountain View, USA
ataly@google.com, ashankar@google.com

Abstract. In this tutorial, we present an authorization model for distributed systems that operate with limited internet connectivity. Reliable internet access remains a luxury for a majority of the world's population. Even for those who can afford it, a dependence on internet connectivity may lead to sub-optimal user experiences. With a focus on decentralized deployment, we present an authorization model that is suitable for scenarios where devices right next to each other (such as a sensor or a friend's phone) should be able to communicate securely in a peer-to-peer manner. The model has been deployed as part of an open-source distributed application framework called *Vanadium*. As part of this tutorial, we survey some of the key ideas and techniques used in distributed authorization, and explain how they are combined in the design of our model.

1 Introduction

Authorization is a fundamental problem in computer security that deals with whether a request to access a resource must be granted. The decision is made by a reference monitor guarding the resource. Authorization is fairly straightforward in closed systems where all resources of interest are held on a small set of devices, and reference monitors have pre-existing relationships with all authorized principals. In these systems, authorizing a request involves identifying the principal making the request, and then verifying that this identity is allowed by the resource's access control policy. The former is called *authentication*, and the latter is called *access control*.

Authorization in distributed systems is significantly more complex as the resources are spread across a network of devices under different administrative domains [22]. Moreover, not all devices and principals in the system may know each other beforehand, making even authentication complicated. For instance, consider the fairly common scenario of a user Alice trying to play a movie from her internet video service on her television (TV). It involves the TV authorizing the request from Alice to play a movie, and the video service authorizing the request from the TV to access Alice's account. The video service may recognize only Alice, and not her TV. The TV must convince the video service that it is acting on Alice's behalf.

With the advent of the Internet of Things (IoT), various physical devices that we commonly interact with in our daily lives are controllable over the network,

© Springer International Publishing Switzerland 2016
A. Aldini et al. (Eds.): FOSAD VIII, LNCS 9808, pp. 139–162, 2016.
DOI: 10.1007/978-3-319-43005-8_4

and are thus part of a large distributed system. These devices range from tiny embedded devices, to wearables, to large home appliances, and automobiles. The promise of IoT lies in multiple devices interacting with each other to accomplish complex tasks for the user. For instance, a home security system may interact with security cameras and locks around the house to ensure that the house is protected from intruders at all times, and all suspicious activity is logged on the user's storage server. Securely accomplishing such tasks involves making several authorization decisions. Some of the key questions that arise are *how do devices identify each other during any interaction?, how do users authorize devices to act on their behalf?, how are access control policies defined?*

Distributed authorization is a long-standing area of research, and several mechanisms have been designed for a variety of settings. However, most IoT devices still rely on rudimentary and fragile mechanisms based on passwords and unguessable IP addresses [19,26]. Indeed, over the last few months, there have been several vulnerabilities and attacks reported on various "smart" devices [1,2,4,5]. A study [19] conducted by HP on the security of several existing IoT devices reported "insufficient authorization" as one of the top security concerns. Besides this, the study found that many devices rely on a service in the cloud for authorization. We stress that proper authorization is paramount in the IoT setting as authorization breaches can impact physical security and safety. At the same time, dependence on internet connectivity can sometimes render "smart" devices unusable. Imagine the consequences of unauthorized access to an embedded heart rate monitor, or being unable to unlock the door right in front of you due to lack of internet access.

This tutorial explores the design of an authorization model for large, open distributed systems such as IoT. The primary guiding principles behind the design of the model are *decentralized deployment* and *peer-to-peer communication*. The model does not rely on any special global authorities for brokering interactions between devices that have a network path to each other. The justification for these principles is manyfold. First, a centralized model assumes all entities implicitly trust the default global authorities. This assumption fails for the enterprise and IoT settings where it is desirable to carve out isolated and fully autonomous administrative domains for devices. For instance, a user may want to be the sole authority on all devices in her home. Similarly, an enterprise may want to maintain full control of its devices with no dependence on any external authority. Second, the central nodes in the system become an attractive target for compromise to attackers. Given the frequent security breaches at well-reputed organizations, users are justifiably weary of having third-party services store more personal data than strictly necessary. Besides this, protecting personal user data from external and internal threats is quite burdensome for the organizations as well. Finally, a centralized model requires that all devices maintain connectivity to external global services, which is infeasible for many IoT devices, including ones that communicate only over Bluetooth, or ones present in public spaces such as shopping malls, buses, and trains, where internet access is unreliable. Moreover, reliable internet access remains a luxury for a majority of the world's population, where routing most interactions through a cloud service can be expensive or simply not possible.

The authorization model presented in this tutorial is fully decentralized, and is based on a distributed public-key infrastructure similar to SDSI [27]. The model supports peer-to-peer delegation of authority under fine-grained caveats [10]. Access control policies are based on human-readable names, and have support for negative clauses and group-based checks. This general purpose model is applicable in various distributed system settings, including, peer-to-peer computing environments, IoT, cloud, and enterprise. The model has been deployed as part of an open-source application framework called *Vanadium* [6], and is thus referred to as the Vanadium authorization model. As part of this tutorial, we survey a number of key ideas and techniques from previous work on distributed authorization, including SPKI/SDSI [18,27], Macaroons [10], and the vast body of work on trust management [12]. We explain how these techniques are combined by the Vanadium authorization model.

Organization. The rest of this tutorial is organized as follows. Section 2 describes the features we desire, and Sect. 3 surveys key technical ideas involved in the design of our model. Section 4 describes our model in detail, followed by an application of our model to a physical lock device in Sect. 5. Section 6 concludes.

2   Desired Features

In this section, we describe features we seek from our authorization model. Many of these features have been considered by prior work on distributed authorization. We use the term "principal" informally to refer to an entity in our system, including, users, devices, processes, and objects, and leave the formal definition to Sect. 4.

Decentralization. As discussed in the introduction, decentralized deployment and peer-to-peer communication by default are the central guiding principles behind this work. The model must not force dependence on special global authorities such as x.509 certification authorities, default identity providers, and proxies that mediate interactions between principals. Instead, we seek egalitarian systems where *any* principal can be an authority for some set of other principals. For instance, a user Alice may become an authority on the identities and access controls on all her home devices. The devices may be configured to specifically trust only Alice's credentials. In general, devices must be able to securely communicate with each other as long as there is a direct communication channel between them. We seek a model that minimizes interaction with globally accessible services, and maximizes what can be achieved with direct peer-to-peer communication.

Mutual Authentication and Authorization. We require all interactions between principals to be *mutually* authenticated and authorized. The principal at each end of a communication channel must identify the principal at the other end (authentication), and verify that it is valid in the context of the communication (authorization). Mutual authentication is essential for both ends to audit all access; we discuss the benefit of auditing later in this section. Mutual authorization is essential whenever the communicating principals are mutually suspicious. Unidirectional authorization often opens the door to rogue entities, leading to security and privacy attacks. For example, when Bob tries to unlock the lock on Alice's front door, the lock must be convinced that it is communicating with Bob, and that Bob is authorized to unlock the door. At the same time, Bob must be convinced that it is indeed sending the request to Alice's front door, and not an imposter device that is tracking Bob's behavior.

Compound Identities. We live in a world today where all users and devices carry multiple identities. For instance, a user may have an identity from social media sites (e.g., Facebook identity), an identity from her work place, an identity from the government (e.g., passport, driver's license), and so on. Similarly, a device would have an identity from the manufacturer (e.g., Samsung TV model 123), and an identity from the device owner (e.g., Alice's TV). A principal must be able to act under one or more identities associated with it, and different identities may grant different authorizations to the principal. The authorization model must seamlessly capture this compound nature of a principal's identity.

Fine-Grained Delegation. The strength of distributed systems lies in multiple computing agents coming together to accomplish complex tasks. This is indeed the promise of IoT. For example, Bob would like to play a movie from his internet video service on Alice's TV and speaker system. In order to enable such interactions, the authorization model must support flexible sharing and delegation.[1] Alice must be able to delegate access to her TV to Bob, and Bob must be able to delegate access to his internet video service to Alice's TV for playing a particular movie. The model must also support delegations across multiple hops. For instance, Bob must be able to easily delegate access to Alice's TV to his friend Carol. Moreover, in light of the decentralization requirement, we would like delegations to work peer-to-peer rather than be mediated by a central authority.

In practice, delegation of authority is seldom unconditional, and thus the delegation mechanism must support constraints on the scope of the delegation. For instance, Bob may want Alice's TV to have access to his internet video service only for playing a particular movie, and only while Bob is present in Alice's house. The TV must loose access as soon as Bob leaves the house. Alice may want the same for Bob's access to her TV.

We emphasize that the delegation mechanism must be flexible and convenient to use. Inflexibilities or inconveniences in the mechanism not only affect the user experience but are also detrimental to security as they push users to look for

---

[1] Some systems choose to distinguish the concepts of "sharing" an "delegation" with the former being a mechanism for a principal to allow another principal to access an object while the latter being a mechanism for allowing another principal to act on its behalf. In this tutorial, we do not make this distinction, and treat "delegation" more broadly as a mechanism for one principal to delegate some of its authority to another principal.

insecure workarounds. For instance, in the absence of a convenient mechanism to share access to an internet video service, Bob may end up sharing his account password with the TV, and as a result give away access to all his account data (e.g., viewing history, purchases) instead of just access to a particular movie.

Auditable Access. In a system with delegation, users should be able to audit the use of delegated access over time. For instance, a user must be able to determine who has access to her devices and who has *exercised* that access. Delegations are ultimately tied to the intention of the human end-user, and software must acknowledge that it is impossible to codify all possible human intentions. This is particularly true when users themselves may be unable to clearly articulate their intentions at the time of delegation. An accurate audit trail is a requirement to detect mismatches between user intentions and their codification. For example, Alice might give Charlie access to her home to come by and walk her dog once a day. Alice's intent is for Charlie to be a dog walker but she cannot possibly know apriori what time Charlie will come by in all future days. Auditing Charlie's use of the authority granted to her by Alice is necessary to detect a violation of the contract between the two. Moreover, this auditing must be fine grained—if Charlie was tricked into running a malicious application on her phone, Alice must be able to pinpoint the exact application that was improperly using the authority she granted to Charlie.

Revocation. Users make mistakes, devices get stolen/compromised, and relationships break. As a result an authorization model must support revocation. For instance, Alice must be able revoke Dave's access to all her home devices when they have a falling out. Similarly, she should be able to revoke all delegations that she made to her tablet when her tablet gets stolen.

Ease of Use. Usability is a key determining factor in the effectiveness of security systems [14, 30]. Systems with complex interfaces and mechanisms often have degraded security, as users tend to look for insecure workarounds when dealing with them. Thus we strive to design an authorization model that can be easily understood and configured by system developers, and lends itself well to simple and clear user interfaces.

3   Background

Distributed authorization is a very mature field with decades of prior research. The Vanadium authorization model is a result of combining various known techniques in order to meet the requirements stated in the previous section. In this section, we provide some background on distributed authorization, and discuss the key ideas involved in the design of the Vanadium authorization model.

In essence, most authorization mechanisms involve a requester presenting a set of credentials (possibly obtained from multiple parties) to a reference monitor guarding a resource which then authorizes the request after validating the credentials [29]. A common paradigm is for the requester to present credentials that establish its identity, which is then checked against an access control policy (e.g., an access control list (ACL)) by the reference monitor. Various mechanisms differ in the type of credentials involved. In mechanisms such as OAuth2 [21], OpenID [3], Macaroons [10], and many others [20,25], the credentials are essentially tokens constructed using symmetric-key cryptography by an issuer (e.g., an identity provider in the case of OAuth2). These mechanisms are simple, efficient, easy to deploy, and are widely in use (particularly OAuth2) for client authorization on the Web. The downside is that the credentials can be validated and interpreted only by the credential issuer. As a result, the credential issuer must be invoked for validating credentials during each request[2]. This is undesirable in our setting.

In contrast, mechanisms based on public-key certificates [9,11–13,23,27,32] do not suffer from this downside. In these mechanisms, principals possess digital signature public and secret key pairs along with signed certificates binding authorizations to their public key. A principal makes requests by signing statements using its secret key and presenting one or more of its certificates. These certificates can be validated and interpreted by any principal as long as it knows the public key of the certificate issuer. Such a mechanism is used for authenticating HTTPS [17] servers on the Web.

Certificate-based mechanisms rely on a *public-key infrastructure* (PKI) for distributing certificates to various principals. Traditional x509 PKI [28], such as the one used on the Web, is centralized with a hierarchical network of certification authorities responsible for issuing certificates. In light of the downsides of centralization, several decentralized PKI [11,12,18,27,32] have been proposed in the literature. A prominent model among these is the simple distributed security infrastructure (SDSI) [27] of Rivest and Lampson. The SDSI model was subsequently merged with the simple public key infrastructure (SPKI) effort [18], and the resulting model is commonly referred to as SPKI/SDSI. In what follows, we briefly summarize some of the key ideas in SPKI/SDSI, while referring the reader to [18,27] for a more comprehensive description.

SPKI/SDSI. This is a decentralized PKI based on the idea of *local names*. Each principal in this model is represented by a digital signature public key, and manages a local name for referring to other principals. For instance, a principal Alice may use the name `friend` to refer to her friend Bob's public key and `doctor` to refer to her family doctor Frank's public key. These bindings are local to Alice, and other principals may chose to bind different names to these keys. However, another principal, say Alice's TV, who names Alice's public key as `Alice` may refer to Bob's public key as `Alice's friend`. Thus names in different namespaces can be linked using the `'s` operator. Local name to key bindings are represented by *name-definition* certificates signed by the issuing principal. Linked names are thus realized by certificate chains. The model also supports *authorization* certificates wherein an issuing principal delegates permissions to another principal.

---

[2] An alternative is for each resource owner to become a credential issuer but that leads to a proliferation of credentials at the requester's end.

Access control policies in SPKI/SDSI specify a list of authorized principals using local names in the owner's namespace. A request is allowed by the policy if the requesting principal is directly authorized by the policy or has a delegation (via authorization certificate) from a directly authorized principal. For instance, Alice's TV may have an access control policy allowing the local name `Alice's friend`, and therefore Bob (who has the name `Alice's friend` in the TV's namespace) and any principal delegated by Bob will have access. Authorizing requests involves assembling a chain of certificates (from a repository of certificates) that proves that the requesting principal satisfies the access control policy [16]. The responsibility of assembling the right certificate chain may be placed on the reference monitor or the requester, and various deployments may differ in this choice. The key idea from SPKI/SDSI used in the Vanadium authorization model is that of delegating access to principals by assigning them local names, and basing access control policies on these names.

Caveats on Delegation. There are several mechanisms in the literature on restricting the scope of delegations. These range from simple, coarse-grained mechanisms of adding a purpose and expiration time to delegation certificates, to complex, fine-grained mechanisms of extending delegation certificates with S-expressions capturing application-specific permissions [18], or program code [13] defining how access must be proxied to the resource. Recently, Birgisson et al., proposed a mechanism for restricting delegations using *caveats* [10], which aims at striking a balance between simplicity and expressiveness.

Caveats are essentially predicates that restrict the context in which the delegated credential may be used. They are attached to the credential in a tamper-proof manner, each time the credential is delegated. Caveats are of two types— *first-party* and *third-party*. First-party caveats are predicates on the context in which a credential may be used. For e.g., first-party caveats impose restrictions on the time of request (e.g., only between 6 PM to 9 PM), the permitted operation (e.g., only Read requests), the requester's IP address (e.g., the IP address must not be blacklisted), etc. These restrictions are validated by the reference monitor in the context of an incoming request, and the credential is considered invalid if any caveat present on it is invalid.

Third-party caveats are restrictions wherein the burden of validation is pushed to a third-party, i.e., neither the party that wields the credential nor the party that is authorizing it. A credential with a third-party caveat is considered valid only when accompanied by a *discharge* (proof of validity) issued by the specific third party mentioned in the caveat. This discharge must be obtained by the holder of the credential before using the credential as part of a request. A reference monitor making authorization decisions simply checks that valid discharges are provided for all third-party caveats on the credential.

A third-party caveat can be used for implementing revocation checks by having the discharge service issue discharges only if the credential has not been revoked. The discharge may be short-lived, and thus the holder of the credential would be obligated to periodically obtain fresh discharges from the service. Although this mechanism seems similar to the online certificate status protocol

(OCSP) [24], the key difference is that unlike an OCSP response, fetching a discharge is the responsibility of the principal making the request rather than the one authorizing it. Other examples of third-party caveats would be restrictions pointed at a social networking service (e.g., discharged by checking membership in the "work" circle), or an auditing service (e.g., discharged by adding an entry to the audit log). Discharges may themselves carry first-party and third-party caveats thereby making the overall mechanism highly expressive. For instance, a *parental-control* caveat on a credential handed to a kid may initially point to a service on dad's phone who in some cases may issue a discharge with a third-party caveat pointed at mom's phone. While caveats were originally designed in the context of Macaroons [10], in this work we use them to restrict the scope of delegation certificates in Vanadium.

4   Vanadium Authorization Model

In this section, we describe the authorization model of the *Vanadium* framework [6]. Vanadium is a set of tools, libraries, and services for developing secure distributed applications that can run over a network of devices. At the core of the framework is a remote procedure call (RPC) system that enables applications to expose services over the network. The framework offers an interface definition language (IDL) for defining services, a federated naming system for addressing them, and an API for discovering accessible services. The authorization model is responsible for controlling access to RPC services, and ensuring that all RPCs are end-to-end encrypted, mutually authenticated, and mutually authorized.

Preliminaries. The model makes use of a digital signature scheme (e.g., ECDSA P-256). In particular, we assume public and secret key pairs (pk, sk), and algorithms sign and verify for signing messages and verifying signatures respectively. $\mathsf{sign}(sk, msg)$ uses a secret key sk to produce a signature over a message msg, and $\mathsf{verify}(pk, msg, sig)$ verifies a signature sig over a message msg using a public key pk. For any public and secret key pairs pk, sk, $\forall msg : \mathsf{verify}(pk, msg, \mathsf{sign}(sk, msg))$ holds. We also assume a cryptographically secure hash function (e.g., SHA256), denoted by hash. For convenience, we assume that hash takes an arbitrary number of arguments of arbitrary type, and internally encodes all arguments into a byte array using some lossless encoding technique.

4.1   Principals and Blessings

A principal is any entity that can interact in the Vanadium framework. Specifically, processes, applications, and services that include a Vanadium runtime are all principals. Each principal is associated with a public and secret key pair, with the secret key never being shared over the network. Each principal has one or more hierarchical human-readable names associated with it called *blessings*.

For instance, a television set (TV) owned by a user Alice[3] may have a blessing `Alice / TV`. Principals can have multiple blessings, and thus the same TV may also have a blessing `PopularCorp / TV123` from its manufacturer.

Principals are authenticated and authorized during requests based on the blessing names bound to them. The public key of the principal does not matter as long as the principal can prove that it has a blessing name satisfying the other end's access control policy. We believe that this choice makes it easier and more natural for users and system administrators to define access control policies and inspect audit trails as they have to reason only in terms of human-readable names. Concretely, a blessing is represented via a chain of certificates. The formal definition of certificates and blessings is given in Fig. 1. We use $\langle\ldots\rangle$ to define tuples, colon as a binary operator for forming lists, and empty for the empty list. n ranges over ordinary names not containing /. Certificates, denoted by C, contain exactly four fields—a name, a public key, a (possibly empty) list of caveats, and a digital signature. We discuss the definition of caveats a bit later; for now they can be thought of as restrictions (e.g., expiration time) on the validity of the certificate. We use the dot notation to refer to fields of a tuple, and thus $C.n$ is the name of a certificate C. Notice that our certificate format is much simpler in contrast to x509 certificates [28].

$$
\begin{array}{llr}
n ::= \text{ordinary names not containing } / & & \text{names} \\
C ::= \text{C}\langle n, pk, clist, sig \rangle & & \text{certificates} \\
B ::= C & & \text{blessings} \\
\quad | \ B : C & & \\
clist ::= \text{empty} & & \text{list of caveats} \\
\quad | \ clist : c & & \\
\\
c ::= fc \ | \ tc & & \text{caveats} \\
fc ::= \text{timeCaveat} & & \text{first-party caveats} \\
\quad | \ \text{targetCaveat} & & \\
\quad | \ \ldots & & \\
tc ::= \text{T}\langle nonce, pk, fc, loc \rangle & & \text{third-party caveats} \\
d ::= \text{D}\langle clist, sig \rangle & & \text{discharges}
\end{array}
$$

Fig. 1. Certificates, blessings and caveats

Blessings (denoted by B) are non-empty lists of certificates with each certificate capturing a component of the blessing name. The list of certificates is meant to form a chain such that signature of each certificate except the first one can be verified using the public key of the previous certificate. The first certificate is self-signed, that is, its signature can be verified by its own public key. The public key listed in the final certificate is the public key of the principal to which

---

[3] For ease of discussion, we refer to users and devices as principals; strictly speaking, we are referring to processes controlled by them.

the blessing is bound. This public key is denoted by $\mathsf{pk}(B)$ for a blessing B. The name of a blessing is obtained by concatenating all names appearing in the blessing's certificate chain using /. This name is denoted by $\mathsf{nm}(B)$.

As an example, the blessing `PopularCorp / TV123` is bound to the television's public key pk_{TV} by a chain of two certificates—(1) a certificate with name `PopularCorp` and public key $pk_{PopularCorp}$, signed by $sk_{PopularCorp}$, and (2) a certificate with name `TV123` and public key pk_{TV}, signed by $sk_{PopularCorp}$. The validity of the certificate chain of a blessing B is defined by the predicate $\mathsf{IsValidChain}(B)$.

$\mathsf{IsValidChain}(B) ::=$
    $\mathsf{case}\ B\ \mathsf{of}$
        $C \quad : \mathsf{verify}(C.pk, \mathsf{hash}(C.n, C.pk, C.clist), C.sig)$
        $\mid\ B{:}C : \mathsf{IsValidChain}(B) \wedge \mathsf{verify}(\mathsf{pk}(B), \mathsf{hash}(B, C.n, C.pk, C.clist), C.sig)$

The signature in each certificate of the chain is not just over the certificate's contents but also the chain leading up to the certificate. This means that each certificate is cryptographically integrated into the blessing, and cannot be extracted and used in another blessing. This property does not hold for SPKI/SDSI and many other certificate-based systems, where certificates can be chained together in arbitrary ways. As a result, Vanadium does not face the *certificate chain discovery* problem [16] that involves assembling the right chain of certificates (from a repository) to prove that certain credentials are associated with a public key. A Vanadium blessing is a tightly bound certificate chain containing all the certificates required to prove that a certain name is bound to a public key.

4.2   Delegation and Caveats

Blessings can be delegated from one principal to another by extending them with additional names. For instance, Alice may extend her blessing `Alice` to her TV as `Alice / TV`. The TV may in turn extend this blessing to the Youtube application running on it as `Alice / TV /Youtube`. Since principals possess authority by virtue of their blessing names, delegating a blessing amounts to delegation of authority. For instance, delegation of the blessing `Alice / TV` allows the TV to access all resources protected by an ACL of the form `Allow Alice / TV`.

Concretely, a delegation is carried out by the operation $\mathsf{Bless}(pk, sk, B, n, clist)$ which takes the public key pk_d of the delegate, the secret key sk of the delegator, the blessing B that must be extended, the name n used for the extension, and the list of caveats $clist$ on the delegation. It extends the blessing's certificate chain with a certificate containing name n, public key pk_d, list of caveats $clist$, and signed by the secret key sk.

$\mathsf{Bless}(pk_d, sk, B, n, clist) ::= B{:}\mathrm{C}\langle n, pk_d, clist, \mathsf{sign}(sk, \mathsf{hash}(B, n, pk, clist))\rangle$

It is easy to see that if the blessing B is valid, and the secret key sk corresponds to the public key $\mathsf{pk}(B)$, then the blessing $\mathsf{Bless}(pk_d, sk, B, n, clist)$ is valid. Each blessing delegation involves the blesser choosing an extension (e.g.,

TV) for the blessing. The extension may itself have multiple components (e.g., home / bedroom / TV), and a blesser may choose the same or a different extension across multiple delegations. The role of the extension is to namespace the delegation, similar to *local names* in SDSI [27].

The role of the caveat list (*clist*) supplied to the Bless operation is to restrict the conditions under which the resulting blessing can be used. For example, Alice can bless her TV as Alice / TV but with the caveats that the blessing can be used only between 6 PM and 9 PM, and only to make requests to her video service (and not her bank!). Thus, the resulting blessing makes the assertion:

> The name Alice:TV is bound to pk_{TV}
> *as long as* the TIME is between 6 PM and 9 PM, and
> *as long as* target of the request matches SomeCorp / VideoService

When the TV uses this blessing to make a request to the video service, the service will grant the request only if the current time is within the permitted range, and its own blessing name matches SomeCorp / VideoService.

The caveats in the above example are all first-party caveats as they are validated by the reference monitor at the target service when the blessing is presented during a request. As discussed in Sect. 3 and [10], first-party caveats are validated in the *context* of an incoming request based on information such as the time of request, the blessing presented, the method invoked, etc. We use $\mathcal{C}$ to denote request contexts, and assume a function $\mathsf{IsValidFCav}(fc, \mathcal{C})$ that checks if a first-party caveat fc is valid in the context $\mathcal{C}$.

While the Vanadium framework implements IsValidFCav on some standard first-party caveats (e.g., expiry, method and peer restriction), services may also define their own first-party caveats. For instance, a video streaming service may define a "PG-13" caveat so that blessings carrying this caveat would be authorized to stream only PG-13 movies.

4.3   Third-Party Caveats

Vanadium blessings may also carry third-party caveats [10] wherein the burden of validating the caveat is pushed to a third-party. For example, Alice can bless Bob as Alice / Houseguest / Bob but with the caveat that the blessing is valid only if Bob is within 20 feet of Alice as determined by a proximity service running on Alice's phone (third-party). Before making a request with this blessing, Bob must obtain a *discharge* (proof) from the proximity service on Alice's phone. This discharge must be sent along with the blessing in a request. Thus, the blessing makes the assertion:

> The name Alice / Houseguest / Bob is bound to pk_{Bob}
> *as long as* a proximity service on Alice's phone issues a discharge after validating that Bob is "within 20 feet" of it.

The structure of a third-party caveat and discharge is defined in Fig. 1. Every third-party caveat includes a nonce (for uniqueness), a public key controlled by the third-party service, a first-party caveat specifying the check that must carried out before issuing the discharge, and the location of the third-party service. A discharge contains a signature and possibly additional caveats. It is considered valid if its signature can be verified by the public key listed in the third-party caveat, and any additional caveats listed on it are valid.

The operation $\mathsf{MintDischarge}(sk_{tp}, tc, clist, \mathcal{C})$ uses a secret key sk_{tp} (owned by the third-party) to produce a discharge for a third-party caveat tc if the check specified in tc is valid in the context $\mathcal{C}$. The returned discharge contains the provided list of caveats $clist$.

$$\mathsf{MintDischarge}(sk_{tp}, tc, clist, \mathcal{C}) ::=$$
$$\texttt{case } \mathsf{IsValidFCav}(tc.fc, \mathcal{C}) \texttt{ of}$$
$$\texttt{true : error}$$
$$\mid \texttt{false : } \mathrm{D}\langle clist, \mathsf{sign}(sk_{tp}, \mathsf{hash}(tc, clist))\rangle$$

The purpose of the additional caveats on the discharge is to limit its validity. For instance, in the proximity caveat example, Alice's phone may issue a discharge that expires in 5 min thereby requiring Bob to fetch a new discharge periodically. This ensures that Bob cannot cheat by fetching a discharge when near Alice's phone, and then using it later from a different location.

4.4   Blessing Roots

Since blessing names are the basis of authorization, it is important for them to be unforgeable. Simply verifying the signatures in a certificate chain does not protect against forgery because the first certificate in the chain is self-signed, and thus can be constructed by any principal. For instance, an attacker with public and secret keys pk_a, sk_a can bind the name Alice to her public key using the blessing $\mathrm{C}\langle \texttt{Alice}, pk_a, \texttt{empty}, \mathsf{sign}(sk_a, \mathsf{hash}(\texttt{Alice}, pk_a, \texttt{empty}))\rangle$. She may then extend this blessing with any extension of her choosing using the Bless operation.

In order to defend against such forgery, all Vanadium principals have a set of *recognized roots*. The *root* of a blessing is the public key and name of the first certificate in the blessing's certificate chain. A blessing is recognized by a principal only if the blessing's root is recognized. For instance, all of Alice's devices may recognize her public key pk_{Alice} and name Alice as a root. Any blessing prefixed with Alice would be recognized only if it has pk_{Alice} as the root public key. Similarly all devices manufactured by PopularCorp may recognize the public key $pk_{PopularCorp}$ and name PopularCorp as a root. Devices from another manufacturer may not recognize this root, and would simply discard blessings from PopularCorp.

We use the term *identity provider* for a principal that acts as a blessing root and hands blessings to other principals. For instance, both Alice and Popular-Corp would be considered as identity providers by Alice's TV. Any principal can become an identity provider. In general, we anticipate well-known companies, schools, and public agencies to become identity providers, and different principals may recognize different subsets of these.

4.5   Authentication and Authorization

Client and servers in a remote procedure call (RPC) authenticate each other by presenting blessings bound to their public keys. The Vanadium authentication protocol [7] is based on the well-known SIGMA-I protocol [15]. It ensures that each end learns the other end's blessing, and is convinced that the other end possesses the corresponding secret key. At the end of the protocol, an encrypted channel (based on a shared key) is established between the client and server for further communication. Since the protocol is fairly standard, we do not discuss it here and refer the reader to [7] for a detailed description.

Once authentication completes, each end checks that the other end's blessing is authorized for the RPC. Authorization is mutual. For example, Alice (client) may invoke a method on her TV (server) only if the TV presents a blessing matching `Alice / TV`, and the TV may authorize Alice's request only if she presents a blessing prefixed with `Alice`. Authorization checks involve two key steps—(1) validating the blessing presented by the other end, followed by (2) matching the blessing name against an access control policy.

A blessing is always validated in the context of a given request. Blessing validation involves —(1) verifying the signatures on the blessing's certificate chain, (2) verifying that the blessing root is recognized, and (3) validating all caveats on the blessing in the context of the request.

$\mathsf{IsValidBlessing}(B, \mathcal{R}, \mathcal{C})$, defined below, determines if a blessing B is valid for a given request context $\mathcal{C}$ and a set of recognized roots $\mathcal{R}$. The context is assumed to contain all parameters of the request, including any discharges sent by the other end. Specifically, $\mathsf{dis}(\mathcal{C})$ denotes the discharges contained in the context $\mathcal{C}$, $\mathsf{root}(B)$ is the root of the blessing B and $\mathsf{cavs}(B)$ is the set of all caveats appearing on certificates of the blessing B. A first-party caveat is validated by invoking the function $\mathsf{IsValidFCav}$, and a third-party caveat is validated by finding a matching discharge in the request context, i.e., a discharge whose signature can be verified using the public key specified in the third-party caveat. Additionally, any caveats listed on the discharge are also (recursively) validated.

$\mathsf{IsValidBlessing}(B, \mathcal{R}, \mathcal{C}) ::=$
$\quad \mathsf{IsValidChain}(B) \wedge \mathsf{IsRecognized}(B, \mathcal{R}) \wedge \mathsf{IsValidCavs}(\mathsf{cavs}(B), \mathcal{C})$

$\mathsf{IsRecognized}(B, \mathcal{R}) ::= \exists r \in \mathcal{R} : \mathsf{root}(B) = r$

$\mathsf{IsValidCavs}(clist, \mathcal{C}) ::=$
$\quad \forall c \in clist :$
$\quad\quad \mathbf{case}\ c\ \mathbf{of}$
$\quad\quad\quad fc\ :\ \mathsf{IsValidFCav}(fc, \mathcal{C})$
$\quad\quad\ |\ \ tc :\ \exists d \in \mathsf{dis}(\mathcal{C}) :$
$\quad\quad\quad\quad\quad \mathsf{verify}(tc.pk, \mathsf{hash}(tc, d.clist), d.sig)) \wedge \mathsf{IsValidCavs}(d.clist, \mathcal{C})$

Once the remote end's blessing is validated, the name of the blessing is checked against an access control policy. Access is granted only if the check is successful. We discuss the structure of these policies next.

4.6   Access Control Policies

The syntax and semantics of access control policies in Vanadium has been defined rigorously in [8]. We give a brief overview of the design in this subsection. Policies in Vanadium are specified using access control lists (ACLs) that resolve to the set of permitted blessing names. In order to allow policies to be short and simple, Vanadium allows ACLs to indirect through groups. For example, Alice may create a group $AliceFriends_G$ containing the blessing names of all her friends and add it to all relevant ACLs. This saves her from enumerating the list of blessing names of family members within each ACL, and also provides a central place to manage multiple policies. Furthermore, group definitions may be nested. For instance, the definition of the group $AliceFriends_G$ may contain the group $DaveFriends_G$ containing the friends of Alice's flatmate Dave. Typically, the definition of a group would be held at a remote server, which would be contacted during ACL resolution. The ACL resolver may cache information about groups in order to combat unreliable network connectivity and avoid expensive network roundtrips.

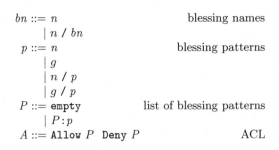

Fig. 2. Access control policies

ACLs may also contain blessing names where one of the components is a group name. Such names are called *blessing patterns*, and are meant to capture a derived set of blessing names. For example, the pattern $AliceFriends_G$ / Phone defines the set of blessing names of phones of Alice's friends. In particular, if the group $AliceFriends_G$ contains the blessing name Bob, then the pattern $AliceFriends_G$ / Phone would be matched by the blessing name Bob / Phone.

Definitions. The formal definition of blessing patterns and ACLs is given in Fig. 2. As before, n ranges over ordinary names not including /. g ranges over group names (i.e., name with the subscript "G"), and bn ranges over blessing names. A blessing pattern is a non-empty sequence of ordinary names or group names separated by /. An ACL is a pair of Allow and Deny clauses, each containing a list of blessing patterns.[4] Deny clauses make it convenient to encode blacklists. For instance, the ACL Allow $AliceDevices_G$ Deny $AliceWorkDevices_G$ allows access to all of Alice's devices except her work devices.

---

[4] The model described in [8] is more general and allows multiple Allow and Deny clauses in ACLs.

Group definitions are of the form $g =_{\text{def}} P$, and thus equate a group name with a list of blessing patterns. For example, the group `AliceFriends`$_G$ may have a definition of the form

$$\texttt{AliceFriends}_G =_{\text{def}} \texttt{Bob}, \texttt{Carol}, \texttt{DaveFriends}_G$$

A given blessing name satisfies an ACL if there is at least one blessing pattern in the `Allow` clause that is matched by the blessing name, and no blessing pattern in the `Deny` clause is matched by the blessing name. For example, when `Bob` is in the group `AliceFriends`$_G$, the ACL `Allow AliceFriends`$_G$ will permit access with the blessing name `Bob` but the ACL `Allow AliceFriends`$_G$ `Deny Bob` will deny it. The default is to deny access, so for example the ACL `Allow Bob` will deny access to `Carol`.

The semantics of ACL checks makes use of the prefix relation on blessing names. Given two blessing names bn_1 and bn_2, we write $bn_1 \preceq bn_2$ if the sequence of names in bn_1 (separated by $/$) is a prefix of the sequence of names in bn_2, for e.g., `Alice` $\preceq$ `Alice`/`TV` holds but `Ali` $\preceq$ `Alice`/`TV` does not.

In order to formalize the ACL checking procedure, we first define a function $\mathsf{Meaning}_\rho$ that maps a blessing pattern to a set of blessing names. It is parametric on a semantics of group names, which is a function ρ that maps a group name to a set of members of the group. We discuss how ρ is obtained later.

$$
\begin{aligned}
&\mathsf{Meaning}_\rho(p) ::= \\
&\quad \textbf{case } p \textbf{ of} \\
&\qquad n \quad\;\; : \{n\} \\
&\qquad |\;\; g \quad\;\; : \rho(g) \\
&\qquad |\;\; n\,/\,p : \{n\,/\,s \mid s \in \mathsf{Meaning}_\rho(p)\} \\
&\qquad |\;\; g\,/\,p : \{s\,/\,s' \mid s \in \mathsf{Meaning}_\rho(g), s' \in \mathsf{Meaning}_\rho(p)\}
\end{aligned}
$$

$\mathsf{Meaning}_\rho$ can be naturally extended to a list of blessing patterns by defining it as the union of the sets obtained by applying $\mathsf{Meaning}_\rho$ to each element of the list, with $\mathsf{Meaning}_\rho(\texttt{empty})$ defined as $\emptyset$. Using the function $\mathsf{Meaning}_\rho$, we define the function $\mathsf{IsAuthorized}(bn, A)$ that decides whether a given blessing name bn (seen during a request) satisfies an ACL A.

$$
\begin{aligned}
&\mathsf{IsAuthorized}(bn, A) ::= \\
&\quad \textbf{case } A \textbf{ of} \\
&\qquad \texttt{Allow } P_A \texttt{ Deny } P_D : (\exists bn' \in \mathsf{Meaning}_\rho(P_A).bn' \preceq bn) \\
&\qquad\qquad\qquad\qquad\qquad\quad \wedge(\neg\exists bn' \in \mathsf{Meaning}_\rho(P_D).bn' \preceq bn)
\end{aligned}
$$

The function checks that the blessing name bn matches an allowed blessing pattern and does not match any denied blessing pattern. Matching is defined using prefixes (instead of exact equality) for both allowed and denied clauses; the reasons however are different.

For `Allow` clauses, the use of the relation $\preceq$ is a matter of convenience. We believe that often when a service grant access to a principal (e.g., with blessing name `Alice`) it may be fine if the access is exercised by delegates of the principal (e.g., with blessing name `Alice / Phone`). Thus a pattern in an `Allow` clause is considered matched as long as some prefix of the provided blessing name matches it. Alternatively, services that want to force exact matching for allowed patterns—perhaps to prevent the granted access from naturally flowing over to delegates—may use the special reserved name eob at the end of the pattern. For e.g., the pattern `Allow Alice / eob` is matched only by the blessing name `Alice`.

For `Deny` clauses, ensuring that no prefix of the blessing name matches a denied pattern is crucial for security. A principal with blessing name bn can always extend it (using the `Bless` operation) and bind it to itself. Thus, from a security perspective it is important that if bn is denied access, then all extensions of bn are also denied access.

Semantics of groups (ρ). We now discuss how the map ρ from group names to members of the group is defined. In Vanadium, groups may also be distributed, in that, different group definitions may be held at different servers. Given this, defining the map ρ becomes complicated for several reasons. Firstly, due to network partitions some group servers may be unreachable during ACL checking and thus their definitions may be unavailable. The definition of a group may depend on other groups, and there may be no overseeing authority ensuring absence of dependency cycles. Finally, group server checks need to be secure and private. For instance, group servers under different administrative domains may be unwilling to reveal their complete membership lists to each other, and may offer only an interface for membership lookups. We refer the reader to [8] for a complete treatment of how these issues are tackled, and explain only the key ideas below.

When group servers are unreachable during ACL checking, we conservatively approximate the definition of ρ for those groups. The approximation depends on whether the group is being resolved in the context of an `Allow` clause or a `Deny` clause. While matching an allowed pattern, unreachable groups are under-approximated by the empty set. On the other hand, while matching a denied pattern, unreachable groups are over-approximated by the set of all blessings. Thus effectively we define two maps $\rho_\Downarrow$ and $\rho_\Uparrow$—the map $\rho_\Downarrow$ is used while defining Meaning$_\rho$ for allowed patterns, and the map $\rho_\Uparrow$ is used while defining Meaning$_\rho$ for denied patterns. The maps $\rho_\Downarrow$ and $\rho_\Uparrow$ coincide when all group definitions are available.

$\rho_\Downarrow$ and $\rho_\Uparrow$ can be constructed by considering the list of available group definitions as a set of productions inducing a formal language. Ordinary names and / are terminals, and group names are non-terminals. For instance, the group definition

$$g_1 =_{\text{def}} \text{Alice / Phone}, g_2 \text{ / Phone}$$

can be viewed as two productions

$$g_1 \rightarrow \text{Alice / Phone}$$
$$g_1 \rightarrow g_2 \text{ / Phone}$$

For $\rho_{\Downarrow}$, no production is associated with a group name whose definition is unavailable. On the other hand for $\rho_{\Uparrow}$, such group names are associated with productions inducing the set of all blessings. Once the set of productions are defined, for any group name g, $\rho_{\Downarrow}(g)$ and $\rho_{\Uparrow}(g)$ are defined as the set of blessing names generated from g by the corresponding set of productions.

While constructing $\rho_{\Downarrow}$ and $\rho_{\Uparrow}$ in the aforesaid manner is infeasible in practice as it requires knowledge of all the group definitions, the key observation here is that checking group membership can be reduced to checking membership in an induced formal language. In [8], this observation and techniques from top-down parsing are used to develop a distributed algorithm for checking whether a blessing name belongs to a group.

4.7 Life of an RPC

We now explain how the various parts of the authorization model come together during the course of an RPC. Consider Alice's house guest Bob who wants to invoke a method on Alice's TV. Suppose Bob has the blessing B_{Bob} with name Alice / Houseguest / Bob, and the TV has the blessing B_{TV} with name Alice / TV. Additionally, suppose that Bob's blessing has a third-party caveat to a proximity service running on Alice's phone. Bob has the access control policy Allow Alice / TV that allows only Alice's TV, and the TV has the access control policy Allow Alice:Alice / Houseguest that allows only Alice and her house guests. In what follows, we describe the steps involved in the RPC from Bob's phone to Alice's TV. We focus on the authentication and access-control aspects, and do not discuss how various network connections are established.

- Bob uses the Vanadium authentication protocol to initiate a connection to Alice's TV.
- As part of the exchange, the TV first sends its blessing B_{TV} to Bob. Bob invokes IsValidBlessing($B_{TV}, \mathcal{R}_{Bob}, \mathcal{C}_{Bob}$) to verify that the blessing B_{TV} is valid for the current context from Bob's perspective and the set of blessing roots recognized by Bob ($\mathcal{R}_{Bob}$). If this step succeeds, then Bob verifies that the name of the blessing (Alice / TV) satisfies his access control policy (Allow Alice / TV). The connection is aborted if any of these checks fail.
- After authorizing the TV's blessing, Bob selects his blessing B_{Bob} (from Alice) to present to the TV. Since the blessing carries a third-party caveat, Bob first connects to the third-party service listed on the caveat to obtain a discharge. The service performs the necessary checks, and if those succeed, it issues a discharge to Bob. Bob (recursively) performs the above procedure for any third-party caveats on the discharge, and once all discharges have been obtained, he presents all of them with the blessing B_{Bob} to the TV.
- The TV invokes IsValidBlessing($B_{Bob}, \mathcal{R}_{TV}, \mathcal{C}_{TV}$) to verify that the blessing B_{Bob} is valid for the current context from the TV's perpspective ($\mathcal{C}_{TV}$) and the set of blessing roots recognized by the TV ($\mathcal{R}_{TV}$). If this step succeeds, the TV verifies that the name of the blessing (Alice / Houseguest / Bob) satisfies its access control policy (Allow Alice:Alice / Houseguest). The connection is aborted if any of these checks fail.

- After authorization succeeds at the TV's end, the protocol is complete and an encrypted channel is established between Bob and the TV. Application data pertaining to the RPC is then exchanged on this channel.

4.8 Practical Considerations

We now discuss some considerations involved in deploying the authorization model in practice.

Managing Blessings. Authorization in Vanadium is based on blessings. A principal may acquire multiple blessings over time, each providing access to some set of services under some contextual restrictions. Consequently, managing these blessings may become quite onerous. The first problem is storing all these blessings while keeping track of the meta-data about where they were obtained from and under what constraints. Another problem is selecting which blessing to present when authenticating to a peer. While presenting all blessings and letting the peer choose the relevant one is convenient, it has the downside of leaking sensitive information, for e.g., a blessing may reveal that Bob is a house guest of Alice. Instead, Vanadium provides a means to selectively share blessings with appropriate peers. Blessing are stored by Vanadium principals using a mechanism similar to cookie jars in Web browsers. All blessings are stored with a blessing pattern identifying the peer to whom they should be presented. This pattern may be set based on information provided by the blessing granter. For example, Bob can add the blessing `Alice / Houseguest / Bob` with the peer pattern `Alice`. Thus, Bob will present this blessing only when communicating with services that have a blessing name matching this pattern. Any other service that Bob communicates with will not know that he has this blessing from Alice.

Blessing vs. Adding to an ACL. The careful reader may have noticed that Vanadium offers two mechanisms for granting access to a resource. For instance, consider Alice's TV with an ACL `Allow Alice` which means all principals with the blessing name `Alice` or an extension of it have access. Alice can grant access to her TV to another principal by either extending her `Alice` blessing to the other principal or by adding the other principal's blessing name to the ACL. The question then is how does one decide which method is appropriate in a given use-case. Granting a blessing is akin to handing out a capability, and thus in a way this question is that of deciding between granting a capability versus modifying an ACL. We recommend the following approach for making the choice.

   The constraints on the access being delegated must be taken into consideration. If the access is meant to be long-lived and unconstrained then modifying the ACL is preferable as it allows the service administrator to audit and revoke access at any time. For instance, Alice may share access to her TV with her flatmate Dave by adding the pattern `Dave` to the TV's ACL. Later when Alice moves out, she can revoke Dave's access by removing this pattern. On the other hand, when the access is constrained then blessing with caveats is a more appropriate choice. For instance, Alice may delegate temporary access to her TV to her house guest Bob by blessing him under a short-lived time caveat.

The choice of how access is granted also affects the subsequent auditability of the delegated access. For instance, when Dave accesses Alice' TV he would use his own blessing (assuming Alice's TV trusts Dave as a blessing root) and his access would be recorded as `Dave`. However, when Bob accesses the TV he would use his blessing from Alice, and thus his access would be recorded as `Alice / Houseguest / Bob`. Finally, we note that the option to change an ACL may not always be available. When Bob wants to grant access to Alice's TV to his friend Carol, extending his blessing to Carol may be his only option as he may not have the authority to modify the TV's ACL.

Revocation. We now discuss mechanisms for revoking access. Revocation is easy when access is granted by adding to an ACL or a group, as it amounts to simply removing the added entry. It is more challenging when access is granted via blessing. One approach is to always constrain blessings with short-lived time caveats, thereby invalidating them automatically after a certain time. Principals would then have to periodically reach out to their blessing granters for a fresh blessing. This idea is similar to "reconfirmation" in SDSI [27]. Using a third-party caveat pointed at a revocation service offers a more systematic way of realizing this idea. The revocation service would issue a short-lived discharge for the caveat only if the blessing has not been revoked.

While such third-party caveats elegantly encode revocation restrictions, they suffer from the downside of requiring blessing holders to periodically connect to a revocation service. Specifically, they introduce a trade-off between how swiftly a blessing may be revoked, and how long things may operate when disconnected. This trade-off may be ameliorated to some extent if devices can recognize when they are offline and use different revocation timeouts in that case. Furthermore, in the home setting, a discharge service may be run on a WiFi access point, thereby requiring devices to maintain connectivity only to the local WiFi network.

5 Application: Physical Lock

In this section, we explain how the Vanadium authorization model may be applied to a physical lock. The application highlights the flexibility and decentralization aspects of the model. A network controlled lock is a common device found in many modern homes today. It allows a user to lock and unlock a door from their phone, and share access to it with visitors. Today, there are a number of manufacturers building locks for homes, garages, factory floors etc.

The authorization model for most existing products involves a global service service in the cloud, often controlled by the lock manufacturer, that is an authority on all credentials used to access the lock. Typically, the service must be accessed during setup and whenever access is delegated. As discussed in Sect. 2, this is undesirable as communicating with global services requires internet access, which may not be perfectly reliable. It can be quite frustrating for a user to be unable to share access to a lock due to lack of internet connectivity at the time sharing is initiated. Furthermore, compromising the manufacturer owned service may allow attacker to unlock all locks managed by the manufacturer. In what follows, we present an authorization model for locks that is fully decentralized, and does not depend on access to an external service or identity provider.

Overview. The key idea is to have the lock be its own identity provider. When the lock is set up by its owner, it creates a self-signed blessing for itself, and extends this blessing to the owner. The blessing granted to the owner is effectively the *key* to the lock. All subsequent access to the lock is restricted to clients that can wield this blessing or extensions of it. Delegation of access is simply carried out by extending the *key* blessing.

5.1   Authorization Details

Consider a user Alice who just bought a brand new lock for the front door of her house. We walk through the steps of setting up identity and access control for the lock. We assume that Alice is interacting with the lock using another device, say her phone.

Claiming a New Lock. We assume that an out-of-box lock device comes with a pre-installed public and secret key pair, and a blessing from its manufacturer of the form `<manufacturer> / <serial no>`. The first step in setting up the lock is for Alice to name the lock and obtain a blessing for subsequently interacting with it. This is accomplished by invoking the `Claim` method on the lock that returns a blessing bound to the invoker's (Alice's) public key.

The invocation is through a Vanadium remote procedure call. The invoker authorizes the lock by verifying that it presents a blessing from the manufacturer with the expected serial number. An unconfigured lock authorizes any principal to invoke the `Claim` method on it, after which it considers the setup process complete and no longer allows invocation of that method.

After the `Claim` invocation is authorized, the lock creates a self-signed blessing with a name provided by the caller. This blessing is presented by the lock to authenticate to clients during all subsequent invocations. The lock then acts as an identity provider and extends this blessing to the invoker's public key (learned during authentication). This granted blessing is called the *key* blessing of the lock. The invoker saves this blessing for subsequent interactions with the lock and also recognizes its root as an identity provider. For instance, Alice may claim the lock on her front door with the name `AliceFrontDoor`. The lock will subsequently authenticate to others as `AliceFrontDoor`, and would grant the blessing `AliceFrontDoor / Key` to Alice (here `Key` is the blessing extension used by the lock).

Locking and Unlocking. Once a lock has been claimed, the `Claim` method is disabled and the lock instead exposes the `Lock` and `Unlock` methods. The methods are protected by an ACL that allows access only to clients that wield a blessing from the lock's identity provider. In the above example, the ACL would be `Allow AliceFrontDoor`, which would be matched by the blessing `AliceFrontDoor / Key`.

Delegating Access. Any extension of the key blessing also matches the ACL for the lock's methods, and thus access to the lock can be delegated by extending this blessing. As usual, caveats can be added to the extension to restrict its scope. For instance, Alice can extend her blessing `AliceFrontDoor / Key` to her house cleaner as `AliceFrontDoor / Key /Cleaner` under a time caveat that is valid only on Mondays between 8AM to 10AM.

Auditing Access. The lock can keep track of the blessings used to access it, even ones that have invalid caveats. Thus, Alice can inspect the log on the lock for auditing access attempts made by her house cleaner. In particular, Alice can detect if the cleaner tried to access the lock outside of the agreed upon time (8AM to 10AM on Mondays) or if there is access by someone who has received a delegated blessing from the cleaner.

5.2 Discussion

We highlight three distinguishing aspects of the authorization model presented in this section.

Decentralized. Each lock is an authority on the secrets and credentials that can be used to access it. No external entity, including the lock manufacturer, can mint credentials to access a claimed lock device. The credentials for accessing one lock are completely independent from those for accessing another. Thus, attackers have no single point of attack to unlock multiple instances.

No Internet Connectivity Required. The authorization model does not require the lock or the device interacting with it to have internet access at any point, including during setup. The model does not rely on any third-party service or identity provider.

Audited. The lock can keep track of when it was accessed, by whom (represented by the blessings). Since blessings inherently capture a delegation trail, the access log also conveys how the invoker obtained access.

Having highlighted the above advantages, we note that decentralization comes at a cost. For instance, the lack of an authoritative source in the cloud makes it hard to recover from loss or theft of blessings and secret keys. Furthermore, users are responsible for managing multiple blessings and keeping track of various delegations they make. We believe that carefully designed user-interfaces and appropriate reset modes for the lock device can help address some of these concerns.

6 Conclusion

This tutorial presents the authorization model of the Vanadium framework [6]. In this model, each principal has a digital signature public and secret key pair, and a set of hierarchical human-readable names bound to its public key via certificate chains called *blessings*. All authorizations associated with a principal are based on its blessing names. In particular, a principal makes a request to a service by presenting one of its blessings (using the Vanadium authentication protocol [7]), and the request is authorized if the blessing name satisfies the service's access control policy.

A notable feature of the model is its support for decentralization and fine-grained delegation. The model does not require the existence of special identity providers that are trusted by all principals by default. Instead, any principal may choose to become an identity provider and create blessings for itself and other principals. Each principal has a choice over which other principals it recognizes as identity providers. Only blessings from recognized identity providers are considered valid. In practice, we anticipate that there will be a small set of large-scale identity providers that most people will commonly use in interactions with the wider world.

Principals can delegate access by extending one or more of their blessings to other principals. The scope of delegations can be constrained very finely by adding caveats [10] to the delegated blessing. In particular, blessings support third-party caveats which allow predicating delegations on consent by specific third-parties. Such caveats elegantly support revocation, proximity-based restrictions, and audit requirements.

Access control policies in Vanadium may indirect through groups whose definition may be distributed across multiple servers, possibly under different administrative domains. While several access control mechanisms support groups, a distinguishing aspect of our design is using groups to construct compound names. For instance, the pattern `AliceFriends`$_G$` / Phone`, with `AliceFriends`$_G$ being a group of blessing names of Alice's friends, defines the set of blessing names of phones of Alice's friends. Such compound names coupled with negative clauses in ACLs make the problem of checking group membership fairly complex, especially when the group server may be unreachable. The Vanadium authorization model mitigates some of the difficulties by making simplifying choices. For instance, group definitions cannot contain negative clauses, and ACLs cannot be reused for defining groups or other ACLs. This tutorial provides a brief overview of our solution, with a more comprehensive description available in [8].

Future Directions. There are several future directions for this line of work. The first and perhaps the most important direction is on making the model and its primitives easily usable by end users. This is paramount to the adoption of the model. Mechanisms for making the model more usable may include designing intuitive user-interfaces for visualizing, granting and revoking blessings, and conventions on blessing names that help write intelligible access-control policies.

Another direction is that of enabling *mutual* privacy in the Vanadium authentication protocol. Currently, the protocol involves the server presenting its blessing before the client. While this is beneficial to the client, as it may choose to not reveal its blessing after seeing the server's blessing, it is disadvantageous to the server. The server's blessing is effectively revealed to anyone who connects to it, including active network attackers. In fact, this lack of mutual privacy is common to many other mutual authentication protocols (such as TLS [17], SIGMA-I [15]) wherein one of the parties must reveal its identity first. In the scenarios considered in this work, the participants may be personal end-user devices neither of which is inclined to reveal its identity before learning the identity of its peer. In ongoing work [31], we are designing a private mutual authentication protocol that allows each end to learn its peer's blessing only if it satisfies the peer's authorization policy.

Finally, one may consider designing mechanisms for securely leveraging external cloud-based services when internet access is available. For instance, a Cloud-based service may be used as a transparent proxy for RPCs, as a revocation and auditing service for blessing delegations, or as a readonly backup for data. In all cases, the goal would be to leverage external Cloud-based services for various tasks while granting them the minimal authority necessary for the task.

Acknowledgments. This work is a result of a joint effort by several members of the Vanadium team at Google. We would like to thank Martín Abadi, Mike Burrows, Ryan Brown, Bogdan Caprita, Thai Duong, Cosmos Nicolaou, Himabindu Pucha, David Presotto, Adam Sadovsky, Suharsh Sivakumar, Gautham Thambidorai, Robin Thellend for their contributions to designing and implementing the Vanadium authorization model. We are grateful to Martín Abadi and Mike Burrows for helpful comments on drafts of this tutorial.

References

1. Fridge sends spam emails as attack hits smart gadgets. http://www.bbc.com/news/technology-25780908
2. Hackers remotely kill a jeep on the highway? with me in it. https://www.wired.com/2015/07/hackers-remotely-kill-jeep-highway/
3. Openid. http://openid.net/
4. Smart meters can be hacked to cut power bills. http://www.bbc.com/news/technology-29643276
5. The Internet of Things is wildly insecure? and often unpatchable. https://www.schneier.com/essays/archives/2014/01/the_internet_of_thin.html
6. Vanadium. http://vanadium.github.io/
7. Vanadium Authentication Protocol. https://vanadium.github.io/designdocs/authentication.html
8. Abadi, M., Burrows, M., Pucha, H., Sadovsky, A., Shankar, A., Taly, A.: Distributed authorization with distributed grammars. In: Bodei, C., Ferrari, G.-L., Priami, C. (eds.) Programming Languages with Applications to Biology and Security. LNCS, vol. 9465, pp. 10–26. Springer, Heidelberg (2015)
9. Appel, A., Felten, E.: Proof-carrying authentication. In: CCS, pp. 52–62 (1999)
10. Birgisson, A., Politz, J.G., Erlingsson, U., Taly, A., Vrable, M., Lentczner, M.: Macaroons: Cookies with contextual caveats for decentralized authorization in the cloud. In: NDSS (2014)
11. Blaze, M., Feigenbaum, J., Ioannidis, J.: The KeyNote Trust-Management System Version 2. RFC 2704 (Proposed Standard), September 1999
12. Blaze, M., Feigenbaum, J., Lacy, J.: Decentralized trust management. In: IEEE Symposium on Security and Privacy, pp. 164–173 (1996)

13. Borisov, N., Brewer, E.: Active certificates: a framework for delegation. In: NDSS, pp. 30–40 (2002)

14. Braz, C., Robert, J.: Security and usability: the case of the user authentication methods. In: Conference on L'Interaction Homme-Machine, pp. 199–203 (2006)

15. Canetti, R., Krawczyk, H.: Security analysis of IKE's signature-based key-exchange protocol. In: Yung, M. (ed.) CRYPTO 2002. LNCS, vol. 2442, pp. 143–161. Springer, Heidelberg (2002)

16. Clarke, D., Elien, J., Ellison, C., Fredette, M., Morcos, A., Rivest, R.: Certificate chain discovery in SPKI/SDSI. J. Comput. Secur. **9**, 285–322 (2001)

17. Dierks, T., Rescorla, E.: The Transport Layer Security (TLS) Protocol Version 1.2. RFC 5246 (Proposed Standard), August 2008

18. Ellison, C., Frantz, B., Lampson, B., Rivest, R., Thomas, B., Ylonen, T.: SPKI Certificate Theory. RFC 2693 (Proposed Standard), September 1999

19. Hewlett Packard Enterprise: Internet of things research study. http://www8.hp.com/h20195/V2/GetPDF.aspx/4AA5-4759ENW.pdf

20. Gong, L.: A secure identity-based capability system. In: IEEE Symposium on Security and Privacy, pp. 56–63 (1989)

21. Hardt, E.: The OAuth 2.0 Authorization Framework. RFC 6749 (Proposed Standard), October 2012

22. Lampson, B., Abadi, M., Burrows, M., Wobber, E.: Authentication in distributed systems: theory and practice. In: SOSP, pp. 165–182 (1991)

23. Li, N., Feigenbaum, J., Grosof, B.N.: A logic-based knowledge representation for authorization with delegation. In: CSFW, pp. 162–174 (1999)

24. Myers, M., Ankney, R., Malpani, A., Galperin, S., Adams, C.: X.509 Internet Public Key Infrastructure Online Certificate Status Protocol - OCSP. RFC 2560 (Proposed Standard), June 1999

25. Neuman, B.C.: Proxy-based authorization and accounting for distributed systems. In: ICDCS, pp. 283–291 (1993)

26. Rapid7. Hacking IoT: A case study on baby monitor exposures and vulnerabilities. https://www.rapid7.com/resources/iot/baby-monitors.jsp

27. Rivest, R.L., Lampson, B.: SDSI - a simple distributed security infrastructure. Technical report (1996). http://people.csail.mit.edu/rivest/sdsi11

28. Santesson, S., Farrell, S., Boeyen, S., Housley, R., Polk, W.: Internet X.509 Public Key Infrastructure Certificate and Certificate Revocation List (CRL) Profile. RFC 5280 (Proposed Standard), May 2008

29. Schneider, F.B.: Untitled textbook on cybersecurity. Chap. 9: Credentials-based authorization (2013). http://www.cs.cornell.edu/fbs/publications/chptr.CredsBased.pdf

30. Whitten, A., Tygar, J.D.: Why Johnny can't encrypt: a usability evaluation of PGP 5.0. In: USENIX Security Symposium, pp. 169–183 (1999)

31. Wu, D.J., Taly, A., Shankar, A., Boneh, D.: Privacy, discovery, and authentication for the internet of things (2016). https://arxiv.org/abs/1604.06959

32. Zimmermann, P.R.: The Official PGP User's Guide. MIT Press, Cambridge (1995)

Author Index

Printed in the United States
By Bookmasters